Turkey

IN MY TIME

IN MY TIME

Ahmed Emin Yalman

UNIVERSITY OF OKLAHOMA PRESS : *Norman*

BY AHMED EMIN YALMAN

Turkey in My Time (Norman, 1956)

Turkey in the World War (New Haven, 1930)

Library of Congress Catalog Card Number 56–11230
Copyright 1956 by the University of Oklahoma Press, Publishing Division
of the University. Composed and printed at Norman, Oklahoma, U.S.A.,
by the University of Oklahoma Press. First edition.

FOREWORD

THIS MANUSCRIPT was started in 1938 and 1939 during a long visit in New York in connection with the World's Fair. I continued to work on it while in San Francisco in May and June, 1945, on the occasion of the United Nations Conference, and tentatively finished it in Turkey in the summer of 1954. Revisions continued to 1956, when the manuscript was accepted for publication.

A brief note on Turkish titles and spelling: Pasha is approximately the equivalent of "Honorable"; Bey, the old form of "Mister"; Hanım, the old form for "Miss" or "Mrs."; Ağa, a term of friendly respect. These titles follow the given name; for example, Kemal Pasha. Formerly written in Arabic script, Turkish has been written in Latin letters since 1928. Certain sounds, peculiar to the Turkish language, require special letters and accents; hence an undotted i (ı) and an almost silent g (ğ); ş (pronounced sh), ç (pronounced ch), c (pronounced j); a circumflex (^) over a vowel lengthens it, and umlauted vowels are the same as in German. These accents will appear only rarely in this book in a proper name or a special idiom.

I wish to acknowledge here the kind assistance extended by my friend Leo Hochstetter, and to express my gratitude to him and to Professor Edward M. Earle of Princeton University and Professor Christine Phelps Harris, curator of the Middle East Collections in the Hoover Institute and Library at Stanford

v

University, for kindly going through the manuscript and making valuable suggestions. I feel especially grateful to Miss Eleanor Bisbee, research associate in the Hoover Institute and Library, former professor of philosophy in Robert College and the American College for Girls in Istanbul, and author of *The New Turks,* for helping me to rewrite the manuscript with regard particularly to the interests of Anglo-American readers.

Ahmed Emin Yalman

ISTANBUL, TURKEY
MAY 1, 1956

CONTENTS

ILLUSTRATIONS

MAPS

Turkey

IN MY TIME

1: THE WORLD

I WAS BORN INTO

Turkey was called the "Sick Man" of Europe for three-quarters of a century. The nickname was not out of place. The Ottoman Turkish Empire, diseased by decadence, was on its deathbed in a relatively healthy world at the turn of the twentieth century. In the first half of this century an amazing reversal took place—Turkey became a healthy nation in a relatively sick world. History chronicles many a sudden development or change as the result of technical discoveries or the growth of military power, but there is hardly another instance of a nation which has so miraculously reversed its role in the world in such a short span of time and by its own will and ingenuity. Of all this I have an inside story to tell.

I am a Turkish journalist, owner and editor of the Istanbul daily paper, the *Vatan*. It has been my fortune to share passionately in this extraordinary transition which occurred in Turkey. While the Ottoman Empire, glorious and respected in its prime but disreputable and hated in its dotage, was breathing its last, a youthful, peace-loving Turkish nation appeared as the healthy and determined heir to the estate. The great powers of the West, particularly Russia, had done everything possible to speed the Sick Man's death, but had not anticipated a healthy heir turning up to foil their plans to partition Turkey among themselves.

During such critical years, young Turkish leaders were very sensitive to every hint of promise for their country. So it was

3

that I, a Turkish student in Columbia University in 1911, took very seriously a prophecy by the French philosopher, Auguste Comte, which Professor F. H. Giddings cited in class. Comte, he said, had foretold that the most far-reaching changes in history would come through Russia and Turkey. This prophecy seems to have come true—in the case of Russia, for evil; in the case of Turkey, I think, for good. From the ruins of one of the most hated and misunderstood nations in the world, new Turkey has emerged as a truly loved and respected nation, trusted to be a stalwart partner in the building of a free and peaceful world.

For me this has meant an intense life of danger and last-minute escapes, always as a part of Turkish and world crises. The first spark of revolution was ignited in me in the 1890's, in the same town and school where, a few years earlier, another native schoolboy started on his way to become the famous Atatürk, founder of the Republic of Turkey. Over fifty years later, in 1952, an unbalanced Turkish youth, indirectly Communist-inspired, shot me because my paper was "too modern" for his quasi-religious tenets. From a bed in a hospital, where five bullets were removed from me, I saw in retrospect the strange, kaleidoscopic patterns of Turkey's career and mine. Two years later, in 1954, I returned for the sixteenth time to the United States of America, where I had received my early education in democracy. Then, Turkey had been struggling for constitutional government while still politically paralyzed by her traditional psychology of imperial despotism. This time I returned in the entourage of the first democratically elected president of the Turkish Republic, Celâl Bayar.

Despite exciting extremes in my personal experience, I share the feeling that something more than the fullness of any individual life is required for an autobiography if it is to interest more than one's self and immediate friends. But it has been my

4

destiny to share in public as well as personal ways in the development of the newborn Turkish Republic, which has already altered history and has potential importance to all the world: This seems reasonable justification for the pages that follow. I think, too, that the remarkable degree of mutual confidence achieved in Turkish-American relations, for which I can claim to have done some pioneering, may have point, as may also a Turk's-eye view of the menace of Turkey's border-neighbor, Russia, with whose threats, tactics, and wars Turkey has had the most painfully intimate experience for centuries. I am glad to be able to present these, along with direct observations on other world powers, from the angle of responsible journalism.

To Western eyes the world into which I was born in 1888 would appear to belong in a chapter of the *Arabian Nights*. It was a shattered world always on the brink of chaos and crisis, where the new and the old, the exotic and the shabby, were in continual clash, and where international greed and palace intrigue found their most favorable breeding grounds.

Looking farther back into history, the Turks are seen in a bitter struggle for survival in their original home in Central Asia. Forced to migrate by intermittent droughts, the Turks showed remarkable vitality and dynamic energy as they wandered far and supplied various countries of Asia with royal dynasties and ruling classes. When the founders of the Ottoman Empire invaded Asia Minor in the thirteenth century because of such a period of drought, they found there a well established empire of Selçuk Turks who, moving from the deserts of Turkestan, had invaded Asia Minor in the eleventh century, established their capital in Konya, and maintained an enlightened rule in large parts of Asia Minor for two centuries. The Ottoman Turks became heirs to the Selçuk rule and proceeded to build up their own empire, not on the basis of mere passing conquest, but by means of a machinery of assimilation, tolerance, and

5

justice which offers strong resemblance to the American melting pot. Professor A. H. Lybyer, in his *The Government of the Ottoman Empire in the Time of Suleiman the Magnificent,* gives an interesting picture of the methods which enabled the Ottoman Empire to survive for centuries in much-contested territories with a most heterogeneous population.

In the seventeenth century the struggle between the forces of unselfish public service and those of self-interest, intrigue, and fanatical bigotry became ruthless. Persons fit and able to rule were still numerous, but everything was set for their elimination. Nevertheless, there were short interludes when strong men like Mustafa Köprülü, a grand vizier who died in 1689, and Mehmed Köprülü, who died in office as grand vizier in 1756, temporarily succeeded in stemming the course of downfall. In 1950, Fuad Köprülü, a worthy descendant of these Turks of high ideals, became the foreign minister of the Turkish Republic.

At the end of the seventeenth century an English clergyman said, in the introduction to a book he wrote on Turkey, "God can perform all sorts of miracles, but even God cannot achieve the miracle of making Turkey survive for another year." Yet, the miracle happened. Turkey, which had missed the impetus brought about in Western Europe by the commercial and industrial revolutions and had lost its own commercial advantages as a result of the discovery of the sea route to India, began to put forth increasingly serious efforts to adjust herself to progressive methods. By 1855, the regeneration of the country had proceeded so far that Turkey was accepted as a partner of the Western European countries in a war against reactionary and imperialistic Tsarist Russia. The peace treaty, signed in Paris in 1856, recognized Turkey as "an equal member of the European Concert of Powers."

It was then that the golden period of modern Turkish his-

6

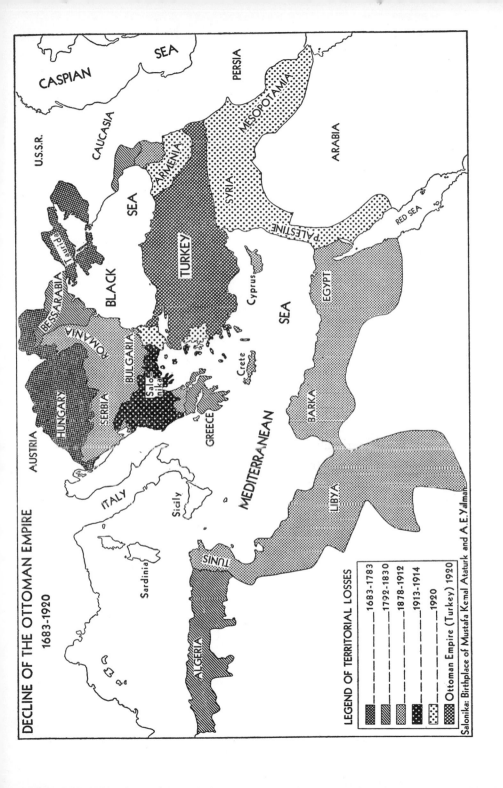

DECLINE OF THE OTTOMAN EMPIRE
1683-1920

LEGEND OF TERRITORIAL LOSSES

1683-1783
1792-1830
1878-1912
1913-1914
1920
Ottoman Empire (Turkey) 1920

Salonika: Birthplace of Mustafa Kemal Ataturk and A.E.Yalman.

tory started. Able and public-spirited men arose in every field of endeavor. A new literature, new drama, and freedom of discussion marked the period in spite of the continued abuses and intrigues of the palace. Men in public life did their best to discover gifted youths in order to train them as future statesmen, administrators, and writers. It was indeed a most animated period, full of ideals and zealous determination to realize them.

This crescendo of cultural zeal and political furor was the prelude to my lifetime. Russia was determined to become the chief heir to Turkey, whose symptoms of recovery and progress were not to Russia's liking. Intrigues in what was known as the "Eastern Question" were perpetrated in order to embarrass Turkey, to make her unpopular in the eyes of the world, and to arrest her internal progress. The vast territories owned by Turkey were strategically so important, and contained such rich natural resources, that all the great powers took a close interest in the Sick Man's health. Sometimes the powers competed with each other for exclusive heritage of the dying empire; sometimes they reached secret agreements to divide the future spoils. At any rate, the interest in the Eastern Question was so grave that it deeply affected the internal politics of the European countries involved. For instance, England was politically split by its Conservative party, which wished to keep the Ottoman Empire alive as an exclusive sphere of British influence and a protective fence along the British imperial routes of communication, and its Liberal party, which stood for an agreement with Russia to liquidate the Ottoman Empire.

At a most critical moment, when the survival of Ottoman Turkey seemed to be at stake, the reform party organized a plot and, in 1876, dethroned Sultan Abdul Aziz, a despotic ruler and willing subject to the reactionary elements actively supported by Russia. The reformers brought to the throne Prince Murad, a freemason, a sincere intellectual, and a true progressive who

8

was expected to proclaim a constitutional regime, to establish a program of equal citizenship for all the different racial inhabitants of the Empire, and to usher in a period of fundamental reforms on a secular basis by liquidating the last theocratic features of the government. Unfortunately, the gentle-minded prince, who ascended the throne as Sultan Murad V, lost his mental balance as a result of the suicide of his uncle, Abdul Aziz, the dethroned sultan. The reformers were obliged to dethrone the reliable, democratic ruler on whom they had staked all their hopes for a bright future.

The next man in the order of succession, destined to rule till 1909, was Prince Abdülhamid. He was known to have an unreliable, scheming character and despotic inclinations. However, he readily accepted all the conditions of the reformers and actually proclaimed a liberal constitution, giving citizens of all races and religions equal opportunities and proportional representation in a parliament composed of a senate and a chamber of deputies.

This despotic-minded Sultan, however, used the Russian war in 1877 for a pretext to establish his personal, absolute rule. He dissolved the parliament and exiled or eliminated all public-spirited men of vision. He formed a government mostly of corrupt men, blindly devoted to him for the advantages he lavishly bestowed upon them, while the country was more and more impoverished and doomed to retrogression.

I was born into this world of conflicts and repressed reform movements—and right in Salonika, the feverish center of the Macedonian question with all of its entanglements.

Macedonia was the area north of the Aegean Sea which included the Turkish provinces of Salonika, Monastir, and Kosova, and contained a mixed population of Turks, Albanians, Greeks, Bulgarians, Serbs, and Vlachs (Rumanians). The neighboring Balkan states were in open conflict for the possession of Mace-

9

donia. Encouraged by various great powers, their "protectors," certain native groups were not only involved in political intrigue in the area, but were engaged in actual fighting by organized bands.

At the same time, Salonika was the city where the underground revolutionary movement for Turkey's regeneration and democratization made its headquarters. The extremely stimulating atmosphere of this environment was to produce, later on, Mustafa Kemal Atatürk, one of the boldest revolutionaries of history.

Ours was an old, patriarchal type of house in the heart of Salonika. Besides the immediate family, our household included an elder brother of my father, his wife, two orphan nieces, a man servant in the part of the house called the *selâmlik,* which was for male visitors only, and several other servants, mostly liberated Negro women, in the *harem* part of the house to which only intimate members of the family and female visitors could be admitted.

Our immediate family had an addition almost every two years until we children numbered seven: four girls and three boys. My mother was not very strong, so every other year we had a wet nurse in the house, usually with her own baby. Mine had been a Circassian; my brothers and sisters had Turks, Greeks, and Albanians. The wet nurses became very attached to the family they had served and kept coming back with their children, who were called our "milk brothers" and "milk sisters." It was a relationship taken rather seriously for one's entire life. Also, in the winter months there was always a young Albanian or Bulgarian boy to do errands. These boys, without work during the winter months in their mountain homes, were brought to the city to be hired for the season.

This made quite a crowd in that house kept safe and private behind high walls and without any outside windows on the first floor. It became more crowded at certain hours of the day when the wall gates were opened to the boys and girls of the neighborhood who came to get water from the large reservoir in the garden. Salonika had no central water system in those days. Well-to-do families had acquired rights to certain private springs, but the Turkish feeling of charity was so sensitive about the free distribution of water that every house with such a water supply gave poorer families in the neighborhood a chance to share it. As everybody was in a hurry, there were constant quarrels over who would be first. The queue system was certainly not known at that time. It was necessary for a member of our family to do police duty and threaten to close the gate in order to prevent the Turks, Greeks, Bulgarians, Jews, Serbs, Vlachs, and Albanians of the neighborhood from vilifying each other and starting racial strife. We could witness the now well-known Macedonian problem enacted day after day in our own garden.

That was not the only conflict surrounding me. The strife between the old and the new was ever present in our house. My uncle, who had absolute authority in the house, was a most gentle person. He not only believed in, but actually practiced the best traditions in Islam. I never saw him lose his temper. When he had particular reasons for being angry with someone, he would say, *"Allah iyiliğini versin"* ("Let God be merciful with him"). These words sounded like an awful sort of cursing to my ears, in spite of their gentle meaning. When I tried them on boys at school as a curse, I drew a big laugh. For some time the phrase was used as a nickname for me. The other children really knew how to curse.

My uncle was punctual in his five daily prayers and observed every other religious rule. In addition, he was extremely conservative in his outlook and in his manner of life. The Turks had been obliged, in 1830, by reform-minded Sultan Mahmud II to accept Western dress in all its details except the headgear. In the latter detail, Sultan Mahmud did not dare to go from the universally worn turban (tarbôosh) directly to the European hat. He compromised by making the Turks adopt the red fez, which was of Venetian origin.

In spite of the general use of European dress since 1830, the conservative mind discovered ways and means to remain on the defensive against new styles of dress. To begin with, my uncle, by one of his inexplicable convictions, objected to white collars and ties. A colored shirt with attached collar was, for him, the extreme limit of westernization in dress to which he felt that one could go without falling into conflict with religion. According to the traditions of the prophet, he wore a beard. His views, strictly puritanical, made him presuppose a world where adventure, travel, change, excitement, and amusement had no place. Religion and the careful preparation for the eternal after-life gave him all the contentment he desired. Occasional excursions to admire God's nature were the limit of his pleasures. He objected to the theater, music, drinking, card playing, and photography—all new inventions which he considered part of Satan's world. In short, he was sort of a hard-shelled Baptist of a Muslim.

This uncle of mine had no children. Since his only child died shortly after birth, he adopted me, naming me after his deceased son. Until the age of fifteen, I slept at his bedside, constantly under the sweet influence of this saint, my inherent dynamism entirely subdued, yet without a feeling of revolt. In the simple life he led, my uncle could save money from his salary as the registrar at the deeds office, and he invested his savings in real estate. With his income from both sources, he insisted on paying all the food expenses of the large household, not allowing my father, his younger brother, to have a share in that expense, although my father always had a larger income than my uncle had.

In sharp contrast to my uncle, my father was a progressive, perhaps even a revolutionary. Following the latest fashions in dress, he wore the highest possible white collars and attractive ties. My father abhorred a beard, prayed only once or twice a year, on the occasion of special holidays, and then merely in the way of a social duty. He did not take fasting seriously and enjoyed music, the theater, innovations, adventure, change, and travel. Unlike my uncle, he ridiculed the prejudice against photographs and kept a large assortment of pictures of himself, his children, and his friends. At the early age of seventeen he, with a few friends of his age, had taken the initiative of establishing a literary weekly, *Gonce-i-Edeb* (*Blossoms of Literature*), which took a veiled stand against the conservative world.

As the first child, I was quite spoiled by everybody in our well-crowded house, and I developed into a freedom-loving youngster. My worst nightmare was the prospect of school. I simply refused to go in spite of the gorgeous ceremony arranged at that time for school beginners. I was warned that I would become a *hamal* (a porter bent double under incredibly heavy loads on his back) if I did not attend school. I immediately seized this opportunity to declare that my great ambition in life was to become a *hamal,* so I did not need to go to school. One day my mother's old Negro nurse, whom we all called "grandma," seized me by force and dragged me to a primary school, where I remained for one year; then for four years in a more progressive school. After that I was made to enroll in a military academy where my father was a teacher.

13

2: DOWN

WITH THE SULTAN

"**L**ONG LIVE the Sultan!" Three hundred of us stood at attention under the Turkish sky.

"Long live the Sultan!" One more cry to go, and school would be over for the day.

"Long live the Sultan!" The officer of the day blew his whistle, and boys in navy blue tunics ran in all directions.

This was in the military preparatory school in Salonika. I was a pupil in the very school where that genius, Mustafa, later known under the names of Mustafa Kemal, Gazi, and Atatürk, had received his primary education a few years before.

The daily routine of shouting "Long live the Sultan!" did not mean anything to most of us. It was just the mechanical ending of another day.

It did mean something to a few of us, I discovered, when I heard a small boy whisper, "Down with the Sultan!" instead of shouting the prescribed salute. He was a melancholy boy. I had an affection for him because of his sad looks and because he was without friends, and I often sought his company. I felt excited about that radical whisper of my friend. Vaguely aware that it meant something terrible, I related the incident to my father, who was one of the few civilian teachers at the school.

"Don't repeat it to anybody else," he said. "It will be dangerous for the boy, dangerous for all of us. The father of that boy is exiled by the Sultan. That's why he feels that way."

Exiled? I knew about a cousin of my mother's who also was exiled. Then I knew vaguely about "secret and dangerous books." I had heard, too, of "secret and pernicious papers." At the age of nine, my mind grasped the idea that there were two separate worlds inside my country. One world pretended abject homage to the Sultan and lavishly distributed titles, decorations, and red plush honors. The other world despised the Sultan and secretly read books and papers written against him. Frequently the offenders were caught and exiled. Often there were little children, like my friend, who suffered, too, and became bitterly aware of the widening breach between the two different worlds.

I saw one thing clearly. The world of the Sultan was based on lies. They made us lie when we shouted, "Long Live the Sultan!" three times every day. There was pretense all around us. In those days (1897–1908), Salonika was the center of Macedonian terrorism. There were endless successions of "bomb incidents," mainly organized by Bulgarian terrorists to undermine Turkish rule in Macedonia and to prepare the ground for a Bulgarian invasion. There were also continual plots and armed encounters with terrorists inside the city. Such incidents, which all the inhabitants witnessed, were reflected by the official paper of the city in flowery paragraphs such as,

Admirable public order prevails in the province of Salonika due to the unceasing bounty bestowed on this country by our august sovereign, Sultan Abdülhamid II, our unequalled benefactor, the shadow of God on earth.

Before I was much older, I had learned to decipher the simple code. The length of the paragraph was in direct proportion to the enormity of the incident. A first-class bombing or other trouble on a really grand scale would pull as many as four or five columns of superlatives describing "the unparalleled bounty of the Sultan."

None of us saw the political struggle and ferment clearly at that time. Only later were we able to discern the true proportions of the conflict. Here was a class desperately defending an inherited ornamental existence, pivoting around and depending on the Sultan and his princes. The members of this class were determined to continue their arbitrary rule, their splendor, and their exotic physical pleasures. They intended to allow no moralist interference. Although legally prohibited, slavery flourished in the palace in a shameless form. Millions of people were enslaved to satisfy a few men's lust for debauchery and pomp. A feudal system, based on service and favors, functioned throughout the palace and the government. In its fight for survival, the palace frequently stimulated jealousies among foreign powers. The silence of newspapers and public men in some countries was bought with money, concessions, and decorations. This machinery was always geared to meet an immediate crisis; tomorrow could take care of itself.

Dangerous as it was and futile as it seemed, there were even then public-spirited men fighting against the Sultan and his system. Since 1878, most of them had been forced to live and carry on their activities outside of Turkey. In Paris, London, Geneva, and Egypt, they wrote and published books and papers which were secretly poured into the country in a steady stream, bringing fresh vitality to the discouraged groups of thinking people at home. Novels, plays, poems, and historical works which had been published by forceful and cultivated men of letters in the interlude of comparative freedom between 1865 and 1876, the works of men like Şinasi, Nâmık Kemal, and Ziya, were read secretly and often memorized.

When Abdülhamid II came to power in 1876, arbitrary rule had triumphed over freedom of the press. Many popular journalists had died in exile, hardly realizing that their works would be read secretly in later years and would inspire and encourage an increasing number of young men to take their place in opposition to the Sultan and in defiance of his shrewd spy system. Some of the new fighters escaped to foreign countries. Others, less fortunate, were exiled to distant provinces of the empire. Since no paper was allowed to political prisoners en route to exile, they covered the walls of wayside inns in Asia Minor with their poems and songs. Successive occupants of the rooms in these inns learned the poems and songs by heart and carried them to the most distant corners of Asia Minor.

During the reign of terror in Istanbul there was one poet who, in spite of the intricate spy organization and the system of arbitrary exile, gave continual secret expression to his disgust for the palace rule in his poems. He was Tevfik Fikret, the widely loved and esteemed poet, who was professor of Turkish language and literature in Robert College (the American college established in Turkey in 1863). His position in an American institution saved him from persecution. Abdülhamid preferred not to attract foreigners' attention to his baiting of liberal thinkers. Fikret's poem, "Fog," described the despotic regime vividly; and, secretly whispered, the poem found an enormous audience.

I continued to breathe this atmosphere of revolt. My father had started, in 1897, to publish the literary weekly *Mutalea* (*Contemplation*). Tevfik Fikret and other poets preferred to send their best poems to this weekly because the censorship was milder in Salonika. This gave my father an opportunity to remain in close contact with these men of advanced modern views, and he often repeated in my presence their utterances against the misrule of the Sultan. After one of his trips to Istanbul, he came back with a poem by Tevfik Fikret intended for secret circulation and written in the poet's handwriting. Fikret's poem, titled "What Is the Use?," related how he had been invited to the palace and warned to forget about progress and to keep to the old path. The palace favorites kept saying: "What is the use of having schools, books, science, hospitals, and factories for this impermanent existence in a temporal world?" The poet ended by saying: "And what is the use of having you, your state, and all this worldly existence, as long as they mean only darkness, slavery, misery, and humiliation?"

This autographed poem soon disappeared. I hid it so that I, too, could have a revolutionary secret. I rejoiced in being the possessor of a "pernicious, dangerous paper." I soon gave up all sorts of games and concentrated my whole interest on publishing a weekly paper of my own. I named it *The Intention* and spent my holidays in writing it by hand. The paper stated that it was published in the printing plant of Hand-Thumb and Company. It contained poems, political articles, and a serial— all, of course, with little sense and coherence. However, I had my subscribers in the family and, as a by-product, a feeling of independence and delight in "earning" my pocket money.

I relate these incidents not to pretend that I was a promising lad, but just to indicate the stimulus at work in the life of a Turkish boy on the eve of the twentieth century, in the very environment where Atatürk was born and where he was exposed to the all-important influences of his life.

I was carried away by the revolutionary undercurrents, although I was only an average boy. As to Atatürk, he was an incomparable exception, a huge force by himself. If men can be classified from the point of view of being good and bad conductors of social energy, it must be stated that Atatürk was a unique conductor. At an early age he fully absorbed and assimilated the spirit of revolt and the dynamism preached in the patriotic poems of Nâmık Kemal and Tevfik Fikret. He absorbed all the stimulation in the air of our native city of Salonika and became a magnet for all the forces of regeneration. His personality continued to grow and grow under the pressure of cataclysmic social events.

I had to leave school just two months before graduation. I had a nervous breakdown. In the military school the stimulation to work, the highly competitive atmosphere, together with the consequences of depriving myself of games in the open air in order to write my paper, *Intention,* and to read all sorts of books, proved too much of a burden for a youngster's constitution. The family doctor recommended that I be sent to one of the foreign schools in Turkey.

In the meantime, Turkey's victory in the Turkish-Greek War of 1897, caused by the agitations and revolts sustained by the agents of the Greek government on Crete (then a Turkish possession) with a view to appropriating the island, had been an easy one. After the war the Sultan became more despotic than ever, and the publication of any literary work was strictly forbidden. Forced to close his paper, my father moved to Istanbul, alone at first; then had his entire family follow him. I spent the next six years at the German school in Istanbul.

The atmosphere in Istanbul was quite different from that of Salonika. The system of espionage in Istanbul was such that everybody lived as quietly as possible. Only the professional revolutionary dared to read forbidden books or express an opinion in public about the misrule in the country.

There were few Turks in my school. The competition with non-Turks was very keen. I felt almost transplanted to a foreign environment, so I concentrated on the school work. Besides, I now felt much more like a boy and took part in games without entering in my diary in the evenings, "Shame! A day wasted in playing!" as I did when I went to the military school.

As soon as I finished the German school in 1907, I was lucky enough to find the best possible post for observing conditions in the country: I became a journalist. My impatience to enter newspaper work was such that, after receiving my diploma, I could not wait until the end of the ceremonies. With a letter of introduction from Hüseyin Cahid Yalçín, now the dean of Turkish journalism, I scurried off to the two leading newspapers of the day. The *İkdam* explained that they had no place for children, but the *Sabah* consented, in spite of my eighteen years, to try me as a translator of English, which I had learned in the German school.

In those days nobody in Turkey thought of making a living by journalism alone. Every journalist had a secondary occupation to help pad his income. I found a place in the translation bureau of the Ministry of Foreign Affairs. At the same time, I enrolled in law school. So I had many opportunities to view from various angles the disintegration of Abdülhamid's authority and the impatience of the great powers (mainly Russia, Great Britain, France, Austria-Hungary, and Italy) to get their share of the crumbling empire as soon as possible. In the meantime, Germany had assumed the role played formerly by Great Britain, that of trying to maintain the Ottoman Empire for its own exclusive sphere of influence.

For a year (1907–1908), I had a unique journalistic experience under the most trying conditions, for not only were we subjected to strict official censorship, but to censorship of the censors. The work of the second series of censors was further scrutinized by palace officials and spies, who were eager to discover material for highly prized secret reports and new favors.

In spite of these conditions, the journalists themselves were staunch idealists who resorted to all sorts of devices to make the reader read between the lines and to foment a secret spirit of revolt. None of them would write a single word in praise of Abdülhamid, for they considered this to be dirty work. Each paper employed two special men to do the "dirty work." The inside life of a newspaper afforded the most enlightened schooling a young man could hope to find in those days. Several of my colleagues on the paper were connected with secret Young-

Turkish (Young Turk Committee of Union and Progress) activities. Personal sufferers at the hands of the palace, dignitaries, and spies, they knew how to describe vividly the conditions in the country. From them I received the proper training for hating despotism in its manifold forms.

On July 24, 1908, the Turkish papers published, without headlines, without any display, an official notice of three lines to the effect that orders had been given for the proper authorities to proceed to parliamentary elections. This was the way Sultan Abdülhamid announced to the public his surrender to the rebellious Young Turks, so named because they were trying to regenerate the old Empire by democratic reforms. As the great mass of the Turkish population had not been informed of the revolution in the western sections of European Turkey, the subversive activities of the Young Turk organizations outside of Turkey and the Young Turk Committee of Union and Progress, which had the bit in its teeth, the news came to them like a bolt from the clear sky. Was it safe for them to believe that an era of liberty had dawned? Would it not be dangerous to open their long-sealed mouths?

The official yearbook of the Ottoman Empire had kept publishing scrupulously, year after year, the charter of the short-lived constitution granted to the people in 1876. This allowed Sultan Abdülhamid to claim that he was living up to his initial oath inasmuch as constitutional rule existed in Turkey officially, but was just indefinitely suspended because "the people were not yet ripe for it."

In the meantime, the Young Turks, mostly outside of Turkey, had kept fomenting the spirit of revolt in underground and subversive activities. The first Young Turk paper, *Hürriyet* (*Liberty*), started in 1862 in London, was followed by others in different European capitals, all smuggled into Turkey by taking advantage of the foreign post offices in Turkey (British,

21

French, Austrian, Russian, German, Italian) which, under the system of "capitulations," independently handled their respective mails. Originally a privilege granted to French residents by Sultan Süleyman I in the sixteenth century, this system was subsequently extended to all major nations, first by charters voluntarily signed as an act of hospitality, then more and more reluctantly under foreign pressure on the weakening Ottoman government. Although this system was useful to Turkish reformers, for the purpose of smuggling in revolutionary literature, the abolition of the "capitulations" was one of the objects of the Young Turks, because these made foreigners a privileged class, exempt from taxation and under the sole jurisdiction of their own consular courts.

It was the fashion among patriots in the Turkish university to carry on secret communication with Young Turk revolutionary committees outside of the country, the medical faculty becoming the stronghold of the spirit of revolt. This ferment, however, produced no direct results in the capital. The effective blow came from the European provinces of Turkey. There, military officers and public servants, many of whom were also Young Turks, witnessed the bloody strife between Bulgarian, Serb, Greek, and Rumanian bands, who were fighting both against each other and against the Turkish authorities. The Turks caught their fighting spirit and learned some of their methods. International intervention in Macedonia, where a control commission had been established and a *gendarmerie* reform launched under the supervision of officers from small neutral countries, had created in Salonika a relatively free environment favorable for secret organizations. The prosperous, foreign Free Masonic Lodges afforded convenient opportunities for meeting. The British policy, which had been swinging between opposite attitudes towards Russian aggression, one of moral resistance

22

and one of surrender in return for material advantages, again swung suddenly towards complete surrender to Russian aspiration at the meeting between the Russian and British rulers at Reval in 1907. Turkish patriots decided that the hour of action could not be delayed, since the danger of dismemberment was thus added to the internal troubles. As the first gesture, several military units retired to the mountains. The entire army in that region followed suit. The Sultan decided not to accept a civil war; he appeared to surrender to the demands for democratic government, but he was hardly sincere, and, if left to himself, would have tried to get by with mere words.

We journalists decided to take open action against this hypocrisy and to electrify the public. We staged a small revolution of our own in Istanbul. Famous writers in disfavor with the Sultan were all invited to write patriotic poems and articles welcoming the new liberty. We held the first street demonstrations, called a meeting of all sorts of writers, and organized a press association. Decisions were made immediately to communicate to the public the excitement of the new era. We spent the night in newspaper offices without sleep. The censors, who came there timidly and sheepishly, were told in unmistakable terms that their shameful role had ended.

The papers which appeared on July 25 were nothing but a fervent outcry of joy. The effect was amazing. The sleeping city became at once ablaze with excitement and enthusiasm. The streets were filled with noisy crowds, listening joyfully to revolutionary speeches. People belonging to different races and religions took delight in fraternizing with one another. The slow flat presses could not publish enough copies, and the demand was such that a paper, ordinarily costing one cent, sold for as much as forty cents.

On the following day the enthusiasm increased. A general

craze for self-expression seemed to spring up. Everyone was inclined to celebrate the "end of the nightmare of despotism and oppression" by speaking and writing prolifically.

The third day of the revolution I found myself transferred to the *Yeni-Gazete,* a newly established and sensational daily. I advanced rapidly on that paper. It took only months to be promoted from translator to assistant news editor, then to chief editorial writer. At twenty I was managing its editorial policy. The paper soon turned out to be one of radical opposition to the Young Turk Committee of Union and Progress, because the latter early developed a new sort of dictatorship as "saviors of the nation and guardians of its liberty." The magical metamorphosis expected from the proclamation of a constitution had not materialized. The Young Turk revolutionaries deposed Sultan Abdülhamid in 1909, and seized control of public powers. But the three who took the lead, Cemal, Enver, and Talaat, and their government soon became more and more unpopular and, in turn, displayed despotic tendencies.

I was terribly attached to the paper. As a very bashful man, it was the only love of my youth. That love was misplaced. Following the French tradition of venality and the example of some other Turkish papers, *Yeni Gazete* soon gave up its idealistic character and accepted money from foreign sources for unpatriotic aid to powers eager to prey on Turkey at any hour of need or panic. The proprietor, a glittering personality of Bohemian inclinations, became very unscrupulous indeed. He did not mind receiving money from conflicting sources at the same time, but the paper was divided into watertight compartments. The "special stuff," written to earn the foreign subsidies, was taken care of by a man who called himself the "political director" of the paper and who received a good share of the money. We, the innocent journalists, kept pursuing lofty ideals in other sections of the paper.

During the years following the Young Turk revolution, I went to Italy with a large group of Turkish politicians, journalists, and businessmen. We had been invited by the Italian Colonial Institute, which received us with lavish hospitality, sending a luxurious ship to take us to Italy and bring us back. We traveled in special trains and received as much honor and attention as royalty. Everywhere there were large crowds ready to cry, "Long live Young Turkey." It came out later that the whole trip had been arranged by Italy, as part of fifth column work, to fool us regarding Italian designs on Tripoli in Africa, then a Turkish possession. The idea was to give us a false sense of security and make us withdraw our troops from Tripoli, which Italy was about to attack. I was fooled with many others. I came back to write article after article about the peaceful intentions of Italy. As a result of the general press campaign, the Turkish government considered it safe to retire the bulk of the military contingents in Tripoli. As soon as this was done, Italy attacked without even bothering to invent an excuse, and fighting ensued. It was the beginning of World War I, just as the Japanese aggression in Manchukuo was the beginning of World War II.

3 : AMERICAN-TRAINED

JOURNALIST

THE LOCALE for my observations was suddenly changed from an Istanbul newspaper office to Columbia University in New York City. This is how it happened. The responsibility of political direction of an opposition newspaper in a chaotic country proved to be a burden too heavy for a young man of my age and experience. In addition, I was studying at the law school and still held my position in the Ministry of Foreign Affairs, where I made translations for the president of the senate. Translating the internal regulations of England's House of Lords was one of the dull tasks which seemed torture to me in my busy life. In order to do justice to all my duties, I was drawing on the very capital of my health. Moreover, I was earning too much money for my age, and I had some "friends" all too ready to teach me how to spend it. My work was bringing diminishing returns in things worth more than money, for I was on the way to physical and mental collapse.

Just at that time, Columbia University, displaying special interest in the Young Turk experiment with constitutional government, announced five scholarships for Turks. The Turkish government held competitive examinations for these scholarships. Without hesitation I entered the examinations, recognizing this as an opportunity to make a fresh start and to equip myself for a more efficient newspaper career. We five winners left for America in February, 1911. Three and one-half delightful years in America followed while acquiring a useful academic background and an inside view of American life, which contributed greatly to my efforts later for closer Turkish-American relations.

I say most gratefully that America gave me more valuable contacts and experiences than many foreign students are lucky enough to receive, and these contacts proved a sound foundation for development of my understanding of America in subsequent visits. It was my good fortune to study under F. H. Giddings, professor of sociology; James Harvey Robinson and J. M. Shotwell, professors of history; and Talcott Williams, dean of the Pulitzer School of Journalism, four penetrating minds with broad outlooks. Turkey has a legend about an angel named *Hızır* who rescues people when they least expect it. To me, each of these professors was an American *Hızır*.

Professor Shotwell gave me two invaluable keys to the gates of knowledge—a purely scientific approach to religion and a vivid sense of economic factors in history—both of which enabled me later to grasp certain basic problems of my country, where religious authority and superstition have stubbornly resisted change, and where economic leadership had been left almost wholly to the minority non-Turkish population. Professor Giddings, with whom I did my major work in sociology, inspired me with rational views of past ages and future possibilities which later often rescued me from falling into the errors of shortened perspectives and emotional irrationalism, always imminent in crises such as my country has undergone in my lifetime. From Professor Robinson, who did not hesitate on occasion to use his independent views to shock his youthful hearers, even at religious rallies, I learned how to disturb convictions, not destructively but constructively.

My chief *Hızır* was Professor Williams. He himself had been born in Turkey and had lived there for sixteen years, and the opportunities he arranged for me to see American life were part of his service to the country of his birth. He sent me, in his stead, to conventions of the National Editorial Association at Colorado Springs and Houston, in order to put me in touch with small-town journalists; and, during my vacations, he arranged for me to spend several days with many first-rank American newspapers. Thus he opened the way for me to visit many communities and, also, introduced me to many visitors of note in his own home.

Those were not the days when nearly a thousand Turkish students were studying in scores of American universities, as was the case after World War II. This was before World War I, when we five Turks, four Muslims and one Greek Orthodox, were literally a curiosity to Americans. Consequently our experiences were both amusing and enlightening. We had landed in America feeling like hunters in a world of new ideas. Soon, however, we had the queer sensation of being hunted ourselves. Consider these experiences: We were told that it was our duty to attend a World Students' Conference in Pocono Pines, Pennsylvania. Not wanting to fail in our duty, we went to Pocono Pines, where we quickly gained the impression that the conference was a highly organized hunting party for Turkish, Syrian, Greek, Chinese, and Hindu souls, with a special premium for capturing Muslim souls. After several days of church services five or six times each day, we Turks played hooky one fine day and picnicked on an island, but were called to account for our desertion. We confessed that we had had more religion than we could take. The chief, in our presence, chided the assistant in special charge of Turkish souls, saying, "You have offered these fellows more of Jesus than they could digest in one dose." The chief admonished him to dilute the "dose" with better understanding of our own interests, in order to make it easier for us to assimilate it.

This lesson on the "proper dose of Jesus" helped me later to provide digestible doses of new ideas for my readers. The soul hunters demonstrated an intense devotion and sincere zeal, from which we gained many a good pointer on how to intensify our efforts later for causes in our own country.

Another year, in company with Professor Williams, I attended the Student Volunteer Convention at Kansas City, Missouri. There I saw thousands of students assembled for religious conquest. Islamic areas, painted in black on huge maps, were the special objectives. The capture of Muslim souls seemed to be very costly in effort and money per unit. The great fundamentalist of the day, William Jennings Bryan, then secretary of state, came in person to offer the students an "invincible" argument to silence skeptics. Of those skeptics not immediately convinced by Biblical miracles, the soul hunters should ask, "How about the black cow eating green grass to produce white milk?" Even medical students of that day found the argument convincing. Pioneers such as Dr. Samuel Zwemer, one of the most famous missionaries to Islam, who entered the field in Syria in 1890, vehemently incited the students to undertake personal conquest. Yet when I met Dr. Zwemer personally, he smilingly asked me, "Don't you feel sure that Jesus and Muhammad greet each other cordially when they meet in heaven?"

Other speakers warned the "conquerors" against succumbing to the sorrow of Muslim families broken by the conversion of one or two members while the rest stayed loyal to their old faith. This attitude disturbed me, and years later I was reminded of it, by contrast, in a conversation with an Armenian Christian, Mr. Ohannes Ferid, then eighty-six years of age and retired from a high post in Turkish public service. In his youth in his home town, Aintab, he had taken lessons from a Muslim religious teacher, Hasırcıoğlu, and was so deeply impressed that he decided to become a Muslim. His teacher's reply was, "If you do so, I will never again allow you to kiss my hand as your teacher. All religions can be good instruments of salvation. Conversion only means disrupting family ties and causing sorrow to those who brought you up and love you."

My American teacher, Professor Williams, by his personal example of devotion and tolerance in private and public life, produced in me a lifelong distaste for all abuses of religion which engender discrimination, intolerance, and hatred. It had been far from his mind to influence me religiously when he took me to the Student Volunteer Convention and gave me behind-the-scenes glimpses there. He considered it part of my journalistic training; and his ideals of clean, independent, fearless journalism have carried me through many conflicts with authorities in my own career.

The cliché, "Terrible Turk," frequently tested our tolerance and humor as students in America, but on one occasion we were happily able to turn it to good advantage. Ahmet Sükrü Esmer, who many years later established and developed the Turkish Information Office in New York City, joined me for a short vacation in the town of Castine, Maine. The population then was about two thousand. Most of the residents apparently felt that the invasion of two Terrible Turks, rumored in advance, warranted a run on the hardware store for locks for house doors and even for the town's one-cell jail, hitherto unlocked. We, however, were already in Castine, living unobtrusively. The Congregational minister's wife, Mrs. Patterson, was surprised to find two young men sitting on a hillside reading a Sunday paper article about the American College for Girls in Istanbul. She was amazed further to find that they were interested in this article because they were the Terrible Turks. She took the risk of inviting this terrible pair to a missionary tea at her home, where she also had invited an Armenian girl from Boston to tell of the plight of the Armenians in Turkey.

When we arrived at her house, there was apparent tension among the guests, especially some sturdy youths protectively solicitous for the Armenian girl meeting Turks unexpectedly. Much more unexpectedly, she broke through their line and ran to us, laughing and talking Turkish. She told us that she had pretended fear so that we could surprise them. This gave all three of us the opportunity to explain that the worst troubles between Armenians and Turks had been provoked by foreign powers, mainly by Tsarist Russia, in order to set the stage for conquest to "protect the Christians." We told them that in the Aintab region in southern Turkey, where her family had lived, interreligious exchange had so united us against bigotry that we shared a common stock of anecdotes ridiculing it, whether on the part of Muslim *hoca* (teacher), Christian priest, or Jewish rabbi.

If there had been no foreign interference, and if a man with Atatürk's vision had held the reins a century sooner, millions of Armenians, Greeks, and Arabs would still be in Turkey, where their families had lived for untold generations, and they would be pursuing a peaceful common course. The Balkan states, temporarily freed from foreign interference between the two world wars, recognized that their hatreds of each other had been foreign importations, that in reality they had similar mentalities and common sources of pleasures and pains, and that they could co-operate for peaceful aims. They began to fulfill this hope when they founded the Balkan Entente, in 1934, which might have led to federal union if World War II had not revived the distorted relations known as the Eastern Question. But, before World War I, when the Armenian girl was helping two young Turks to explain their common troubles to Americans in a Maine parsonage, the Eastern Question was acute. The two Balkan wars, 1912–13, had been stirred up, and Turkey had lost my native province of Salonika and the adjoining provinces;

and then had regained a very small fraction of territory around the ancient Ottoman capital of Edirne (Adrianople).

The Eastern Question so interested one of the guests at the tea in Castine, a Mr. Kimball from Wichita, Kansas, that he and his wife invited me to visit them in Kansas. Wichita became my second home, where I spent most of my spare time in the United States. I attended club, church, and school meetings, became an active member of the Monday Club, which discussed social problems, and was a frequent visitor at the *Wichita Eagle*. Whenever I saw the sign at the railroad station, "Watch Wichita Win," I shared the citizens' pride and enthusiasm. Years later, when I revisited Wichita, I was most proud to see that Wichita had "won"; it had boomed into a thriving aeronautic center.

I left America, on the eve of World War I, with a store of brand-new ideas, intent on applying them for the benefit of the Young Turk regime. The horizon for Turkey and for a crusading journalist in Turkey appeared bright. The two Balkan wars were just over. The sweeping defeat of Turkey in Macedonia had proved to all Turks that, in spite of the sop to their pride in regaining Edirne, something was wrong with their system. The air was full of self-criticism. New ideas seemed to be welcome. My clear vision of the future, however, was soon clouded by the terrible tragedy of World War I.

To even a very young man familiar with Balkan conditions, the news of the murder of the Austrian crown prince by a Serbian terrorist was sensational. The news reached me on shipboard. On landing, I hastened to Paris, where I spent a month with my sister and my brother-in-law, who was the Turkish consul general there. I was present at the Bastille Day parade of that July, 1914, during the day-by-day suspense under the gathering war clouds which broke in that very month. The French gave me the impression of feeble shadows of human beings whose cheer and energy had all been sapped. I found a different situation when I reached Berlin. There the tone was aggressive and arrogant. The people's wild enthusiasm for a fight could almost be touched by hand. I happened to be at Potsdammer Platz when mobilization was proclaimed. One rarely observes individual enthusiasm so compounded in a mass that nothing could stem or contain its volcanic force.

On an Italian ship on the Mediterranean Sea, as one of the many persons taking the last chance to reach home after railway connections across Serbia to Turkey had been cut, I had my first glimpse of combat. A little south of Greece I saw shots fired by some English war craft at a fleeing German cruiser which easily outdistanced its pursuers. I was not aware at the moment that this unimpressive display was decisive in the fate of Turkey and, to some extent, in the entire course of history. The incident was serious because anti-British feeling had become intense in Turkey in 1914, when England sequestered for her own use two warships under construction for Turkey in British shipyards. The Turks had raised the money for those ships by popular subscription, and British refusal to deliver them on completion was deeply resented. Germany promptly offered two of her cruisers, the *Goeben* and the *Breslau,* and I had witnessed the *Goeben*'s escape from British guns on her way to Turkey. The Turks enthusiastically added the German cruisers to the Turkish fleet by technical "purchase." Without the gift of the *Goeben* and *Breslau,* Enver Pasha, one of the leading instigators of the Young Turk revolution of 1908, who later took office as minister of war at the age of twenty-six and was the driving spirit of the small war party in Turkey, would not have found the courage to force the country into the war as a satellite of Germany. The Dardanelles would have remained open, giving an opportunity for free communication between the Western powers and Russia.

Hence huge Allied forces, pinned down by two million Turkish fighters on distant fronts, could have been concentrated against Germany and Austria.

When I arrived in Turkey, I could see no trace of the peaceful paths of opportunity about which I had dreamed during my years in America. In their place I seemed to see a single dark field of folly and stupidity. To illustrate this I need merely recite my own experience in the ensuing few months. On the day I arrived, I joined the new courses for reserve officers in the superior military school, and my service lasted that day only. Nomination to an assistant professorship of philosophy at the University of Istanbul immediately exempted me from military service. All teachers had exemption. The stupidity in my case was that when I personally informed the minister of education that I had not studied philosophy in America but had studied sociology, statistics, and history, he remarked to a visitor present, "Young men today want to teach only what they already know and are too lazy to try teaching what they don't know." Then he granted me this concession: "I will not nullify your assistant professorship in philosophy at the university but will add sociology there, and also appoint you professor of statistics at the School of Civil Service. But there will be no additional salary."

The professorial salary was about $40 a month, whereas the same government department had provided me with $100 a month as a scholarship student in America! But since only 50 per cent of each salary was paid during the war, my actual salary was $20 a month. I had ample excuse to supplement it by resuming newspaper work. However, the teaching afforded me close association with Ziya Gökalp, who then occupied the chair of sociology and had almost the vision and role of a Biblical prophet in the Young Turk revolution. He was one of the most influential members of the central council of the Union and Progress party which ruled wartime Turkey, largely in secret

34

for not even the party knew many of its council's decisions. To Ziya Gökalp, more than to any other one man, belongs the credit of producing both historical facts and the inspiration to revive native pride in the early traditions of Turkish culture and constructive Turkish rule. This was the pride which Atatürk later employed so successfully in uniting the Turks to save their heritage when it was slipping from the Sick Man's grip into the avaricious hands of the great powers.

The organ of the Union and Progress party was the Istanbul daily, the *Tanin,* and within a few months I became the news editor of this paper. I found very little to edit beyond official communiques because the wartime scarcity of newsprint from our usual sources, Germany and Austria, had reduced the daily editions to only four small pages. Moreover, censorship was extremely strict. My job gave me hardly a taste of real journalism. My one important assignment was to ghostwrite an interview with War Minister Enver Pasha, who was actually a dictator, without even consulting him about its content. This "interview" was inspired by an alarming rumor that those exempted from military service by payment of a special, high military tax would be called to service anyway. Civilian and military authorities agreed that this must be casually and tactfully denied in a statement of Turkey's war aims and the military situation. My three column "interview," putting into the Minister's mouth the words I thought a dictator would say, was approved by him without a change. This seems to have been the chief reason that I was selected to go to Germany as the only war correspondent sent from Turkey.

4 : MY COUNTRY

AND GERMANY

 My FIRST month in Germany, May, 1915, was devoted to surveying general conditions. As a Turk, and thus the German newspapermen's only "brother-in-arms" among the foreign war correspondents, I was offered opportunities to visit the most advanced posts on any active front. This made the American correspondents in Berlin envious. Among them were United Press's Carl Ackerman, my classmate and friend from Columbia, and another friend of mine, Raymond Swing, then representing the Chicago *Daily News*.

My sector-to-sector visit of the western front began at Priest's Wood and ended in Dixmunde on the North Sea. At Priest's Wood, after a successful German attack, I first saw French prisoners being taken to the rear and the arrested life in the trenches where death stopped this one's hand raising food to his mouth and that one's hand penning a letter to his mother. The survivors acted like automatons in a sort of lethargy between life and death, while the French artillery was counterattacking the Germans in the captured trenches. Near Thiaucourt my special privilege as the guest of the division commander, who had been a German military attaché in Istanbul for many years and who felt a sentimental attachment to Turkey, enabled me to violate the rule that war correspondents should not fly. From a small observation plane I witnessed an aerial duel near Verdun. Aloft for the first time, with "harmless" clouds of flack around us, I discovered that in our fear of death the "form" matters much more than the result itself. A man may go into hysterics about one form of death and stoically face another. In a rowboat on a swelling sea, I am a person who can feel frightened to death and be unable to hide panic. But in that airplane, a target from the air and the ground, I was one of that fraternity of newspapermen who, like soldiers, can face any sacrifice for the sake of their duty. The only sensation I felt in that relatively fragile World War I plane was the joy of being able to convey vividly to the reader a firsthand impression of the soldier's danger in the air. Yet my story would live for only a few hours.

I was completely absorbed in this aerial view of war. In battle, as viewed on the ground, you faced an enemy world; it was the task of your own war machine to kill or capture as many as possible of the detestable fellows obstructing your own nation's pursuits. Death held absolute sway in the no man's land between you. In that inhuman realm of primitive barbarism, every human sentiment was out of place on either side. Seen from the air, both sides of no man's land were scenes of equal human stupidity. The men on both sides were the same unhappy instruments of their respective war machines; they had the same thoughts of home and kin, the same desire to continue their young lives to the natural end. On no man's land all petty passions and hatreds were suddenly stopped in the common brotherhood of death. The aerial view of the enemy trenches offered nothing to incite a feeling of hostility; the people there were as blind on one side as on the other. Both were trying to win something illusory while losing, every minute, values which could never be replaced.

Safely landed from this first flight, I found myself at least partly sobered from my war intoxication. The large French population in the conquered territory ceased to appear as merely

37

enslaved people. I recognized for the first time why they were going about like shadows. In defeat, they were suffering a most humiliating experience as human beings, so they made themselves unobtrusive in order to minimize contact with their conquerors. I began to seek contacts with all classes of Frenchmen where our press headquarters were, and I also visited their primary schools. It seemed to console them to meet a stranger who spoke their language and was not a German. Their apathy cleared momentarily as one or another said, "We expected you Turks to be on our side. Why are you fighting us?"

Why? If I could know it myself! I tried to explain that war is a dangerous epidemic, and we, the Sick Man, could not resist contagion. While our body was weakened by former wars and internal strife, a few individuals in our government felt free to play with our destinies without asking us, and in the face of the fact that our huge neighbor, Tsarist Russia, was an enemy sworn to absorb us.

Next, I set myself to studying the admirable organization of the German commissariat. Going methodically from large supply centers to the local units, I saw everywhere German ingenuity carried to perfection. Then, I went into Belgium, starting at Thielt, the army headquarters of the crown prince of Wurtemburg. There, for the first time, I could observe German political war measures. Fraternization with the Flemish population was fully encouraged for the purpose of rendering future absorption into Germany "voluntary and easy." After a canal trip to see the short Belgian front, I went to Brussels to obtain an interview with General Bussing.

In contrast to the French area, which was just a slice dismembered from the mother country, I found Belgium a complete living organism. Instead of lifeless shadows like those in France, these unsubdued but proud people walked in the open. I went to a vaudeville show and, to my surprise, found that every

*Ahmed Emin Yalman as a political hostage
on Malta. The beard was the fashion
among the political prisoners.*

A group of opposition journalists tried in 1925
before an extraordinary court
for "undermining the authority of the government."

act had satirical quips against the conquerors and reassertions of the Belgian national spirit which the audience applauded enthusiastically. The whole show was an open demonstration against the German occupation. I congratulated one of General Bussing's aides, a well-known German novelist, on the tolerant attitude of the German authorities.

"The Belgians are great children," he replied. "Let them demonstrate and feel important and self-satisfied. That eases the pressure and saves us many serious troubles."

In Brussels I tried to see Herbert Hoover, there in charge of American war relief, but his secretary informed me that the absolute neutrality of Mr. Hoover's position did not permit contact with journalists. I finally managed to meet Mr. Hoover in America twenty-seven years later. Carl Ackerman, who had become the dean of the Columbia Graduate School of Journalism, obtained a ten-minute appointment for me. After we started to talk about world problems, Mr. Hoover, by then a former president of the United States, gave me four hours of his time, canceling all his morning appointments.

From Belgium I rushed east to be in Warsaw on the very day of its occupation. On the eastern front, I found that I, as the Turkish correspondent who had been a privileged and escorted guest on the western front, had to take my chances as a "military person" with the rest of the foreign correspondents and find my own transportation in a military train slowed by track repairs after Russian destruction, so I reached Warsaw three days after the occupation. At that stage of World War I, the city could not determine whether the Germans had freed it from the Russian yoke to stay free or simply applied a new yoke to wear. At any rate, gay promenaders strolled freely in the streets, and some restaurants served, without ration cards, all you cared to eat. After a rugged trip with the other correspondents, by truck or afoot like common soldiers, sharing their field rations and their fatigue, we entered Fort Novogeorgievsk with the spearhead regiment. The fort, considered impregnable, fell with almost no fight. Several generals and sixty thousand men were made prisoners.

The first sight there appalled us. More than one thousand horses had been herded together and machine-gunned to keep the Germans from using them. Dead, wounded, and terrified horses were revolting evidence of butchery. So were the similarly butchered geese. The ammunition stores were, of course, destroyed. Only men, apparently, had not been slaughtered; any human casualties appeared to be the result of vodka. The mingling of Russian and German officers was too unusual and interesting for us to admit our fatigue and leave. I saw there clearly that men and materials are not the chief factors in a fight. The will to fight and skill in the high command are the main factors; for without those, armies and equipment mean only so many prisoners and so much booty for the enemy to appropriate, or to destroy.

The next weeks passed with maximum variety and minimum comforts and a prime opportunity to study the soul of the German fighting man on whom my government was staking our national future. I witnessed a parade in the presence of Kaiser Wilhelm II, was quartered with young division staff officers, shared weary marches, wrote my fresh impressions at the cost of nights of sleep, went for a week at a time with no chance to undress or wash (but gained one chance to sleep thirty-six hours without interruption), and transferred from regiment to regiment. Finally, I was with the army of von Hindenburg in the Korno-Vilna sector. One Austrian and one German correspondent and I took a hard-earned rest in one of the best villas of Vilna, but it was soon interrupted by word from von Hindenburg himself.

The German Field Marshal had refused to receive war

correspondents. Knowing this, I had written to him, "If I go back to Turkey without an interview with you, I am sure to be hanged in front of my newspaper office." My device worked. Von Hindenburg invited me to be his personal guest at his headquarters. This was partly because he was amused, but largely for a deeper reason. He was the only German war hero popular in Turkey. His paternal personality appealed to the Turks, and he knew it. Von Hindenburg had been bombarded with presents from all classes of Turks and with invitations to visit Turkey. He seized upon my request as an occasion to convey his warm regards to his many friends in Turkey.

At dinner, on the night of my arrival, he was wearing all of his Turkish decorations. He made me sit on his left and Dr. von Dernburg, former minister of colonies just returned from a propaganda mission to New York, on his right.

He smilingly asked me,

"Is it true that you would hang before the door of your paper if you returned without speaking with me?"

"Most decidedly true," I said with great solemnity, "so now I feel like a resurrected man."

"Well," he replied, "I resurrected you to tell your readers that my heart is always with Turkey. If I ever go abroad, my first trip will be to Turkey. This I promise definitely."

Von Hindenburg liked to eat and drink and enjoyed the wide variety of rare delicacies which he received as gifts. But when I offered him a Turkish cigarette, the army chief surgeon jumped from his seat with a warning signal to the Marshal not to accept it. Von Hindenburg ignored the warning and calmly lit the cigarette.

After dinner we retired to his private rooms. We were four, including Erich Ludendorff and von Dernburg. Ludendorff had been my idol, but upon engaging in conversation with him, I immediately felt a revulsion against him. He seemed to be trying to mask extreme pride and bitter ambition under a cloak of bashfulness and reserve. His character impressed me as being very similar to that of our own dictatorially ambitious Minister of War, Enver Pasha. His first words to me were:

"At your age you should be serving at the front. Why do they let you go about as a civilian journalist?"

"I am a university teacher on leave, and all teachers in Turkey are exempted from military service."

"The very men they should not exempt!" he snorted.

Ludendorff became more friendly during the conversation and explained for the benefit of Turkish readers why final victory would be ours. I was not supposed to publish his comments, but to introduce the spirit of them into my own writings. After our short talk, during which he remained standing, he bade us all good night. Von Hindenburg, with a fatherly glance after him, said, "The poor chief! He must go and work."

We sat down and started to drink Moselle wine, von Hindenburg's favorite. I emptied glass after glass with him until three o'clock without feeling any physical effects. Keen interest proved to be far stronger than any effect of the drink. Von Hindenburg was telling his own story: how he had seen crowds of fleeing refugees when East Prussia was invaded by the Russians, and as a retired general had heard their painful story; how he had determined to fight against the invaders in any capacity; and how he was offered the management of the campaign. He was a fine raconteur and told, for example, the story of the Mazurya battle in terms of an amusing hunting tale. He spoke throughout as a good man and a good soldier—Prussian style.

Then von Dernburg started to tell about his experience in America, which turned out to be a complicated attempt at propaganda from an entirely wrong angle, although he did not know he was wrong. Instead of telling Americans in a modest way the simple story of all the Germans fighting with their backs to the wall in a blockaded country, he seemed to have proceeded in an arrogant fashion to try to incite anti-British feelings. The Americans whom he thought he influenced that way were not real ones, but mere creatures of his imagination.

In him I saw with my own eyes the type of German politician and diplomat who, despite his bustling energy, undoes the work of the soldier and plays the very game of the enemy by his blundering. In my opinion, there was just one man among the wartime diplomats who understood America well and who had a constructive view. He was von Bernstorff, who became ambassador to Turkey after being ousted from Washington. I was, at that time, the editor of the Istanbul daily, *Vakit*. My knowledge of America and the affinity of our views drew us together. During his stay of about one year in Turkey, I saw him at least once a week. We would talk for hours on end about the United States. He spoke as a scholar discussing and reinterpreting past affairs rather than as an ambassador commenting on current problems, but his interpretations shed light on current affairs.

After my weeks on the eastern front, there came days of anticipation in the south of Hungary at the headquarters of Field Marshal von Mackensen. A stoic and a puritan, this marshal wanted his officers to remain aware of the spirit of sacrifice in time of war and to keep away from every enjoyment not available also for the common soldier. The food at his mess, where he ate regularly with his officers, was hardly different from that of the common soldier. Von Mackensen paid no attention to war correspondents attached to his army, except once when he said to one of our group, a well-known German writer by the name of Gomoll:

"I recognize you. You are the son of my barber in Berlin during my days in the War Academy. You used to help your

43

father in the shop after school." Poor Gomoll did not know whether he should take this as a sign of friendship or an insult.

The general offensive against Serbia was brewing. The German aim in this large-scale operation was to establish direct contact with Bulgaria and Turkey, Germany's then weakening partners. The Turks were in a desperate position on the Dardanelles front, and the Bulgars' lukewarm interest in the war needed to be fired up. The Germans also had exaggerated hopes of importing various foodstuffs and raw materials from Turkey and Bulgaria. The stubborn and heroic Serbs, left without help by the Allies, could not be expected to withstand alone the violent German drive for any length of time, especially as there was also some Bulgarian pressure from the south. So I saw Belgrade and the northern part of Serbia conquered and pillaged.

Upon learning that, by a short trip from Ada-Kaleh, an island in the Danube River at the very point where Hungary, Serbia, and Romania meet, I could soon observe an event most important to Turkey, I sped there. The island itself peculiarly interested me because it had remained, strangely enough, a part of Turkey after all three of the countries conjoined there were freed from Ottoman rule. It was forgotten in writing some of the peace treaties; from others it was omitted purposely because no one of the interested parties would consent to let this strategic point go to either of the other two. In the hands of Turkey, but more than one hundred miles from the home country, this small island did not seem so dangerous. In physical contact with three different nations, the island resisted all outside influence and remained a living museum of the Turkey of the seventeenth century. At moments there I believed that somebody was staging a continuous historical pageant. Today, Ada-Kaleh belongs to Romania.

On the day of the promised event, I left the island and went by horseback along the Serbian shore of the Danube and came face to face with a Bulgarian advance guard from the south. At that moment no more exciting news than this could have been received by Turkey. It meant that communication between Germany and Turkey had been re-established. As the first man to travel from the north on the reopened Berlin-Istanbul road, I was granted the privilege of telegraphing this big news to Turkey, which, without ammunition, was still trying to defend this road, almost with naked bayonets alone.

In all, I made four trips to Germany during the war, returning to my own country for only brief periods between them. In the summer of 1916, again as a war correspondent, I accompanied a Turkish army corps dispatched by Enver Pasha to Galicia to help the German and Austrian armies. The Turkish soldiers found the living conditions on the Galician front a great contrast to the unspeakable privations they had suffered on the Turkish fronts. The German soldiers' rations of food, tobacco, and clothing, which the Turks shared in Galicia, were a privation for the Germans, but abundance for the Turks.

"This is not like war," several of our soldiers insisted to me. "This is a pleasure party with plenty to eat, tobacco regularly, warm clothes, and shelter, and you get attention immediately when you are wounded. What more can you expect?"

I continued my observations in Germany for a month that summer. In 1917, I revisited Germany, Austria, and Hungary, this time in a group of six Turkish editors especially invited by the German government, which had us visit the western front and Belgium and also the Tyrol front. Finally, I spent the summer of 1918 in Germany on my own initiative, to continue my study of developments.

I would like to sum up my impressions of the German war effort—whose lot our government had chosen to share. What that cost us will be apparent in a later chapter. I unhesitatingly assert that the German effort in World War I was an unsurpassed human achievement. It was heroic, efficient, well calculated, and well organized—at least during the first two years. During this period the impression was that the selfish side of human nature had been eliminated from German life. Men who did not use their bread cards, in order that others might have more, were not an exception. Men went to war without fear and faced all sorts of sacrifices readily. Families took the news of the death of their children, one after another, most stoically. The organization at the fronts and in the rear was geared to the last degree of efficiency without the slightest waste, always substituting ingeniously for materials in short supply. The transport system east, west, and south worked like a compact, well-built machine. Morale was so high that no one doubted final victory; no adverse propaganda could penetrate the German mind.

The Germans in World War I were not worse in dealing with conquered people than any others under the same circumstances. They went to the last allowable limit to exploit any country at their mercy. The limit of exploitation was set by the cultural consciousness and unseen resistance of the conquered people themselves. The Germans behaved relatively well in Belgium, as I judged not only by my observations there, but also in comparison with what I saw of the Inter-Allied occupation in Turkey after the Armistice. They showed less reserve in northern France, still less in Poland. In Serbia, the behavior of the German soldiers could not be differentiated from that of any neighboring armies. Pillage and individual excesses were more frequent there than on other fronts. Even in Turkey, an allied country, many of the Germans often acted as arrogant as in a conquered land.

After the second year of the war, you could feel a change in everything in Germany. The climax of overstressed effort had been reached and passed. An era of diminishing returns set in.

Individuals became aware that they existed apart from the group, and they tried to see to it that their families were better treated than other people. There were more and more men who thought it clever to buy or sell on the black market. As a matter of fact, supplies legally distributed were becoming more and more scarce and inferior in quality.

Given the same efficiency of organization and the same firm will for victory which existed during the first two years, Germany should have won the war in Western Europe after the Russian fronts disappeared, but it was no longer the same Germany. Germany was numbed by extreme fatigue from an exaggerated effort under big doses of political and psychological stimulants. The body did not react any more to pressure and self-discipline. Factional differences and personal rivalries became bitter again. The German defeat took the form of internal disintegration. It was not primarily a physical failure. It was rather a psychological reaction against an overinflated spirit of sacrifice and privation.

At the end of the war Germany was ready to be cured forever from militaristic diseases. The world had a unique opportunity for general disarmament and for establishing a real peace by consent of the conquered. Instead, there were shortsighted politicians who overlooked this unique chance; they kept provoking and harassing the defeated and humbled Reich until the militaristic disease had a terrible recurrence and became an uncontrollable epidemic. Without the unbelievable stupidity and shortsightedness of some foreign powers, Germany could hardly have overcome so soon its state of lethargy and discouragement.

After seeing a Germany capable of sublime effort and self-abnegation, and then a Germany sick of militarism, one cannot but deplore that energies of such a high quality should have been misdirected again towards aggression. Instead, these energies could have been channeled towards co-operation, recon-struction, and stability in a peaceful world. This constructive direction of energies would have meant a gain almost propor-tionate to the price of World War I, and would have averted the necessity of paying the greater price of World War II.

5 : I MEET

MUSTAFA KEMAL

BETWEEN my trips to Germany during the war, I naturally tried to study the ever changing situation in my own country. I also tried, through the press, to keep the Turkish people posted on the true course of the war. Therefore, imagine my excitement when, on a return trip from Germany in 1917, a fellow passenger whispered in my ear,

"You know, Mustafa Kemal is on this train."

There were reasons to whisper. Mustafa Kemal, to whom many years later a grateful National Assembly gave the family name of Atatürk (Father Turk), was already the secret war hero of Turkey. He was the one general always successful in action and hence feared by those in power. Consequently, the secret police watchfully obstructed contact with him and marked as "suspected persons" any who tried to see him.

When I heard that the great mysterious man was on the train, returning from a short cure in Karlsbad, I thought it a singular opportunity to meet him without the attention of the secret police. I went to his compartment and introduced myself as a journalist and also the son of one of his teachers in the military preparatory school in Salonika. Fortunately he was familiar with my journalistic work and vividly remembered my father as one of the few civilian teachers who had always given this exceptional pupil special attention. The conversation immediately became very cordial, and he did not hesitate to tell me his views.

The real enemies of Turkey, Mustafa Kemal explained to me, were the shortsighted men in power in Turkey, the leaders who had proven themselves incapable of recognizing facts and acting accordingly. The Young Turk triumvirate, Enver Pasha, Talaat Pasha, and Cemal, and their appointees, through their own lack of ability and perspective, had decided that Turkey could not save herself without foreign alliance. Losing sight of every essential of independence, they had committed Turkey to German command. All active chiefs on Turkey's general staff and in her army were Germans. They were running Turkish participation in the war to relieve pressure on the German fronts and to reduce the already deficient and seemingly helpless Turkey to a colony. That Turkey was bleeding too much meant nothing to the Germans, except that an enfeebled Turkey would be easier prey for them.

"Our own men in high office are gamblers, staking Turkey's destiny on the turn of the single card of final German victory," Mustafa Kemal said. "They are not aware that, at this moment, they have lost the war, because Germany has lost the initiative and even the will to succeed."

This categorical assertion startled me. My journalistic sense of responsibility to maintain national confidence and the spirit of resistance against an enemy had kept me writing about "final victory"; and I had persuaded myself that it was possible. Whether a German victory would be a Turkish victory, too, meaning the survival of an independent Turkey, was another and, to me, a startling question. Enlightened minds in Turkey, conscious of this danger, had been shelving their apprehension of the future because the chivalrous Turkish character was not attracted by the idea of forsaking an ally during a fight and making a separate peace. To hear, all of a sudden from a man who should know, that the German defeat was already certain was bitter for me. Mustafa Kemal had been convinced of this by his visit to the German front, a few months before our conversation, in company with the Turkish prince who, in 1918, became Sultan Mehmed VI. He had not hesitated to make von Ludendorff and some others feel that they were either fooling themselves or fooling the people.

Upon arrival in Turkey, Mustafa Kemal addressed a private report to Enver Pasha, the minister of war. In this report, September 20, 1917, which is an example of his clear vision and daring, he repeated all the statements he had made to me in the privacy of the train. Here are a few passages:

"There are no bonds left between the present Turkish government and the people. Our 'people' are now nearly all women, disabled men, and children. For all alike, the government is the power which insistently drives them to hunger and death. . . . Public life is full of anarchy. Each new step taken by the government increases the general hatred people feel against it. All officials accept bribes and are capable of every sort of corruption and abuse. The machinery of justice has entirely stopped. The police forces do not function. . . . Neither the people nor government employees have any confidence in the future. The will to live rids even the best and the most honest of every sort of sacred feeling. If the war lasts much longer, the whole structure of the government and dynasty, decrepit in all its parts, may suddenly fall to pieces.

"The end of the war is not near. The other side has more power to resist than ourselves. Yet the Germans are devoid of all initiative; they seem to say, 'Come and defeat us if you can.' The key to the termination of this war is not in our hands. . . . Most of our army formations are at one-fifth of their prescribed strength. The Seventh Army, our only organized force, has been shaken without firing a single shot at the enemy. . . . The

51

Fifty-ninth division, at full strength, consisted 50 per cent of men too weak to stand on their feet, and the rest were under-developed youths between seventeen and twenty and used-up men between forty-five and fifty years old. The best organized divisions lose half their numbers by desertion or sickness before they reach the front. The army cannot remedy this situation; it is the result of general conditions. . . .

"Our military police hereafter must be wholly defensive, aimed at saving the life of every soldier possible. We should not hand over a single man for foreign governments' purposes. No Germans should be employed in the service of Turkey. What is left of the Turkish army must not be endangered senselessly for the personal ambitions of a von Falkenhayn [the highest ranking German officer in Turkey]. The writer of this report is personally ready to accept any subordinate position but believes, in principle, that no German should have direct control of hundreds of thousands of Turkish lives. The Germans should not be given the means to prolong this war to the point of reducing Turkey to a colony in disguise."[1]

This foresighted leader also said: "Pessimism is a danger in itself. Positive and sweeping measures must be taken to improve the Turkish outlook. Our government's power must be redirected solely to safeguarding public interests; and private interests must be subordinated to putting in order our police forces, courts, food distribution, and economic organization. If home conditions are healthy, local defeats at the fronts cannot shake our national structure from its foundations."

The only result of this report was to increase suspicion and bad will against its author. With youthful defiance, Enver Pasha became more obstinate in his reliance on Germany. He ap-

[1] This report is quoted by Hüseyin Hüsnü in his *Yildirim Ordusu*. These passages are condensed from the English translation in Ahmed Emin (Yalman), *Turkey in the World War* (Yale University Press, 1930), 262–63.

pointed General von Falkenhayn commander of a new army group in Palestine (then a part of the shrinking Ottoman Empire), as bold proof of his indifference to Mustafa Kemal's courageous report. Enver's relations with the Germans became so close after this that the Germans started to call Turkey "Enverland." You could see "Enverland" stamped even on boxes of ammunition sent to the Turkish Army.

My talk with Mustafa Kemal on the train changed my entire outlook. Instead of feeling we were on a seaworthy ship heading towards final victory, I became aware that we were on a doomed floating wreck. The problem before us was how to salvage all possible material and moral assets.

After my career as war correspondent for *Tanin,* I had become editor in chief of *Sabah,* the morning paper on which I had started my journalistic career as a translator at eighteen. My signed stories from the various war fronts had made a sufficient name for me to become an editor in chief just two and one-half years after graduating from Columbia University. My pen was free at *Sabah.* The owner was an Armenian who had settled in the south of France after being a close palace favorite during Sultan Abdülhamid's despotic rule. The business manager of the paper was too well satisfied, when we raised the circulation from two thousand to sixteen thousand within a few months, to interfere with our editorial policies.

Thus, in a favorable position to follow the inspiration of Mustafa Kemal's views, I started in a subdued tone, raising it gradually and tactfully, to draw attention to the war abuses and their consequences. War profiteering, curtailing for the benefit of the few the narrowing opportunities to secure food, clothing, medicine, and other necessities; the breakdown of moral values as a result of bad examples among the newly rich; individual scandals in selling transportation permits; secret speculation in goods, all of which the government was supposed to have requisitioned for public benefit—all these were subjects which I methodically dealt with in an ever louder and firmer tone.

Against all expectations, this got me into no serious trouble with the government. The censors, themselves part of the exploited multitude, sympathized with our line of attack. The government, not wishing to identify itself with abuses which it pretended were against its wishes, took no action. Furthermore, I was shielded and encouraged by Ziya Gökalp, the outstanding idealist in the government circle and my chief at the university.

This exposé, however, caused my first severe conflict with private interests. A campaign purely in the public behalf was incredible to such private-interest parties, to whom altruism was a mere mask for selfish motives. Their mildest supposition was that I was seeking either personal notoriety or a profitable sale of my paper; their worst, that I was the tool of rival speculators or of enemy powers. Because they badly needed to silence me in order to continue their abominable abuses, they tried offers of material gain and invitations to join the pleasures of the newly rich, then threats and reports to the police that I was conniving with the enemy or with a secret political opposition group to undermine government authority and prestige.

Nevertheless, while the abuses continued under the impotent government of the Young Turk triumvirate and the ineffectual Sultan, an extraordinary intellectual awakening was developing in Turkey, something quite incongruous in a period of war, disintegration, and misery. Turkish idealists had long cherished a dream of "enlightened despotism"—to overcome resistance to progress by the still dominant adherents of a theocratic government controlled by religious law under a ruler who was both temporal sultan and religious khalif (caliph). A small group of enlightened Union and Progress party men, guided by Ziya Gökalp, took advantage of their all-powerful, single-party control to usher in certain fundamental reforms.

54

To begin with, an initial calendar reform synchronized the solar months of the Greek calendar, then in use in Turkey, with the months of the Western calendar. (The full Western calendar was not adopted until 1926.) This facilitated commercial and cultural interchange with the West. Nineteen German professors were enlisted to reorganize the University of Istanbul. German and Austrian experts were engaged to help plan the reform of all public services. Intensive intellectual activity, long suppressed by the Sick Man's unhealthy suspicions, was released in newly organized cultural clubs called the Turkish Hearth (*Türk Ocağı*). Above all, the groundwork was laid for secularizing civil law and limiting religion to purely spiritual matters.

Critical resistance to this reform movement, strangely enough, came from Prince Said Halim, the grand vizier of the very government which was supposed to be carrying out the Union and Progress party's policies. A member of the Egyptian dynasty and a fierce conservative, the Prince was in office as a Turkish citizen because Egypt was, prior to World War I, a tributary of the Ottoman Empire. He engaged in a duel with Ziya Gökalp, using as his weapons the booklets which he published under the pen name of "Mehmed." However, such indirect attacks could not stop the progressive movement. The progressives openly protested against that prime symbol of conservatism, the veiling of women. A revolutionary change towards the free association of men and unveiled women was accelerated by the necessity of employing women in government bureaus during the war. This soon became a matter of course in the Hearths and in private social gatherings. Social activities of the two American colleges, Robert College and the American College for Girls, aided the new trend to a large extent. Yet war weakness and confusion and corruption prevented any consistent progress. The Turkish people had to wait for a greater crisis to bring them to the revolutionary pitch necessary to abandon old traditions and support a progressive leader of true power and vision. That crisis was to develop as part of the World War I aftermath.

During the later months of the war, I often escaped from the confusion of internal politics and friction by taking social refuge among the Americans living in Turkey. The American colleges maintained a neutral atmosphere into which I withdrew from time to time. Also, I had become a close friend of the American ambassador, Abram I. Elkus, a man of tact and noble character, and his private secretary, Mr. Alsberg, a former newspaperman, and with certain officers on the *Scorpion,* the small United States Navy ship attached to the embassy. One of these officers, Ensign Stewart F. Bryant, became my constant and very agreeable companion. He repeatedly asked me, "Why don't you start a paper of your own inasmuch as you have been so successful with somebody else's nearly defunct paper?"

Why not? There were in Istanbul, it is true, some old, established, well-capitalized papers with their own buildings and rotary presses. But, after all, one needed neither a whole building nor a rotary press to publish the two pages a day which was the limit for any daily during the wartime paper shortage. Also, it was an opportune moment for me to start a paper of my own because my father, who was embittered when a higher post due him as the oldest and most experienced chief in the Court of Auditing was given to an outsider, wished to retire from public office. In him I would have an efficient business manager, and with me he would have an occupation and livelihood. I persuaded a fellow journalist to be my partner. In the depreciated currency of that period, our combined financial resources were the equivalent of about $400. We discovered a complete printing plant, closed at a loss years before but still with two flatbed presses, complete typesetting equipment and fonts of type, and four rooms for editorial and business offices, which we could rent for $100 a month.

Obtaining a permit to publish was more difficult since the government had been refusing new permits. Moreover, my critical articles in *Sabah* had attracted enough secret hostility in government bureaus to make me a rather undesirable applicant from the government standpoint. My good friend, Ziya Gökalp, came to my rescue by explaining to the grand vizier, Talaat Pasha of the Young Turk triumvirate, that he himself would write articles on social reforms for my paper, whereas he had not felt inclined to write for any of the existing papers. Thus my first paper, *Vakit* (*Time*), was born about eight months before the end of the war; and my last trip to Germany during the war was as its editor.

We had luck. *Vakit* was a financial success from the first, and war censorship was abolished on June 11, 1918, a few months after our paper appeared. Our profits permitted us to move to more spacious quarters and buy new type and machines, and we could take full advantage of the new spirit of tolerant discussion and criticism in order to lift all sorts of curtains and denounce obvious evils.

The government had had to lift its censorship to provide a safety valve for the dissatisfactions over the conduct of the war and uncontrolled abuses which were on the verge of violent outburst. No proclamations, threats, or appeals could stop the flood of desertions from the army. Gangs of deserters and outlaws had become the real masters of the country outside of the largest cities. The government, sensing its helplessness, belatedly saw that it must take the public into its confidence and let grievances be aired before the war's end in order to reduce the storm bound to break at the end.

The day after censorship was lifted, I published a direct

attack against the government's general policy. The substance
of it was as follows:

"The war-imposed burdens on our people have exceeded
reasonable bounds because the government has served private
interests above public interests. It is best to tell the truth now.
Tomorrow it may be too late. The economic chaos in this country is already known to both our allies and our enemies who
even believe that it is fivefold or tenfold worse than it is. We
doubt very much whether the bad impression created in Germany and Austria by our selling at two or three hundred piasters
the necessities of life which we bought from those countries for
five or ten piasters can be dissipated by any stubborn silence.
Permitting public discussion will prove the existence of a desire
for improvement. The government has finally recognized that
silence is not a remedy."

This article brought to my office to offer me his encouragement a remarkably brave and able man named Celâl, whom I
had hoped to meet some day. As the delegate of the Union and
Progress party from İzmir (Smyrna), he had opposed his party's
conduct of public affairs during the war. He was later known as
Celâl Bayar, and he was destined to become the third president
of the Republic of Turkey.

One scandal, exposed by our reporters, was the sale, at 6,000
per cent profit, of ten carloads of sugar secretly imported from
Austria at five piasters a kilo and sold in Turkey at three hundred piasters. The former minister of education, who was implicated in the scandal, was the very man who, at the beginning
of the war, had criticized me for "wishing to teach what I already knew and not what I did not know," when he made me
assistant professor of philosophy. This scandal was brought up
in the parliament by the deputy, Ali Haydar Midhat, the son of
the Midhat Pasha who had dethroned Sultan Abdul Aziz in
1876, and who had almost succeeded in modernizing Turkey

then. (Afterwards, in exile in Arabia, Midhat Pasha was strangled in his prison by agents of Sultan Abdülhamid II.) Although the men involved in the scandal were close friends of the rulers, the latter found no way out of seizing the sugar and distributing it to the public at cost price.

The *Vakit* did not stop with the civilian administration, but openly attacked the abuses in the army commissariat. Illicit trade in transport permits was revealed in its grim details, and no name was spared. The government made a show of taking punitive action and experimenting with new economic measures in the public interest. Among other measures, a "chaining back" of speculation was tried. Every speculator was to restore all merchandise to the man who sold it to him, that seller again to the previous one, and so on until it could be sold finally to the public at a reasonable commercial profit. This measure, which lent itself to humorous newspaper stories, succeeded only in attracting public attention, and had no constructive results because, in all the cases studied, the merchandise involved magically disappeared during the chaining back.

The end of the war found Turkey in full awakening and in a most self-critical mood, but the sickness of the government in Istanbul had advanced too far to admit any lasting improvement.

6 : LAST ACT

OF THE TRAGEDY

T<small>ALAAT</small> P<small>ASHA</small>, the grand vizier, returned from a visit to Germany in September, 1918. He invited the representatives of the press to see him, and he tried to give them an optimistic picture. "Huge fresh armies are being organized among the Turkish minorities living in Russia," he said. "They have so far been spared the fatigue of the war; they are zealous; they are warlike. It is a mere question of time before they arrive at the Palestine front. Besides, a loss of Arab provinces is not so important when compared with the bright prospects which are awaiting Turkey in the east as a result of the collapse of Tsarist Russia."[1]

Talaat had a charming personality and was known to be a man of great self-control. He was a quick-witted joker, reputedly able to find a temporary way out of every complex situation. One such instance occurred during a visit of the young Austrian emperor to the Sultan. The Emperor was to attend a parade of Turkish troops in the Sultan's presence. The Sultan was late in arriving. The royal guest felt insulted and communicated his bitter feelings to Talaat Pasha through his chief aide-de-camp.

---

[1] This was during the revolt of the Arabs under Lawrence. Talaat's statement reflects the Young Turk leaders' inclination towards a policy of Pan-Turanism, namely an ambition to reunite all peoples of Turanian stock, of which the Turkish-speaking peoples form the largest group. More of them were, and still are, in Russia and neighboring countries than in Turkey. Later, the Turkish Republic renounced irredentism and prepared itself to support a larger population, welcoming Turkish-speaking immigrants who were dissatisfied or unsafe elsewhere.

Talaat replied in a confidential tone: "We Turks and Austrians are almost neighbors, and we are very congenial, whereas the Prussians are so stiff and un-understanding. The Sultan is going to be late for an hour today, but he was two hours late at a similar function when the German emperor visited him. So, please don't mention today's very short delay anywhere. If the Germans hear about it, they will raise trouble, pretending that the Sultan showed favoritism for Austria." The poor Austrian aide was at a loss to decide whether he should feel angry or honored on behalf of his sovereign.

In spite of his joking disposition, Talaat could not camouflage his worries at our press conference. His jokes were overdone, and his optimism sounded false. A few days after this, when I managed to see Talaat Pasha alone, he was an entirely different man. He had laid down his mask and was showing his true face.

"No use concealing the facts," he said. "Our position is desperate. At this moment my feelings are those of a patriot, no more a party man. In my heart I was always a nonpartisan patriot. When I worked for the success of the Young Turk revolution, as a secretary in the telegraph office in Salonika, I never thought of engaging in politics. I was dragged in by circumstances beyond my will. The difficulties we had to face were of such a nature that a temporary way out always seemed the only way. Union and Progress party men dominated everything. We should have given a reasonable and reliable opposition a chance to form and function, but we were blind and have missed our opportunity. Now we face chaos. I am speaking openly with you because I know you to be an honest journalist. I feel sure that you will not allow yourself to be carried away by partisan feelings, but will abide by your patriotic duty whatever comes to pass."

Such words from the lips of Talaat were enough to reveal

the true measure of desperation in our situation. At the same time I was deeply impressed by this admission of failure from one of the strongest men of the Young Turk staff. Talaat was undoubtedly one of the leading actors in the war tragedy, but even in the minds of his opponents he was not identified with a villain's role. He had never abused his power for personal ends. On the other hand, he was hardly the man to guide a ship in troubled waters. His quick mind allowed him to skip around troubles, but he never showed a capacity to engage in a long-range policy with true comprehension of existing facts.

When the enemy forces, on the north, split the Bulgarian Army and, on the south, sweepingly defeated the Turkish Army in Nablus, Palestine, the end for us came into sight. On October 2, the minister of the interior retired; on October 9, the entire war cabinet resigned. On October 10, a cabinet composed of honest and mostly nonpartisan patriots came into power.

Talaat struck a sincere tone in the proclamation he made in the name of his party. He openly pleaded guilty: "The war has lasted beyond expectations," he said. "It has led to abuses in transport and in business, as well as in food distribution. It is impossible to deny these things today. It was the task of the government to punish such acts. This has not been done. The persons responsible for this neglect are known; we are to be blamed, and we have to bear the full responsibility.

"The reason for our neglect is quite clear. The abuses had become too general. Many officials, many soldiers, and merchants were implicated. If we had arrested and punished all these people, we would have been deprived of too many co-workers whom we needed. Therefore, we put off investigation and punishment until the end of the war. . . . Our policy is defeated. It is impossible for us to retain public power in any form whatever. Therefore, we have not only resigned office, but we also step down from the leadership of the party."[2]

The last act of the war was decisive and sharp. The Union and Progress party held a convention, found itself guilty, and decided to dissolve itself. A new government signed an armistice at Mudros with British Admiral Galithorp on October 31, 1918. About the same time it was learned that Talaat, Enver, and Cemal, the three men responsible for Turkey's entry into the war and for the actual conduct of the war, had fled to Russia, and Talaat had gone from there to Germany.

The curtain of the last act of the war fell in Turkey on a scene of indignation aroused by this flight. These three men had gambled blindly with the destiny of a nation, and had entered the war without any excuse, without any obligation. They had caused millions to be killed, a whole country to be devastated, and moral values to be destroyed. When nothing was left, they retired, merely saying, "Sorry! We really were wrong!" As if this expression of regret was enough to make up for all the lost stakes! Then, rather than give an accounting of their deeds and face the consequences of their responsibility, they simply fled to foreign countries.

There was an epilogue to the tragedy. Enver fell while organizing a revolt of the Turks in the Trans-Caspian area against Soviet authority. Talaat and Cemal were shot, the former in Berlin, the latter in Baku, by Armenian political agents.

What was still called Turkey on the map was a sadly neglected remnant of a once vast empire, the homeland of the Turks themselves, consisting of Istanbul and its European hinterland, about the size of New Hampshire, and Asia Minor or Anatolia, somewhat larger than Texas. From the populace no marked reactions to the dissolution of the Empire was noticeable, nor did there seem to be any will for national survival.

Just imagine our situation. Several great powers, physically and morally capable of coercing a weak people, were determined

2 Ahmed Emin (Yalman), *Turkey in the World War*, 267–68.

to do away, as quickly as possible, with the Sick Man of Europe. These powers met no resistance in occupying Turkey militarily and were in no mood to show any degree of leniency. Still, those very victors acted with such disregard of facts, used means so contrary to their own purpose, that the lethargic kinfolk around the Sick Man's deathbed, themselves infected by enough poisons and germs to cause a natural death, were stimulated to fresh vitality, regained their will to survive, accumulated fresh energy, and miraculously recovered a national health which soon exceeded that of their conquerors. Such an unusual exploit in self-defeat was performed by the Allied Powers in Turkey with the British directing the moves. It was really a rare drama, showing how far human stupidity can go; and it also contains many a lesson which should not be lost to humanity, although learning by actual experience is not the forte of governments in general. When governments plan to be stupid, they can create marvels. The policy followed in Germany after World War II, in the face of the Russian menace, is a new example of shortsightedness.

Let me tell our story from the beginning:

After a pretense of national unity until the war's end, our attention concentrated on the possible attitude of our approaching "conquerors." By the armistice terms, they were expected to arrive at any moment. The armistice was signed in Mudros by the English representative, alone, in the name of the Allies. The British government seemed to be playing the leading role in Turkish matters. On the other hand, there was in Turkey an old tradition of veneration of everything British, a tradition passed on from generation to generation since the days of our alliance in the Crimean War (1855) against Russia. When something went amiss in British-Turkish relations, even the common people in Turkey used to think: "The British are certainly right, and we are wrong. They see so far. They have such great experience. They are so just, so much attached to the idea of liberty! One should have implicit confidence in what they do. If you want to hang yourself, be sure to use a British rope because it never breaks."

With these thoughts in the backs of their minds, people were asking themselves: "Will the English behave really in such a hostile way as the tone of their press makes one fear? Is nothing left of the old English friendship with Turkey? And what about the Englishmen as traditional friends of liberty, justice, and fair play? Can they fail to assert themselves in the long run?"

I had communicated my burning anxiety and my curiosity regarding the British approach to the Turkish situation to my personal friends, Lieutenant Babbit and Ensign Bryant of the U.S.S. *Scorpion*. Like all open-minded Americans who were residents of Turkey for an extended time, they felt and acted as good Turks in those troubled days. They offered to help me to discover the British attitude as early as possible. We decided to dine at Pera Palace Hotel, where a shipload of British officers were expected. We wanted to contact them on the very night of their arrival and find out how they felt towards the Turks before they were poisoned by the views of the dissatisfied minorities in Turkey who could not be expected to manifest a patriotic solidarity with the majority at the hour of extreme crisis.

That night, like the Three Musketeers, we were ready to indulge in foolhardy adventures. In the Pera Palace dining room we sat at a table facing a party of English officers. In order to make me feel less depressed and bashful, and more lionhearted, my two American friends made me absorb large quantities of Turkey's strong national drink, *rakı*, called "lion's milk" because it turns milky when water is added and has a powerful effect. At the opposite table sat a group of those Englishmen who can be so congenial when they are not required, in foreign environments, to wear masks of caste, convention, or policy.

Also aided by abundant drinks they were rejoicing that the fighting was over; it was so pleasant to be in "Constantinople" (Istanbul) as victors, the objective for which such a valiant effort had been tragically defeated at the Dardanelles. All these officers were from General Wilson's occupation headquarters.

We soon met them, and they became so friendly that we felt like full-fledged members of the British staff ourselves. These officers fulsomely praised the fighting qualities and chivalrous spirit of the Turks at the Dardanelles. They would also see to it that the brave Turks received fair play now. I left the party with a feeling of relief and reassurance which I quickly communicated to all my friends. I was soon to discover that my impressions were quite wrong. The tone of British relations with the Turks was not to be decided by individual military officers. Official government policy was quite different. So the three Turkish-American musketeers, who believed themselves to have won a small diplomatic victory, had in reality only attended a pleasant, insignificant drinking party.

The fate of Turkey had been decided in all its details in a series of secret treaties signed by Great Britain, Russia, France, and Italy. These had been revised after the Russian Bolshevik revolution, but as far as Turkey's destiny was concerned, no changes had been made. There was to be a Turkish government with limited sovereignty over the central part of Anatolia; the Arab provinces of the old empire would become semi-independent mandated territories; the Cilician region in southern Turkey, including Adana, Maraş, Urfa, Aintep, would go to France; the hinterland of Antalya with Muğla in southwestern Turkey, to Italy; and the eastern section to the Armenians.

The British government, under Lloyd George, represented the agelong Turkophobe traditions of the British Liberal party. The Turkish nation could expect no mercy from such a government. In addition, Eleutherios Venizelos, the Greek prime minister, and Sir Basil Zacharoff, the munitions merchant-prince, had acquired a great deal of influence in Lloyd George's immediate circle. Both of them, being clever Greeks with great imagination and energy, had decided that the miraculous hour had come to make true the "Big Idea" of a Greek empire to dominate the entire Near East politically and economically. Lloyd George accepted the Greeks as trustees and executors of the British policy in the Near East. In reality it meant putting all resources of the British power at the disposal of two highly imaginative Greek empire-promoters. There is also the gossip that a marked affection of Lloyd George for a Greek lady born in İzmir, later married to a wealthy Englishman, bore some influence on the British policy.

As a result of the orders received from London, British officers were to abstain from any contact and fraternization with progressive and patriotic Turks, to treat them just like enemies in war, and were asked to confine their contact to the minority communities and to the members of the Liberty and Entente party which, prior to its dissolution by the Union and Progress government in 1913, had acted as a tool of British policy. Some of its members had been exiled; the most influential ones had taken refuge in Western countries and, during the war, cooperated with the Allied Powers in disseminating defeatism among Turkish soldiers. After the war, both the exiles and the refugees returned to the British- and French-occupied city of Istanbul, where they formed the "Association of Friends of Great Britain," to serve, blindly, British political designs. Allying themselves to Sultan Mehmed VI, whom subsequent events made the last reigning member of the Ottoman dynasty, they constituted, except for short intervals, the Turkish incumbents in political office during the occupation.

This antipatriotic, antidemocratic Turkish government in Istanbul offered no resistance to signing the Treaty of Sèvres, one of the "peace" treaties dictated to the nations defeated in World War I. For the Allies, there was just one disturbing factor —Great Britain seemed to want to neglect some obligations of the secret treaties so far as France and Italy were concerned, and to secure for itself, under the guise of a Greek invasion of the western parts of Asia Minor, the dominant position in the Near East. As France and Italy aimed, also, to secure for themselves a bigger share than that assigned to them by secret treaties, rivalries, jealousies, and intrigues sprang up among the occupying Allied Powers almost from the first day.

On one point the Allied Powers agreed fully. They all wanted to destroy all Turkish social bonds, to kill the progressive spirit, to foment religious reaction, and to make of the Turks individual slaves chained to the past. The fact was entirely overlooked that the Turks were a nation with a reviving national consciousness, that their patriotic leaders had displayed in their long fight against the Ottoman dynasty, after it became arbitrary and corrupt, a wide-awake spirit of sacrifice, and that many of them had learned the necessity of immediate and complete readjustment to the requirements of progress and civilization.

The attitude of Great Britain constituted, in this regard, a most unexpected change of roles. The policy carried out in the name of Great Britain was exactly the same as the one devised fifty years before by Tsarist Russia with a view to hastening the end of a slowly dying Turkey. Soviet Russia now pretended to have become the standard-bearer of progress, while England elected to follow in the footsteps of Tsarist Russia by abdicating its historic role and influence as a protector of liberty and progress.

Sultan Mehmed VI and the ruling clique around him were in full sympathy with the British reactionary policy. It meant for the Sultan a possibility of maintaining a safe, easy, and pleasurable palace rule, in a golden cage, without having to bother about the complications of a democratic system. It meant also foreign protection against new risings of patriotic reform parties.

There was nobody among the British living in Turkey who could detect the anomaly of the situation and the danger connected with it from the British point of view. The people back in England had no accurate or adequate information about what was going on in Turkey. If you had told them the facts, they certainly would not have believed them.

The actual scene in Turkey was a curious one. In Istanbul, cultured human beings seemed to be reduced to colorless men interested only in animal appetites, intrigue, and destruction. The Levantine residents were the predominant influence, while White Russian refugees and the rather poorly selected non-Turkish residents of Turkey in the foreign occupation service, notably some Circassians who had attached themselves to the palace, re-enforced this influence. The controlling military authorities were called "Inter-Allied," but they really formed enemy camps ready to betray each other.

Istanbul, under occupation, gradually became a sort of Sodom, breeding an environment most favorable to cunning, corruption, and intrigue. Although large co-ordinated Allied offices were opened and generals were on hand, one would hear of a mere British captain or some other minor and anonymous figure who ran the inside show. Nobody could discover the source of such figures' power, yet they could act as political intimates of the Sultan, dictate his decisions, overthrow cabinets, make laws, form secret bonds with unpatriotic Turkish elements, and employ and pay huge numbers of spies.

The Inter-Allied occupation of Turkey after World War I was an experiment which proved fully that the foundation of a peaceful edifice cannot be laid by an extended military domination, but that such methods are liable to stimulate developments directly opposed to those intended. Peace cannot be engendered by a warlike mentality geared to the spirit of retaliation and revenge.

7: AMERICA: OUR

INFORMAL ALLY

Wand HEN THE British authorities revealed themselves as merciless enemies of the very existence of Turkey, the eyes of patriotic Turks turned to America. There was a special reason for this: An armistice had been accepted readily because President Wilson's Fourteen Points had promised an equitable peace. The twelfth point said: "The Turkish portions of the present Ottoman Empire should be assured a secure sovereignty."

Now that the European victors were entirely disregarding the Fourteen Points, the obvious thing to do was to assert them as loudly as possible. The Turkish papers of patriotic tendencies, which included all but two newspapers, agreed among themselves to publish every day, on their first page with as much emphasis as possible, Wilson's twelfth point. The idea was to remind the Americans of their moral responsibility and to urge them to defend their principles, which had been used by their European allies merely as bait for a quick armistice.

This was not the only reason that Turkish eyes were turned to America. The antinationalist Society of Friends of Great Britain advocated the idea that England should receive an exclusive mandate over Turkey. It was a veiled approach to make Turkey a British protectorate. Where was there a way for Turkish patriots to counteract the effects of such movements and to save the national existence and independence of Turkey? There seemed to be none.

The French were secretly offering their support and encouraging the formation of a rival Society of the Friends of France. However, the double-faced policy carried out by France was not one to win confidence. While the French were trying to make friends with patriotic Turks in Istanbul, they had militarily occupied the southern parts of the country, set aside for them by secret treaties. In Cilicia, Colonel Bremont, the French commander, had joined hands with some terroristic Armenians to exterminate the Turks in order to reduce the country to a colony. Educated Turks disappeared mysteriously. There was no end to oppression.

Moreover, the French prisons in Istanbul rivaled the English ones in horrors. The French also advocated a strange educational policy in Istanbul. They spread the idea that all modern Turkish primary schools should be closed, the old mosque schools should be revived, and colleges using French as a language of instruction should be established. It was the old imperialistic device for rendering the masses in a hoped-for colony docile through religious control, and for educating, by the invader's standards, too limited a number of young men ever to turn their training effectively against that invader.

With France so unreliable, there remained Italy. The Italians were viewed by us as the only reliable participants in the Inter-Allied occupation of Turkey. They were well controlled, and they tried to be just. A patriotic Turk, needing a place of refuge from injustice or imposition by the unpatriotic government in Istanbul, could obtain convenient citizenship papers and passports to Italy by claiming, sometimes without proof, that his father was born on the Aegean Islands belonging to Italy or in Tripoli, which Italy had seized in the 1911 war with Turkey after much less fair conduct than she was displaying during the occupation of Turkey. This passport liberality became an advantage later for Turks endangered by the Greek occupation of

İzmir. Still, the general impression was that the Italians in Turkey were following this conciliatory course because of the resentment resulting from the British denial of the spoils of war promised to Italy in secret treaties. The Italians were trying to make friends and gain influence with the Turks while waiting the chance to get their share of war spoils, but they were no match for the British in power and prestige.

The United States of America was such a match. It had power, prestige, and influence; it had no imperialistic designs in Europe and could be trusted to carry out a mission of peace and progress. Growing numbers of Turks came to the conclusion that co-operation with America was the least dangerous and most hopeful course. Such a course would do away with the effects of the rivalries between European nations, would save Turkey from partition, and would supply expert guidance for a period of years. Such co-operation with a good number of American experts could not but prove advantageous from the standpoint of rapid development of the country. Halide Edib Hanım, well-known writer and courageous patriot, was the moving spirit of this project. I was also one of the goodly number of active promoters.

Eventually, selected representatives were invited to hold a meeting to discuss the whole situation. The result was a Turkish "League of Wilsonian Principles," as the first step toward a unilateral agreement with the United States, but members did not agree exactly in their interpretations of "co-operation" with America. For some, co-operation meant a free mandate so that the United States would have full power to run things. Others, and I was among them, wanted a temporary arrangement for American aid in reorganization and in forming bonds of mutual tolerance between the various elements in our heterogeneous population which, for centuries, had been distinguished by religious divisions called "millets," each inwardly governed by its own patriarch, who was appointed by the sultan-khalif. Too, it was felt that the presence of the United States, in some capacity, in the Near East would protect the integrity and independence of Turkey and would force avaricious European powers to curb their selfish interests. The idea was not well received by patriots who had not attended the first general meeting of the League of Wilsonian Principles. They took it to mean submission to foreign tutelage and an abdication of true independence.

Professor Esat Pasha, a well-known eye specialist and a courageous patriot, had organized a body called the National Congress, composed of representatives of all political associations existing in Turkey, with a view to formulating one strong platform for defending the rights of the Turkish nation. I was sent to this congress as the representative of the League of Wilsonian Principles. Although I am a poor orator, I forgot my timidity in the heat of discussion and succeeded in presenting the purposes of that organization convincingly. Esat Pasha and the National Congress eventually adopted the program of the Wilsonian League.

It is most significant that this Turkish-American co-operation, which seemed so desirable at that time, has finally materialized after a second world war. If co-operation had started at that time, it would have helped to develop and unite the Balkan–Middle East region materially and morally. It could have re-directed the entire trend of events in Europe and western Asia towards peace and progress without costing the American people anything materially. The whole matter amounts to this: The idea of unavoidable American responsibility in the destiny of the entire world—rightly grasped by Woodrow Wilson as historically necessary, but a responsibility very badly managed politically—is being carried out today after three decades of delay, with heavy costs and losses as the price of outdated isolationism.

While discussions about co-operation with this or that victorious world power continued, the men who later actually saved Turkey maintained the position of patient observers of all attempts to find a way out. Throughout that period, Mustafa Kemal took a definite stand on only one question. He tried to save the parliament which had come into being and had started to function, though timorously, after nearly a century of aborted reform movements for a parliament to check the absolutism of palace rule. This parliament was one to represent all sections and peoples in the Empire; it included members from Yemen, the Hedjaz, Palestine, Syria, and Iraq, and it also had Greek, Armenian, and Jewish members. If it were to be dissolved, the re-election of another parliament would be impossible. Had there been an honest government, mindful of the real interests of Turkey, to co-operate with it, the parliament could have been a useful instrument for securing a just peace from the victors. Its dissolution, as planned by Sultan Mehmed VI and by the government taking orders blindly from him, could only mean more chaos, more helplessness, and more arbitrary acts on the part of the Sultan. That is exactly why the Sultan and his confederates, composed of British authorities and antinationalist and corrupt elements in the country, had made up their minds to proceed to an immediate dissolution of the parliament.

Mustafa Kemal asked me to come see him in his apartment in the Pera Palace Hotel, where he dictated an interview, very tactfully formulated, pointing out the advantages of the parliament and the disadvantages its dissolution would bring about. This interview was an important step at that moment, for Mustafa Kemal was a man of great prestige, the leader who had been responsible for the victory over the British at Gallipoli on the Dardanelles and the only commander who had kept his army intact and undefeated during the final disintegration. In this period of general agitation against the wartime government his voice carried weight, also, because he was known to have been treated as a dangerous opponent by the narrow, self-seeking circle at the head of the Union and Progress party during the war.

Guided by Mustafa Kemal, I engaged wholeheartedly in a campaign against dissolution of the parliament. But our effort was futile because the Sultan and those who cast their lot with his were relying on British battleships in Turkish waters and armed forces on Turkish soil, while the Turkish patriots had no physical forces on which to draw. It was a clear case of foreign interests' allying themselves for selfish ends with native elements of reaction and dissolution against patriotic, though unarmed, advocates of national survival and progress. England's attitude towards Turkey was an omen of the approaching moral bankruptcy of British world policy and the consequent disappearance of the old British prestige.

At that time it was my luck to make another contact which was to become highly significant in the continual interweaving of my country's and my own destiny. The Sultan's grand vizier and minister of war, after the downfall of the Union and Progress government, was Field Marshal İzzet, a capable and honest man. His first official act was to appoint as undersecretary of war and president of the Commission for the Preparation of Peace a Colonel İsmet, then only thirty-five years old. Hearing much from İzzet Pasha about İsmet Pasha's fine character, enthusiastic idealism, and superior mental qualities, I was anxious to meet him. One day İsmet Pasha, himself, called me and set an hour to see me at my office and discuss the role of the press in the preparations for peace.

In our conference, I found him a man whose exceptional mind impressed one immediately, and I admired him deeply. What a relief to know we had such a man concerned with the problems and future of Turkey. He purposely ignored the immediately adverse conditions and planned and acted with farseeing vision. But little could I, or anyone else, anticipate then that, within another five years, this young colonel would command new armies, defeat greater invasion forces, and negotiate and sign the Peace of Lausanne, voiding the dictated and unjust Treaty of Sèvres! Nor could anyone foresee then that, as İsmet İnönü, he would become the second president of the Republic of Turkey. For on the day of the meeting with Colonel İsmet in my office, the Ottoman Sick Man was still in his death throes, and the Republic of Turkey did not even exist.

While Turkey was in this plight of foreign occupation and divided domestic leadership, our declaration of love for America did not go unreciprocated. American newspapers took more and more interest in news of Turkey. American correspondents and representatives of various interests in America visited Turkey with open minds, studied our situation, and invariably showed us sympathy and understanding. To the dismay of the British, the American press and visitors were instrumental in breaking the blockade of silence which muzzled Turkey. Through the publicity they gave to Turkey and Turkish problems, individual Americans, like Constantine Brown of the Chicago *Daily News* and Clarence Streit[1] of the Philadelphia *Public Ledger,* took active part in the Turkish movement to regain independence.

Then came the King-Crane commission. It was sent to Turkey to prepare a report for President Wilson on public sentiment in Turkey, especially with respect to the Arab provinces. The commission was also to report the kinds of risk involved for America in assuming a general mandate over the Ottoman Empire, including European Turkey, Anatolia, Syria, Iraq, Lebanon, Transjordan, Hedjaz, Yemen, and the eastern provinces of

---

[1] For some time Mr. Streit, then of the Philadelphia *Public Ledger,* later of *Union Now* fame, ran a column in my paper entitled "If I Were a Turk," and occasionally I wrote for his publication, *Freedom and Union,* under the title "If I Were an American."

Turkey which were claimed for the Armenians. Many of us were given a hearing at the American Embassy. The rumor went around afterwards that the members of the commission, including Professor A. H. Lybyer of the University of Illinois, who had taught at Robert College and published a book on Süleyman I's reign, were inclined to believe that an American mandate, not only for Turkey proper but for the entire Ottoman Empire, would be a great service for peace.

In this period, the British suggested a way out, which, if adopted, would certainly serve their purpose of completing the dismemberment of the Ottoman Empire with American consent. It was that old Constantinople (Istanbul) and some chosen hinterland should be organized as an independent cosmopolitan state under the presidency of Herbert Hoover. Mr. Hoover, approached on this question by President Wilson, expressed the view that no such decision should be reached without a thorough investigation, and suggested General John G. Harbord to head a large group of investigators. As finally comprised, the group included Brigadier General F. R. McCoy, who later became head of the Foreign Policy Association in the United States, and a long list of experts, both military and civilian. The Harbord commission made a thorough investigation. It also visited Sıvas, where the Turkish nationalists held an early congress and where General Harbord had a long discussion with Mustafa Kemal about the latter's designs and plans for the future.

Although no form of mandate over part or all of Turkey obtained final approval in the United States, it was the only country which brought a deep sympathy and understanding to the movement of regeneration and independence in Turkey. The choice of Rear Admiral Mark Lambert Bristol as American high commissioner must be mentioned as one of the few favorable outside factors against thousands of adverse ones in the first phase of the Turkish "National Struggle" (*"Milli Mücadele"*). Admiral Bristol, an exceptional example of a brilliant and chivalrous American navy man, had a deep sense of justice and unusual courage in assuming responsibilities. He reached decisions quickly in cases which he considered right, regardless of the inconvenience he might incur for himself.

His activities from the beginning to the end of our struggle for independent national existence amounted, in effect, to almost an informal alliance between Turkey and the United States. The excellent American Hospital founded in Istanbul in 1920 was renamed the Admiral Bristol Hospital in 1945, by which time, under the able direction of Dr. Lorrin A. Shepard, it had become a seventy-bed hospital in new and modern buildings. Maybe the Turks, someday, will recognize Admiral Bristol as one of the heroes of their national struggle and erect a suitable monument to express their appreciation. Be that as it may, this American's concern for Turkey's fate in the critical years, 1919–23, can be considered the introductory phase of Turkish-American co-operation during and after World War II and, subsequently, in mutual defense against aggressive gestures by Communist Russia. Admiral Bristol's persuasive words and constructive actions contributed greatly to the negotiation of peace in the Balkans and Middle East, where he saw, instead of a "powder barrel," a potential stronghold for international peace.

8 : TIME FOR

GREAT LEADERSHIP

THE IRRATIONALITY of the unpatriotic government in Istanbul was bringing the Turkish patriots closer every day to open revolt. They were fast becoming ardent nationalists, not in the narrow sense of a phobia against foreigners, but in the fundamental sense of anti-imperialism. They had had enough of subject nations' troubles, but were unshakably determined upon the survival of the Turkish nation under a Turkish government. Anyone opening press channels for leaders to protest against the Istanbul government's corruption and its subservience to the occupation authorities was, of course, suspect; and I fell into that category.

During the early period of the World War I armistice and occupation, nearly everything I did and said served only to make me an increasingly undesirable person in the eyes of the new men in power, who were Sultan Mehmed VI, his ministers, and the British authorities. For one thing, they noticed that I was always in close touch with the Americans in Istanbul and always sought the company of visiting American journalists. I was known, also, as an active promoter of the League of Wilsonian Principles.

Secondly, I was frequently seen with Prince Mecit, the crown prince who eventually succeeded Mehmed VI as khalif after the sultanate ended. This man was a living protest against the corrupt environment into which he was born. He led a monogamous family life and disdained the endless possibilities of physical luxuries and excesses to which birth and old palace traditions entitled him. He had always sought the company of men of letters and concentrated his interests on books, music, and painting. During the armistice he was the only member of the Ottoman dynasty, other than Prince Selim, who openly took a stand against the dynasty and its policy. Sultan Mehmed considered him his worst enemy, so I was committing a double offense in seeing him regularly and in taking every visiting American journalist to the palace to meet him. I maintained similar relations with Prince Selim, who was not an educated man like Prince Mecit, but shared his common sense and national loyalty.

Thirdly, I was openly attacking the Sultan and his clique as enemies of not only the independence but the actual existence of Turkey. And I also hinted at specific doings by the clique which were supposed to be taking place in complete secrecy. Strangely enough, the government could not enforce censorship. The Sultan's wraithlike government lacked authority, and the Union and Progress politicians, who wielded whatever power remained, had been so furiously attacked for curtailing the liberty of the press that for them to impose effective censorship would have been self-incriminating.

Fourthly, I had written an open letter to the president of the senate, Ahmed Riza, an early Young Turk leader, reminding him of his years of exile in Paris in heroic opposition to Ottoman despotism. For him to be on the Sultan's side now because he had a personal feud with the Union and Progress party, I told him, was unworthy of his glorious past. His response was an invitation for me to see him in person. He assured me that he had been only temporarily deceived by the Sultan's attitude and now fully recognized his sovereign's unpatriotic game. Ahmed Riza's own attitude as president of the senate was of great importance at that critical moment. His radical shift to the nationalist side, which coincided with my open letter, deeply annoyed the Sultan.

There was a fifth reason for hostility towards me. Some of the new men in office were seeking primarily for personal advantage. Their shady dealings grew into the intricate chain of corruption extending from scandals in the flour mills to the bread loaves for Istanbul homes. I had a fine source of information about this in the person of Dr. Celâl Muhtar, former minister of food distribution. He incited me to expose, in vigorous attacks, the specific men responsible.

Small wonder, then, that I received warning of "something" about to happen to me, "openly or treacherously." The warning came from Dr. Besim Ömer, who, as a physician, went regularly to the palace, and whom I saw frequently at meetings of the Children's Protective Society, of which he was the head. He informed me that the Sultan had demanded, in the presence of various palace and government dignitaries, "Is there no way, is there no one to protect me against the attacks and offenses of this Ahmed Emin?"

Dr. Muhtar, with his usual sense of humor, tried to reassure me by frequent taunts such as, "What have you to fear? The most they can do is to put you in prison. What do you need in prison? Something to kill lice, some fresh yoğurt, eggs, and butter. I promise to supply you daily with all this." I must say that he did not keep his promise after I was arrested, but Dr. Muhtar deserves to be known for his works. Respected in Turkey as a practical economist as well as a world-famous specialist in skin diseases, he had made a fortune by his own practical ideas and by living a simple life of many privations. During the war the distributing organization which he created as one of the managers of the Red Crescent (the Muslim counterpart of the Red Cross) produced wonders. Immediately after the fall of the war government, he was made a cabinet member in charge of food distribution. Alas, he considered it safer to avoid my company in prison, and perhaps he was right. He admitted this later when he invited me to a lavish luncheon, a rare invitation from him.

All my "offenses" finally brought two civilian policemen to the newspaper office to inform me that the director of police had something to tell me. Two men bringing such a summons suggested rather more than a mere invitation to be told something. I was annoyed at first by the interruption, then was relieved that the expected had happened, and finally felt the journalist's zeal for a new story, which very likely would produce fresh justification to attack the government.

At police headquarters nobody had anything to tell me. A disagreeable looking fellow searched me for arms, and another led me to a cell, clean and light but bare except for a cot and a chair. The prospect there was exercise three steps each way and no food unless relatives or friends brought it. Very shortly, however, a policeman opened the door and disappeared, but Colonel Halil, the new police director, whom I recognized from his pictures, appeared.

"Your arrest," he informed me, "was merely a coincidence in the arrest of many others with whom you have nothing to do. Your name was listed by mistake. You can be released after the two days necessary to correct the list. I have explained to the minister of the interior that I cannot accept responsibility for arresting you without legal justification. Please consider yourself my guest for two nights, and don't tell the others you will be released."

"What others?" I asked. "I am in a solitary cell."

"You will meet them," he said.

A few minutes later all cell doors were opened, and sixty bewildered men met on a spacious open terrace. I saw Prince

Said Halim, a former grand vizier, two former Sheiks-ul-Islam (religious dignitaries) who had been members of a former cabinet, senators, deputies, and other high officials.

"Why are you among us?" they asked me.

"Oh," I explained glibly, "They offered me the chance to be the only journalist to get the inside story of this affair."

The men present had all shared in the responsibility for the war, and they fell to discussing their respective shares. All of them certainly had an account to render, and some deserved heavy punishment. However, their illegal arrest by a corrupt government under orders of the Sultan and enemy officials turned them all into martyrs and heroes. Those who had been in the wartime cabinet immediately held a secret "cabinet meeting" to decide what they would do. A former legal adviser of the Ministry of the Interior and other experts among the prisoners were called to join their parley. They were gay and confident because of this almost unbelievable chance to gain credit and esteem by favorable comparison to their antinational and knavish successors in office. Moreover, we had a good time telling jokes and enjoying the food provided from the prisoners' own homes. There were also touching reunions with worried family visitors.

The government wanted to give this arrest an atmosphere of secrecy and terror. Newspapermen were kept at a distance. The public was agog to know what was going on behind the prison walls. Retiring to a cell corner, I wrote my impressions— one of the most successful scoops of my journalistic career. I gave an intimate and humorous picture of my first day in prison with former celebrities. A cook, bringing someone's evening meal from his home, smuggled it to my paper.

The next morning, the story exploded like a bomb. My inspiration from American journalistic tactics turned the planned effect of terror into one of general ridicule. The Sultan and his

ministers were furious and held each other responsible for the
folly which had resulted in inside access to the prison story. That
very afternoon I was evicted from the prison as an "undesirable"
and sent under escort to the Acting Commander of Istanbul,
Colonel Fehmi.

He received me most cordially and told me: "I have an
order from the minister of the interior to exile you as a man
dangerous to the military zone of Istanbul. I do not take my
orders from him, and I am not willing to carry out illegal orders
even from my military superiors. So I release you to go wherever
you like."

I thanked him heartily, but he added, "Don't try to play
the naughty child with more 'dangerous' articles. At least don't
sign your articles for some time. Just don't put me and my police
colleagues in a difficult position."

I followed his advice—for a few days. Then I signed my
articles again as if nothing unusual had happened. But word of
the government order for my exile spread far, and I received
invitation after invitation from Turkish towns beyond the military zone to select one of them for my place of exile. Sensibly
enough, although my place of exile had been decided, nobody
in the police or military would enforce an order in illegal form
from a weak and despised government. Finally the minister of
the interior issued his personal written order to the police station
nearest to my newspaper office. Then I was taken back to the
same prison as before, but I was alone there this time, my former
associates having been transferred to a special military prison.
The same dreadful policeman who had searched me before
spent the evening with me deploring my arrest. The next morning the police escorted me to the governor of Eskişehir, who was
to provide another police escort to my destination for exile, the
town of Kütahya in Anatolia.

In Eskişehir I learned that the postwar government had

85

placed new men in top positions but not yet in lower positions. The governor spent an hour advising me to meditate in exile on joining the conservatives in trying to restore the absolute rule of the palace. Then he turned me over to the local director of police, from whom I learned that he and all officials below the governor were in the patriotic camp. He "released" me to a group of lawyers and teachers, who welcomed me cordially to Eskişehir and entertained me lavishly. I began to feel that the pulse of the Turkish people was beating strongly, even under the nearly dead hand of the Sick Man.

A similar welcome awaited my arrival in Kütahya with my police escort. The director of police there asked me to feel entirely free, even to leave if I wished. He was ready to accept the whole risk and responsibility. I stayed three months, joining provincial officials on their tours of duty to many towns and villages and enjoying local festivities with Dr. Esat Pasha, a fellow exile. Dr. Esat Pasha was president of the "National Congress", the association of representatives of private groups, previously mentioned in Chapter VI, which met to voice national aspirations while the very word "national" was tabooed by the authorities in Istanbul.

One day the head of the Kütahya telegraph office whispered to me exciting news. "I just heard over the wires," he said, "that Mustafa Kemal Pasha has resigned his post as inspector general of the army in Anatolia in order to engage in open revolt against the Sultan and the Allied Powers. The palace is in great panic. He is likely to be outlawed and summarily condemned to death by a court-martial."

I instantly recalled words that I had heard years before in an oil field in Texas. Watching the drilling, someone had said, "A fool came. He did not know that the thing could not be done. He went ahead and did it." How quickly those words came back to me with the telegraph operator's whispered news! That

86

Atatürk asking a schoolboy about the meaning of the victory after freeing Anatolia from Greek invasion.

Atatürk (carrying silk hat), as president of Turkey, on his way to open the Grand National Assembly in Ankara.

United Press Photo

The Istanbul water front in 1947.

whisper was in May, 1919, when the Greek armed forces had landed unopposed in İzmir under cover of British navy guns in İzmir harbor. Inevitable incidents, almost simultaneous with the landing, brought on violent opposition.

The end of the world had come as far as we Turks were concerned. The outlook was entirely hopeless. The Sick Man was living his last hours. An agony lasting for four centuries, since the first mortal infection of decadence after the reign of Sultan Süleyman (1520–66), was ending. Backed by British might, fresh armed forces from a neighbor state had landed to overwhelm our exhausted and disarmed population.

And now, suddenly, a man stepped forward, claiming in the name of the Turkish people their rightful heritage. This act of defiance was at least a ray of hope, coming so unexpectedly. I felt the need of solitude to think this over. I climbed to a hill-top and set myself to thinking.

"Anything but passive death and blind submission," was my first reaction. Yet success seemed out of the question. This man, challenging all the victorious powers in actual physical control of Turkey, challenging also the authority of the Sultan rooted in tradition and fanaticism, seemed to be forgetting a great many things. Did he not know that the Turkish armies in excess of two million men, mobilized in World War I to obtain for Turkey a new lease of life, had failed completely, that they had been disarmed and destroyed? Was he not aware that the Turkish people were worn out and resented any new effort? That even words like "nationalism" and "patriotism" were becoming irritating clichés to all whose weariness blinded their vision?

Yet there was one fact that nobody could forget, and I found myself concentrating on it as I looked out over the scene of my exile: Mustafa Kemal was not just anybody. He had to be taken seriously. Ever since the Young Turk revolution, ten years earlier, he had proved on every occasion that he was a man of more than ordinary vision, that he could make quick decisions at critical moments and courageously bring brilliant success out of a hopeless situation.

On occasions such as the crushing of the counterrevolution of Sultan Abdülhamid, maneuvered with the help of Dervish Vahdeti, a Turkish lawyer from Cyprus and a secret agent of the British intelligence service specially trained for this purpose; in the War of Tripoli against Italy and again on the Arab fronts in World War I, where Turkey suffered defeat but Mustafa Kemal's advice proved correct and his action saved our armies; and at the Dardanelles, where his lightning decision and heroic action turned back the British: in all these crises, Mustafa Kemal Pasha had proved to be a living force by himself. Why should he not be equal to even this crisis and again make history by his own initiative? Once more I thought of Comte's prophecy of startling social changes bound to come from Russia and Turkey. I descended from the hill feeling like a new man.

I looked up my friend, Dr. Ziya, Kütahya's director of health services, a sincere patriot, and said to him, "We are at a turning point in Turkey's destiny! Let us celebrate by drinking lots of *rakı.*"

"Did you have a pleasant dream last night?" he asked.

"Maybe a dream now," I replied. "But there are dreams which come true." And this dream, through strange sequences of events, came true beyond the boldest expectations. The sentiment in the country changed so suddenly and violently that the government felt obliged to let us political exiles return to the capital. Our reception in Istanbul by delegations with flowers and speeches turned into an antigovernment demonstration to the dismay of those in office.

In Anatolia, Mustafa Kemal Pasha achieved things which cannot be explained in terms of usual human conduct. Immed-

88

iately after he was allowed to leave Istanbul, May 17, 1919, for Samsun on the Black Sea, all the members of the clique around the Sultan, as well as leading representatives of the foreign occupation forces, suddenly realized that a blunder had been committed and that it was dangerous to allow a man of Mustafa Kemal's disposition and character to go to the interior with unlimited powers as an army inspector general. Torpedo boats were dispatched to stop his steamer and force him to return. It was a queer race for the destinies of Turkey, the Near East, and Europe.

The movement for regeneration and independence started by Mustafa Kemal followed these initial steps: He landed in Samsun on May 19, the very day that the Greek forces landed in İzmir, and a day now widely celebrated in Turkey as Turkish Youth Day. Visiting the commanders of all the army units still existing, even in skeleton form, in Anatolia, he reached a secret agreement with them concerning future common action. Then he resigned his army commission and, as a citizen, took part in the convention or "National People's Congress," which met in Erzurum in eastern Turkey to discuss the survival of Turkey as a responsibility of the people themselves. He was elected president of the congress.

As a second step, another congress was held in Sıvas, in the north central part of Turkey, to draft the National Pact. The purpose of this Pact was the liquidation of the Ottoman Empire by proclaiming the independence of the provinces inhabited wholly or in large part by Arabs, and by setting the minimum boundaries of a Turkish homeland inhabited wholly or mostly by Turks. Furthermore, the National Pact recommended cooperation with a Western power for the sake of introducing basic reforms in the governmental machinery. The Western power in mind was the United States.

One of the clauses of the National Pact paved the way for

the organization of an "Association for the Defense of the Rights of Asiatic and European Turkey." Consequently, the National People's Congress became the *de facto* revolutionary government of all unoccupied Turkey. The congress moved its seat of operations to Ankara so it could be in closer touch with the outside world than was possible from occupied Istanbul. The Sultan's government tried to make a stronger stand and condemned Mustafa Kemal and his close followers to death. However, as the revolutionary government in Ankara kept gaining ground, the Sultan reconsidered the matter and tried for reconciliation.

New free elections for a parliament were held. After much discussion, and against the advice of Mustafa Kemal, it was decided that the newly elected parliament should meet in Istanbul instead of Ankara. This parliament accepted and ratified the National Pact, making it the basis of the Turkish peace policy, and proceeded to work zealously to unify and regenerate Turkey in preparation for the coming peace conference. These activities were disturbing to the foreign powers which had already planned the final doom of Turkey, so they decided to tighten the occupation of Istanbul in the strictest military sense and to crush the nationalist movement for independence. But already the Ankara government was organizing military resistance against the Greek invasion and making its own contacts with separate Allied Powers, as it insisted on speaking for Turkey at the peace conference in place of the disloyal government of the Sultan in Istanbul.

It is difficult to surmise what course history would have taken if Mustafa Kemal Pasha had been arrested in that May of 1919. Turkey, instead of becoming a center of order and peace, would have become a center of terrible strife and conflict. There certainly would have been some other form of Turkish resistance to the verdict of death. This, in the long run, would have made Turkey an aggressor state on the crossroads between Asia and Europe, siding with aggressors. Also, world conflagrations would have resulted from the heat of "Big Power" rivalry to inherit Turkish territories. On the other hand, it is doubtful whether the genius and energy of Atatürk could have produced such abundant results if the adverse British policy, the Greek occupation of İzmir and the subsequent fighting, the policy of conquest and domination followed by the French in southern Turkey, and other plans and acts of dismemberment had not created a favorable ground for daring action.

9 : PRISONERS

OF THE BRITISH

O<small>N</small> M<small>ARCH</small> 16, 1920, the day when full military occupation replaced the regime which had left some initiative to Turkish authorities, Istanbul offered a very sad spectacle for a Turk. British soldiers raided and closed the parliament, arrested and deported deputies, and took over every military post. Individual Turkish soldiers who attempted any resistance were instantly killed by British units parading in the streets. The British seemed to have set the stage for an atmosphere of terror. Nevertheless, our people's moral resistance seemed almost organized.

The whisper went around: "Don't feel terrified. British oppression will not spread beyond the range of their naval guns. These soldiers you see landing are always the same ones. They parade and are taken back secretly aboard their ship. Then they land again. It's to create the impression of a huge force at hand."

Such whispers indicated a remarkably vigorous national spirit. I felt somewhat relieved. Earlier that day I had received an urgent invitation to spend the night at the home of Dr. Abdülhak Adnan,[1] a member of the parliament and a very active and influential nationalist. His wife, Halide Edib, was the leading feminine nationalist. I had declined, despite his insistence that it was essential for me to come that particular night. Some years later he explained that he had received, under oath

[1] After the 1934 law requiring surnames, Dr. Adnan became Dr. Adnan-Adıvar.

of secrecy, word of the British military occupation and what it would mean. He had taken measures to escape with his wife and wished to give me the chance to go with them. Very stupidly I missed my chance to escape to Ankara and spend usefully there the next two years which, instead, I wasted as a political hostage in Malta.

In a council at our newspaper office on our editorial policy towards the occupation, we accepted a suggestion of Ruşen Eşref, former Turkish ambassador in London, who said, "Since we cannot comment on actual events in any sense contrary to the British purpose, let me write daily editorials about the old public fountains in Istanbul, their donors, their inscriptions, and so on. The public will grasp the idea of avoiding and, thereby, registering antagonism to the current course of events."

The following evening I went to the island of Heybeli, about eight miles, by ferry boat, for a night's rest at the home of my friend, Sabri, who, to me, represented a typical John Citizen. I found him in a sadly hopeless mood. The next morning a member of my newspaper staff greeted me at Galata Bridge with the news, "The British police raided your home last night, seized all your papers, and searched for you from cellar to roof. You had better flee!"

In order to find out more fully what it was all about, I went first to the Italian acting high commissioner, who had always been friendly to me. He told me that the decision was taken formally by the Supreme Allied Council but actually by the British authorities. He thought an attempt to escape would be futile.

Then I went to the American Embassy, where I saw my former Columbia classmate, W. W. Cumberland, who was in Turkey on the Harbord commission, and Professor Eliot Grinnell Mears of Stanford University, former American trade commissioner at Athens and Constantinople. Professor Mears was

93

then compiling his book *Modern Turkey,* a symposium to which I contributed the chapter on the press. Both of these friends advised me to give myself up as I had committed no actual offense, and this would show that Turks were not terrified by British oppression.

But Professor Mears also went to consult Admiral Bristol, and returned with this message: "Ahmed Emin Bey has no right to give himself up to be exiled. His people need him in Ankara. I am ready to help him to escape. He will find an official car at the rear of the embassy to take him to a place on the Bosporus where he can find a boat to cross to the Anatolian side, and he can then surely find some way to escape."

As the representative of one of the Allied Powers, a power, however, which had not declared war on Turkey and was not participating in the occupation, Admiral Bristol was indeed taking a heavy responsibility in aiding the escape of a nationalist journalist on the British blacklist. Cumberland and Mears were ready to carry out Admiral Bristol's advice, including the finding of a hat for me to wear instead of my red fez; but on reconsideration of the trouble the Admiral's courageous offer might bring upon him, they persuaded me not to accept it and to give myself up.

I was to discover that it was not so easy to be arrested. Going directly to the British Embassy, a few blocks from the American Embassy, I stated that the British raid of my house signified that I was wanted, so here I was, entirely at their disposal. I was told that the High Commissioner's office in the embassy did not handle such matters, that I should try the military headquarters in the Tunnel Building. The authorities there thought the headquarters of General Wilson in the Krocker Hotel might be the place for arrests. I began to find it quite amusing to apply for arrest in a terrified city. I enjoyed a good lunch in a crowded restaurant, where acquaintances stopped at my table to express relief that the rumors of the raid and the British search for me were not true.

"The rumors are true," I said, "and I am searching for a British authority competent to arrest me." This made each one leave, speechless, as if fleeing a contagion. Maybe some thought I was crazy. One suggested that any Turk would gladly hide me.

"Would you?" I asked.

"You must excuse me. I'm under suspicion myself. Otherwise . . . ."

At the Krocker Hotel I was sent from office to office, and finally returned to the young sergeant to whom I had first explained my mission. "Why are they after you?" he asked.

I explained that it was for loyalty to my nation and refusal to be the tool of hostile conspirators. His response was that no Englishman would arrest a man for loyalty to his country; that I must be seeking protection against my own people, and he would like to help me. He summoned another kindhearted sergeant to confer on it, but I left and dashed to the Turkish police headquarters. The new police director had been a fellow journalist and had eventually turned against the Union and Progress party. He very kindly explained that my case was hopeless as the order came from higher up; that I should return to Moda, an Anatolian suburb of Istanbul, and apply to the British police station. That station was right next door to my own home!

Stopping a moment at my office, I learned from a reporter that I could escape from Beykoz, a Bosporus village, by asking at a certain drugstore there for a former member of our own staff, Lutfu Arif. By this time, I felt I was crazy to be seeking arrest. I hastened to Beykoz only to find that Lutfu Arif was out on a "big hunting party," and no one could tell when he would return. This meant he was helping others to escape.

Returning to the city, I spent the night at a club in a state of indecision. At my office the next morning I was told that a good hiding place was being prepared for me and that, meanwhile, I could spend one night at the home of another journalist's mother-in-law. I accepted this hospitality, but learned the next day that the hiding place had not materialized. That night I went home to Moda, where I stayed with my parents. I quieted my parents' anxieties, called on various friends who had relatives already exiled to Malta, and collected messages for the exiles. Early in the morning I reported at the British police station next door, but it was not until 2:00 P.M. that the right official would be in, and I was quite free until then. That official assured me that the honor of being exiled for patriotic ideals was enviable in comparison to his duty to exile me. He placed me between two armed guards, who, he assured me, were an "honor guard" that would not humiliate me in public. Yet my father, following us, wept at the sight of his son, a "captive," until I consoled him with the officer's view of my escort. We attracted abundant attention on the ferry and in the streets, for other arrests had been effected inconspicuously. Thus I entered the Arabian Han, a notorious British dungeon.

I was there voluntarily, had insisted upon going, but the dirty, unheated fifth-floor cell allotted to me, with no indication of why or for how long, took all fun out of being arrested. My first visitor, within half an hour, was Captain Bennet of the British Intelligence Service, who, with his perfect command of Turkish, had made himself the confidant of the Sultan and was really, in himself, the whole British show in Turkey.

Most courteously, as if relaxing in a fashionable drawing room instead of actually sitting with me on the dirty bed, he directed the conversation towards conditions in Turkey, bringing in the names of the men in the new antinationalist cabinet in Istanbul and asking my opinion of them. Since they were the most unscrupulous men available, I congratulated him on choosing the best tools for the purpose he seemed to have in mind.

This nearly cracked his composure, but he restrained his temper behind his smiling mask. I obstinately refrained from making any sort of personal protest until he was leaving the cell. Then, calling attention to its condition, I said, "I don't want to discuss your general aims and methods, but don't you find these details of treatment unnecessarily mean and ugly?"

"How can you think for a moment that this is intentional?" he retorted with an odd smile. "I will reprimand those responsible. You will see that you will receive the treatment you merit."

My failure to plead for release seemed to have angered him. And very soon two filthy men were shoved into my cell. This pair explained in broken German that they were Russians arrested as Bolshevik agents, first interned at the Dardanelles, then dragged from prison to prison until transferred to Arabian Han, where they had been shifted suddenly from another cell to this one, which they interpreted to mean that they would be shot the next morning. My interpretation was that Captain Bennet was providing me with their cheerful, sweet-smelling company.

I rapped on my cell door to demand at least a moment's relief and a chance to wash. Flatly refused that, I later asked for food and was told that the evening meal had already been distributed and prisoners could not receive food from outside. During a night of mostly pacing back and forth, I became tired enough to spread on the bed, for sheets, the pages of the London *Times,* which I still had with me. Thus I realized the advantage of reading a journal which used a solid, neat paper. Yet, perhaps symbolic of a free press, those improvised bed sheets refused to stay in place. I learned afterwards that no other Turkish political prisoner was subjected to such indignities.

The next morning, in the prison office, the commander went through my luggage and seemed impressed by the quality of the English books in it and by the manuscript of my chapter for Professor Mears' book. He granted my renewed request for a clean cell, water for washing, and food from outside. I shared my nice, new, spacious cell with two nationalist Turkish secret service men, charged with trying to identify unpatriotic Turks acting as British spies. They, like the two Bolsheviks, were in terror of being shot without trial.

I had only a few hours there before being escorted aboard the light cruiser *Cardiff*. I was silently led below to a passageway, literally as hot as hell, beside the engine room, and was pushed into a windowless cell, airless in spite of its few air vents. I thought I was suffering medieval torture. The instinct for survival kept me pounding on the door. At last the door opened and admitted the ship's doctor.

"Are you going to claim that your health does not allow you to journey to Malta in this cell?"

"Another hour in there and I will die," I said, and I looked it.

"This is the regular accommodation for prisoners of war."

"I am not a prisoner of war. I am a civilian taken from his home during an armistice and deprived of liberty without any charge or trial."

This made him decide to report to the captain. The result of that was an order to let me sleep just outside of my cell, in the passageway, which had a porthole that might be opened later. Even that hellish hot spot was paradise in comparison to the cell. I was soon joined by a red-fezzed unfortunate creature, crying and sobbing, "They will shoot me. Oh my wife, oh my poor daughters!"

"But, man," I said, "they don't bring a fellow onto a ship to shoot him. They do it, with less trouble, on land."

"They told me so," he wailed. "They put me in a truck and covered me with a blanket so I couldn't see where they brought me. I hear them coming now to shoot me."

Terrorized though he had been by someone in the British secret service, he finally told me that his name was Muammer, and that he had been, for the past few months, head of the political section of the police and was accused of trying to identify Turkish spies in the British secret service.

After the ship's departure, the captain of marines, an extremely kind man, took me to Admiral Hope, commander of the light cruiser fleet in which the *Cardiff* was his flagship.

"Tell me the whole story," the Admiral said as we stood on the upper deck. I told him the whole story of the ugly tragedy staged in the name of Great Britain in the Near East. I gave details and offered proof. The Admiral, in sincere indignation, made a single comment at the end: "They say we British are stupid. We really are."

This unexpected statement by an admiral to a prisoner on his flagship confirmed my belief in the noble character and free mind of the individual Englishman. Already, since my arrest, I had received individual expressions of disgust at British policy by Englishmen obeying orders in my case; and in Malta, I was to receive evidence that the individual English officer feels independent and unhesitatingly expresses personal opinions.

The Admiral saw that I had magazines, books, and cigarettes, but my request for a cabin for myself and my terrified companion was of no avail. The ship's captain could not provide a cabin, but he let us use sailors' hammocks in their quarters. Again I attributed this deprivation to the influence of Captain Bennet, which overrode others' good will. All Turks previously deported to Malta had had cabins, even on torpedo boats. However, the experience of living among the sailors was more interesting. Again I found the individual Englishman kindhearted and courteous. On arrival at Malta, when I tried to tip the sergeant of marines, he refused but, without showing offense, said:

"You may tip Greek waiters in Istanbul on your return. I have done only my duty, and I have felt ashamed to keep you always under guard."

A Maltese lieutenant came aboard and led us to a prison called Polverista. It was a camp of Turkish political prisoners.

When I look back now, my actual impression is not of living through a long series of real events, but of seeing an extraordinary dream coherently staged. For each act, some providential power gave me a convenient seat, or a place behind the scenes, or even a minor role on the stage itself. When the curtain lifted on this camp, I became aware that such a scene has rarely been staged, and that it will probably not be repeated anytime, anywhere. Here were all the leading men who had been high in one country's government during a war, except a very few who had escaped.

Here were Professor Ziya Gökalp and other members of the central council of the Union and Progress party, former grand viziers, cabinet members, governors, deputies, and generals. Here were those men who had caused Turkey to enter the war on Germany's side, those who had conducted the war, those who had had to do with Armenian deportations, and those who had maltreated British prisoners of war. I was one of twenty-four deputies, generals, and journalists in a special category of sympathizers with the new nationalistic movement of Mustafa Kemal. We had been arrested and sent there, during an armistice, contrary to all established rules of international relations. This violation had been carried out by certain British authorities in the name of the Allied Powers.

In Polverista we did not suffer the brutalities which made the concentration camps of World War II notorious. Yet our story is unique for the reasons just given and also because all the prisoners were mature men accustomed to comfort, position, and influence. They were really a depressed crowd, many of them for the first time in their lives without assured means of subsistence for themselves and for their families in Turkey. Moreover, they did not know specifically why they were there, how long they would be there, or what would be their final fate and that of their country.

We were assigned haphazardly to about thirty overcrowded apartments of two rooms and a kitchen each, originally intended for noncommissioned officers with families. The whole camp was ringed with barbed wire. An entire detachment of Essex and Lancashire regiments took turns, week by week, in guarding us. My main objection to them was that they shouted through the night, "Number one; everything is all right! Number two; everything is all right . . . !" These regular cries, every night for two years, became a nightmare in themselves.

Imprisoned officers were paid salaries according to rank. Civilians were treated like common soldiers on prisoner-of-war rations of frozen meat, dried vegetables, milk, and marmalade. The prisoners formed messes. Those with independent means employed cooks. Enterprising men among us who needed to make a living, after their government salaries stopped, organized and ran messes for profit. And the rich took care of the few needy.

I belonged to a mess organized by one Übeydullah, a member of parliament and an eternal Bohemian. First he had been a Muslim preacher, then a radical Young Turk. He had fled to America to escape persecution under Sultan Abdülhamid and had sold Turkish candies on Chicago streets. He learned English, spending days and nights in libraries; and after the Young Turk revolution of 1908, he returned to Turkey and was elected a deputy. He had enriched his Turkish sense of humor by spicing it with American wit. The readiness of that wit saved many a troubled situation in a parliament which was always edgy and discordant. Once, when all the deputies were violently agitated over a statement in a daily paper that 90 per cent of them were donkeys, Übeydullah remained perfectly calm.

Asked why he showed no sign of anger, he coolly replied, "I am in the category of the 10 per cent."

To everybody's envy, the British soon released Übeydullah, saying that he was in Malta by error. We were astonished when he reappeared after two months. He had found liberty in enslaved Istanbul duller than imprisonment among so many friends in Malta! He managed to get sent back on a trumped-up charge, and we benefited again from his delicious cooking.

Turkish publications were prohibited in prison during the early months, so Celâl Nuri, the editor of the *İleri,* and I published rival "papers." Each had a staff to take dictation and race to be first to post the news on the camp bulletin board. For important good news, each paper had its public criers. Aside from camp items, we had to depend on short letters from home and foreign language newspapers.

The monotonous camp routine took us to the tennis court every morning under escort. The afternoon started with a walk in the garden and a discussion of the day's news. Then everyone retired to read or study. Ziya Gökalp offered a well-attended course in sociology, and I gave one on statistical methods and social problems. The majority studied new languages. I soon learned enough Italian to translate Italian papers. The evenings were devoted to games, bridge being the most popular one. Two afternoons a week for two hours, we were escorted by an officer and armed soldiers on walks, and once a week on a carriage drive to deserted parts of the island.

This routine taught me many a lesson about our valuations of things. It was amusing to see the keen delight which minor deviations from the routine brought to all these men who had for so long previously enjoyed the independence that comes with mundane success. If there were a sanitarium to teach the value of simple existence for blasé people who require ever larger doses of stimulants to overcome boredom, I think I could qualify as an expert staff member—I know the remedy for the malady. I'll never forget the thrill produced when a kind Irish officer took us, against instructions, through a village street. How we crowed over those who had not gone with us into the world of real human beings outside of barbed wire.

We found that the English officers accepted such precedents as acquired rights, so we acquired the "right" to stop at a village saloon and, eventually, to take tea at Dowdal's Hotel, an English beachside inn, where we saw, for the first time in our exile, fashionably dressed men and women. What a thrill that afforded! We even reached the point of leaving the camp twice a week on parole, then daily, and finally of attending the opera and staying out till midnight. But one day two prisoners, in complicity with a professional smuggler, escaped to Italy. This escape caused a return to strict rules and even stopped the old liberty of leaving the camp under armed escort.

Such close confinement brought out the pessimists who recalled that Boer chiefs were kept on Malta for nineteen years. Others dwelt on their personal worries about a possible Inter-Allied court trial for their participation in the war, Armenian deportations, or maltreatment of British prisoners. These worries inevitably resulted in individual or collective letters to the governor general of Malta, which kept me busy translating them into English. Lack of replies did not deter the writing of new letters, for there was the need to feel that one was at least doing something to save the future. Airing grievances in friendly debates sometimes ended in bitter fights. But fighters were calmed by being reminded that they were victims of the epidemic named "barbed wire disease." Gradually all symptoms of it were charted, and potential victims were diagnosed and warned before it was too late.

It seemed to me most significant that a common hostility to the Sultan's government and the Allied Powers' policy and the common concern for the bitter national struggle going on in Anatolia were not sufficient to silence rival political passions. Those members of the Union and Progress party who had tasted supreme power during the war, and who comprised the majority in Polverista, certainly had an insatiable greed for power. Instead of remembering the endless errors made when they had responsibility, some of the extremists viewed the nationalists fighting in Anatolia as opportunistic usurpers of their power, and they were convinced that they themselves would regain control in due time.

This Union and Progress majority in the prison camp spared no efforts to win elections to the council which took care of our camp administration problems and collective finances and made contact with the British commander. Once a nonpartisan group headed by Fethi Okyar (later the organizer and leader of a short-lived "free opposition" party in the Assembly of the Republic), and including myself, won the elections, and we used our power to improve the prisoners' lot. The old guard was furious and so scheming that we resigned in disgust. They resumed their illusion of power, and we had profited by a salutary political lesson.

Everybody's outlook changed when good news from Anatolia reached us in August, 1921. Mustafa Kemal's newly organized nationalist army had stopped the Greeks' advance inland from İzmir in a battle at the Sakarya River, dangerously close to Ankara. The new national government in Ankara was interested in our destinies and was campaigning to capture British hostages. Our regular letters from home carried past the censors such "innocent" and cheering messages as, "The sheep merchant now has thirty black sheep at his disposal." Thirty more British hostages to be exchanged for us!

The capture of important hostages like Colonel Rawlinson, a nephew of the viceroy of India, along with continued successes by the new Ankara government, entirely changed our situation. We no longer felt that the island of Malta was our cemetery. We felt alive. And, all of a sudden, we began to receive very considerate treatment. It was the first step towards our liberation. By pretending hernia trouble, I even obtained permission to leave the camp and stay in a hotel in Sliema. As my paper in Istanbul had not suspended publication during my absence, without authorization and without censorship, I began to send regular articles signed "A Hermit." These appeared eventually in a column headed, "From a Secluded Corner." I also prepared, and smuggled out, a booklet about the whole Malta scandal, which was published in French and English by the Turkish publicity bureau in Geneva. The British, at last, were ready to exchange us for their own captured countrymen.

I cannot close this chapter without adding a pleasant epilogue. In the summer of 1953, the British Embassy in Ankara invited me to go to Malta, as a guest on a British battleship, to study the new North Atlantic Treaty Organization. What a thrill for a former political prisoner of the British! On disembarking from the battleship, I hurried to Polverista to revive my memories. The buildings had been turned into living quarters for needy Maltese families. Flocks of children followed me on my way through the buildings. There happened to be an ice-cream vender in the garden, and it occurred to me to offer ice cream to the youngsters—to see happy faces where I had seen so many unhappy ones and had suffered so much myself. The total came to 180 portions. I could have had no happier end to the Polverista episode.

10: TURKEY'S

"NATIONAL STRUGGLE"

THE BRITISH-TURKISH exchange of prisoners was not accomplished without trouble. The British voluntarily freed two categories of prisoners on Malta, namely, those held responsible for declaring war against Great Britain and those exiled by mistake with no specific charges against them. But negotiations for the special group of nationalist followers of Mustafa Kemal failed because the Ankara government asked for the exchange of all Turkish prisoners, offering to put on trial in Turkey those responsible for Armenian deportations and for ill treatment of Allied prisoners. England was willing to exchange only the twenty-four in our category, holding the other two categories for trial in English or Inter-Allied courts.

Sixteen leaders in the two disputed categories succeeded in escaping from Malta in a small motorboat. This escape cost those of us left behind a few more days of seclusion and oppression. Finally, however, we were all to be exchanged, and in January, 1922, twelve of the more important men were put on a small ship with a few cabins, the rest of us on a British tanker. We had an exceedingly rough trip, during which we were exposed to the weather when the wind whipped the deck canvas away.

We forgot all our discomforts when we reached Istanbul and were greeted with frantic demonstrations, cleverly managed, though the city was still under foreign occupation. However, we were carried on to ports on the Black Sea for the actual exchange. One hundred Turks were readily exchanged for eight British officers at İnebolu. But the British met an unpleasant surprise at the next exchange point, Zonguldak. The twenty-two British prisoners sent aboard turned out to be six Maltese laborers and their Greek wives and children. They all held British citizenship, and the Turkish authorities were technically correct in exchanging them for us. It had been impossible to get enough "black sheep" without extending the hunt to European Turkey, which was still occupied. The Turkish authorities did not mind playing this sly trick on the British, since the British had been totally wrong, in the first place, in taking us as political hostages during an armistice.

As a matter of fact, we received an unofficial admission of this error when a few of us, who had obtained permission to return at once on the tanker, reached Istanbul. General Harrington's aide-de-camp met us there with assurances that the General regretted all that had happened to us and that nothing similar could happen again. Later, when this young officer, Colonel Blunt, became assistant military attaché at the British Embassy in Ankara, he confessed to me that he had acted then without special instructions but as a matter of decent fairness. Incidentally, he is one of the few Englishmen I have met who cannot be distinguished from a Turk in speaking Turkish.

It was a delight to review what had happened in Turkey during our exile. When I was shipped to Malta in March, 1920, the Greek Army had control of İzmir and some of the hinterland. Thereafter, as I learned in 1922, the Sultan's government in Istanbul made verbal protests. But in the interest of its own survival, the government dreaded a national revival in Asiatic Turkey. Hovering under British protection, it scrupulously avoided even a gesture of violent retaliation against the Greeks. It did feel it wise, or unavoidable, to tolerate local resistance by

Turkish mountaineers, famous for their courage and chivalry, who took up arms to defend their homes in the invaded areas. Both the Istanbul government and the occupation officials tolerated, as "safety valves," huge protest meetings and newspaper tirades in the capital and elsewhere. But the regular Turkish Army, almost entirely disarmed, was not allowed by the Sultan's government to back up the peasants, in any way, in defending their homes and their women's honor.

More resentment than could escape through minor safety valves had welled up in Anatolia and had been channeled into the Association for the Defense of Asiatic and European Turkey. Mustafa Kemal, president of the Association, promptly issued an invitation to the members of the dissolved parliament to meet in Ankara to form the revolutionary government of "the National Assembly." This government was actually formed and, as the *de facto* power in Turkey, went to war against the Greek invaders.

The forces available were a few scattered, disarmed, but patriotic units of the old Ottoman army, refugees from invaded areas, peasants still resisting the advancing Greeks, and a number of guerrillas led by daring bandits more interested in plunder than in patriotism. The new government was exposed every minute to the danger of insubordination and rebellion from these bands, who were in no mood to tolerate any reorganization of a regular army which could become a potential rival force.

There came a time when the nationalist military forces, formed and equipped out of nothing but stupendous popular effort and sacrifice, had to fight simultaneously the Greek Army, several irregular bands, and even certain forces of the Sultan acting in virtual alliance with the Greeks. Although the bandit bands at first had been the main support of the nationalist cause by aiding the peasants' resistance to the Greeks, some later fell under Communist influence, and a few went over to the Greek side. At the same time, the palace and the occupying powers were instigating many local revolts against Mustafa Kemal. That, in spite of this multiple harassment, a nationalist military front was established, and that the new army defeated the well-organized and well-supplied invaders and freed Anatolia and finally European Turkey, too, amounts to a miracle.

I had planned to spend a week in Istanbul seeing my family and attending to matters for my newspaper, and then to leave for Ankara to get acquainted with this new Turkey. But, during the exchange at Zonguldak, the governor of that province had brought to me, on the tanker, a telegram from Yusuf Kemal Bey, the minister of foreign affairs in the Ankara government, to tell me that I was nominated "Director General of the Press and Propaganda." I was expected to land there and proceed immediately to Ankara. This was indeed a sign of confidence in me, and it was a splendid opportunity for service in our national struggle, as we were calling the movement in Anatolia to save Turkey. Nevertheless, my deep attachment to journalism would not allow me to accept a government post. I telegraphed back that I would serve my country as a journalist and come to Ankara to write about the situation at firsthand.

After only three days in Istanbul, I was on my way to Ankara. A trip there always had the character of an adventure, and even more so in January of that year because part of the railway line was held by the Greeks, although their advance had been stopped. Sporadic fighting continued while each side prepared for decisive action. The quickest way to get from Istanbul to Ankara at that time was to travel by steamer to the Black Sea port of İnebolu and, then, to take a horse carriage inland for the six-day trip to Ankara. My attempt to save time by going all the way overland in a Ford truck, belonging to the Red Crescent, failed because an unabating snowstorm forced me to take six days to make the two hundred miles.

Ankara was a most cheerful roost after the dark and bitter armistice days. It is true that there were no hotels, no electric lights, and no conveniences. You had to carry your own bed and find a space for it in the house of a friend. When it was your turn to get a bite to eat in the only restaurant, called "Anadolu" (the Turkish name for Anatolia), you certainly were not carried away by gastronomic delight. Still, you were happy; you did not highly prize physical values. You had a sense of possessing, all of a sudden, a great many satisfactions and dreams, and much else which had been beyond even the horizons of your dreams. Paradise could not be any different or better.

Here, in a little peasant town, a new world was dawning. It was not only a new world for us as Turks, but here you could see the only real resistance anywhere against the international tendencies of folly and stupidity prevalent following World War I. Mustafa Kemal seemed to be the only statesman who had undertaken a fight for real peace, by mutual consent which alone could create good will and realize a profit from the very costly experiences of war.

I felt very anxious to talk with the great man, our daring guide who had led us away from darkness and death. Upon my arrival in Ankara, I heard an almost unbelievable story about him. On his return from the Sakarya battlefield, he was received at the station by a large crowd, headed by turbaned religious leaders carrying green flags with inscriptions from the Koran. (Green is the symbolic color of Islam.) They implored him: "Go with us to the tomb of Haci Bayram Veli (the saint of Ankara), and thank him for the victory he has given us."

This was the new leader's great opportunity to make friends of the religious reactionaries who, up to that moment, had fostered agitation and intrigue against him. The nationalist situation was such that an offer of harmony from any side would be welcome. Mustafa Kemal, however, realized that co-operation with that class of reactionaries would only admit their influence and continue the stultifying compromises which had hitherto killed any radical and loyal progressive effort.

"Go to your homes with your green flags," he told these leaders of reaction. "You have too often stolen, for the benefit of your saints, the victories of my soldiers. I will not allow you to do it again. This victory was won by the sacrifices and valor of the soldiers. We have no debt to recognize towards any saint."

I was told that all you had to do to meet this man was to open his door and walk in when he happened to be in his room at the National Assembly. Not even the intervention of an aide-de-camp or secretary was necessary. These patriots, pronounced outlaws by the Sultan's government, were engaged in a frantic struggle for independence and had no time to spare for formalities and pomp.

Nevertheless, I was not sure that President Mustafa Kemal would remember me from our earlier meeting on the train from Germany, and I preferred to see if my old friend, Dr. Adnan, now vice-president of the National Assembly, would present me. Together we walked to the President's room. A large number of deputies were there, listening to the *Gazi* (Victor), as Mustafa Kemal Pasha was called after the battle of Sakarya.[1] All were smoking and sipping thick coffee.

Dr. Adnan pushed me forward, announcing, "Here I have a deserter. He is the first man who has refused an office offered by the government of the Grand National Assembly. What shall we do with him?"

One of my fellow prisoners from Malta who was present intervened, "Ask him first what he has to say in his own defense."

"If I accepted an office," I said, "I would feel like a deserter

---

[1] Mustafa Kemal condoned the use of this title for some time, and then rejected it because of its religious connotation of one entitled to a special place in paradise because of victories for Islam.

from my country's service. I am a journalist, and I believe I can serve best in that capacity."

I went on to thank the Gazi for our liberation from exile in Malta, and explained that the changed outlook in Turkey made me ask myself every moment, "Am I dreaming?" Our victorious leader expressed his opinion that faithful attachment to one's profession was a commendable excuse. He added that the country needed enterprising and fearless journalists.

The next day, when I called on Yusuf Kemal Bey, who had sent me the notice of nomination as director general of press and propaganda, he urged me to reconsider my decision. He said, "We want to prepare you to be the first ambassador to Washington from the Turkish national government. Refusing the present offer means losing a great opportunity."

Though I thanked him, I explained that I did not consider journalism a steppingstone to other positions, but an end in itself. Then, Celalettin Arif, a leader in the "Second Group," as a newly forming opposition was called, argued with me: "You ought to accept the offer because you enjoy the confidence of both the new government and the opposition. This combined confidence will make it possible to obtain more appropriations for propaganda. We need propaganda badly."

I did not share this view about my place of greatest usefulness. I thought that a man sitting in Istanbul with a full grasp of the new spirit in Ankara could be more useful, through contact with foreign journalists, than a director general of the press coping with red tape in Ankara.

I decided to start on what I considered my mission by securing the life story of the Gazi from his own lips. Dr. Adnan, also a newspaper man in his younger days, said that a surprise visit at the Gazi's residence would be the best approach. It took some effort to get there in Dr. Adnan's open carriage in the cold winter weather on that high central plateau of Turkey. Moreover,

Ankara, at that time, was one of the most retarded provincial towns, with a population of twenty-five thousand. Its most prosperous section had been razed by fire in the last year of the war. Most of the members of the new government were living in small summer homes constructed in orchards and vineyards some distance from the town. Mustafa Kemal had a six-room house on the hill, called "Çankaya," about four miles out of town.

En route I had plenty of time to concentrate on my companion. I have never known a purer type of idealist than Dr. Adnan. Unfortunately, his health did not seem good. He coughed badly, and his back had become a rounded hump in the two years since I had last seen him in Istanbul, the day he tried to have me join him and his wife in escape. They said that an old tubercular condition had recurred.

Although he was one of the best physicians in Turkey, and fully aware of the risks to which he exposed himself by working night and day in this severe climate, he never spared himself. To my repeated requests that he take better care of himself, he answered: "Our individual lives are too unimportant compared with the national task ahead of us. If I stop working and start thinking about myself, I shall feel that I am dying morally and it will be immaterial how soon physical death follows."[2]

His wife, Halide Edib, during the national struggle, was on regular military duty as a corporal attached to the headquarters of the western front—the only woman soldier, though Turkish women everywhere were extremely active in supplementing their men's efforts for the national cause. Corporal Halide took her military task most seriously, but in one letter to her husband she could not resist a joke about her military "influ-

[2] Dr. Adnan-Adivar continued his brilliant activities for thirty-three more years and died in the spring of 1955. During a stay in America after World War II, he received an honorary doctorate from Princeton University.

ence." She asked him, "Are they taking good care of you? If not, tell me and I will file a complaint that a soldier's family is being neglected."

Our unheralded visit to the Gazi was completely successful. He was in a mood to talk about his life, and I took careful notes. This rare story, beginning with boyhood and school days in our home town, Salonika, and finally explaining certain phases of World War I and the national struggle, filled wide gaps in my mental picture. It gave me an almost uncanny feeling to hear from the moving spirit how, in less than two years, the gulf between utter despair and thrilling confidence had been bridged. I found it easy to grasp the fact that the will power, the vision, and the courage of a clear-sighted leader was the immediate source of this miracle. Today, his story is known, in more detail, through books and articles by both Turkish and foreign authors. Then, however, the whole world was eager to learn about this mysteriously daring leader who was resisting the will of victorious powers in his defeated and devastated country.

Even in Turkey, the people knew little about Mustafa Kemal because the war government had discouraged publicity concerning him. Inter-Allied censorship had cut the population of Istanbul off from the real sources of information in Ankara. I could satisfy the wide-awake curiosity in Istanbul and elsewhere by publishing the life story of the new national chief in his own words. I could offer a coherent account of what had happened to arouse the Turkish nation to life. My interview, which appeared as a twenty-column story in *Milliyet*, remains the only published record of the military life of Mustafa Kemal during World War I as related by himself. The Inter-Allied censors showed the good taste not to suppress this story.

I left Ankara to visit the war fronts in Anatolia. I felt very curious to see our fighting forces, forged virtually overnight from remnants of a defeated and disintegrated army. It was an acid test of what Turks are capable of achieving under stress of extreme danger from outside and the inspiration of farseeing and resourceful leadership inside.

To begin with, I must explain that the Turks did not have a high idea of their own capacities. There were various reasons for this. Foreign powers had conducted a successful propaganda campaign for their "right" to interfere in Turkey, on the premise that the Turks were incapable of progress by their own ambition and ability, and were badly in need of tutelage. The Turks themselves had been influenced by this propaganda. The retarded condition of their country seemed to offer sad evidence that this was so. Many of them compared Turkey's condition with that of Western Europe and felt obliged to admit that this gap could never be filled.

Furthermore, the wasteful measures in World War I had not raised the self-respect of the Turks. It is true that there had been heroic tilts against superior Western forces, but the three Young Turk dictators had deliberately yielded Turkey's destiny to German direction and inevitable failure. The Istanbul government's handling of postwar economic problems and spiritual issues had been inefficient and demoralizing. On my way to the front, I reviewed to myself this depressing background of Turkish degradation.

I also called to mind the early days of the national struggle after the Greek landing in İzmir, while I was in exile in Kütahya. All life, then, appeared to have been drained from the nation's arteries, leaving a perfect vacuum. Then this vacuum began to fill. The first transfusion of fresh spirit came along the telegraph wires. As the Gazi himself acknowledged, the obedience of many telegraph operators was the first actual force at his disposal in the struggle for survival. I saw this, day by day, in Kütahya. The telegraph office seemed to connect the community with a spring of vital energy which originated in Mustafa Kemal.

Everyone with any sense of attachment to his country kept returning to the telegraph office, day and night, eager for each bit of news.

When I arrived at the actual front, after my two years of foreign exile, I was amazed. The new army was superior in spirit to the best-organized and well-disciplined troops that I had seen on German fronts. The officers' and soldiers' vitality and initiative could be attributed to the spirit of love and sacrifice engendered to protect their own homes and freedom. Each officer had been carefully selected from a long list of applicants, mostly volunteers from the defeated army of World War I. These officers, chosen on the bases of morality, ability, and courage, did not look down on their soldiers as nonentities whose lives they were free to waste as in previous wars. This strange Grand National Assembly in Ankara, with self-made executive power, sent deputation after deputation to the front to see that the life of every soldier was carefully treasured. Warm winter quarters had been dug behind the trenches. Clothing was adequate, and the food was nutritious, and most of both had been requisitioned from the homes of townsman and peasant alike and transported to the few rail centers, or directly to the fronts, by buffalo or oxcart or on donkey and human backs. Finally, careful medical service was supplied at the front.

I was seeing with my own eyes how far superior in spirit and achievement a co-operating force is, compared to a merely disciplined one. Upon investigation, I found that nearly every soldier, loyally fighting against invasion of his homeland, had been a deserter from the World War I army. Here was an entire army that had saved itself by desertion from sure death by hunger, neglect, sickness, and inhuman treatment, not by enemy bullets. The common story that I heard from these soldiers was this:

"I was sent to fight in lands inhabited by people who did

not speak my language. They spoke Arabic or other strange languages. I did not know why I was fighting. Nothing to eat, drink, or smoke; no leaves from the army; no mail from home for years. We were like so many flies to be killed. The German soldiers, serving on the same front, lived like princes. I felt rebellious. I ran away to save my life. So did other men from my village, and thousands from other villages. We are glad now that we did. If we had not deserted, if we had all died as so many thousands did, who would save our homeland now?"

"In our National Army," they would add, "we all know what we are fighting for. The highest commander is one of us, a big brother, anxious for our welfare. With confidence, we do what he says. When we are wounded, we are impatient to get back to the front."

These simple avowals in friendly conversation revealed the high efficiency natural to a people's army fighting to save their own homes from aggressors. This may also explain the poor performance of the aggressive Russian Army against the Finns in 1939, whereas the same Russian Army thereafter performed miracles of defense against German invaders. One fact is outstanding: the new nationalist Turkey had no tradition, no sacrosanct rules, no red tape to be followed blindly. When this is so, waste motion dies, and functional activity flourishes.

Later on, the new government forgot the very source of its strength and picked up again the whole snarl of red-tape regulations left by the Sick Man—until new regulations could be made. In that interval, special commissions and courts-martial tried, according to old regulations, "misdeeds" in the War of Independence against the Greeks. Officers in that war had assumed responsibility freely and ignored red tape. Consequently, the court-martial report on many of them read: "According to regulations they should be hanged. According to actual service and achievement, they should have monuments erected to them.

117

We feel incompetent to condemn, for instance, the director of an emergency artillery repair shop for stripping rails from a railroad siding to make spare parts for cannons. The government must decide what course to take."

Certain types of persons in the army both helped and hindered in their confusion of old and new values. I saw one such example at Akşehir, where, as elsewhere on my tour of the Eskişehir, Akşehir, and Konya fronts, I again met generals I had known on Malta. At the Second Army headquarters of Generl Yakub Şevki, whom I consider the best exponent of true military virtues, I met Osman Ağa, the commander of the only irregular regiment then left from the early guerrilla fighting. Osman Ağa and his daring warriors from Giresun, a Black Sea province, had been a great help. But in the regular army, he was rather a handicap, and so he was kept near headquarters lest he do harm.

This man was one of the semifeudal overlords, a relic of the past, tolerated and protected by Sultan Abdülhamid II in return for blind fealty and service, and surviving only because the nationalist government could not so soon liquidate all evil vestiges of the past. I had my first quaint taste of Osman Ağa's sense of values when I took a snapshot of his eight-year-old son. When I could not instantly show the finished picture, the boy drew a small revolver and said in genuine anger, "The picture right now or I kill you." The father was amused and proud. His only criticism was that his son did not yet understand that the sacred duty of hospitality took precedence over anger.

Osman Ağa then told a barbaric tale of his guerrilla days in order to convince me of his psychological shrewdness. When his band had ambushed a Greek unit, the Greeks appealed to the British for support. On arrival of the British representative, Osman Ağa made a quick move to deter him from any helpfulness to the Greeks. "Mayor" Osman welcomed the English offi-

Editor Yalman returns from Malatya after recovering from wounds inflicted in an attempted assassination.

Hüseyin Üzmez, the would-be assassin, in court.

*President İsmet Inönü, left, talks with Mr. Yalman
at a press conference just before the 1950 elections,
when Inönü became the leader of the opposition party.*

cer in the name of the town and invited him to a banquet in his honor in the town hall.

"That night," said Osman Ağa, "while the festivities were going on in a large room, I had one of the Greek revolutionary chiefs executed in the adjoining room. We had captured and tried him in a revolutionary manner the night before. I took pains to let the Greeks know what was happening. The next day the Greeks rushed to the house where the English officer was the guest of the town, and added to their other allegations the story of a Greek killed in the room next to the banquet room during the banquet.

"The Englishman, as I knew he would, said, 'Now, I am certain that you are lying. I cannot believe that this could happen without my noticing anything unusual going on in or around that small building. Why should I believe your other stories? I don't need to make any further inquiry.' "

"You know," Osman Ağa added, "the pressure of a strong hand on the throat is sufficient to make one cross the thin line between life and death. I relied on the fact that the Englishman would expect violent death to be spectacular and attract attention." This man certainly had the inspiration of the devil, and I was glad, myself, to flee from his effusive hospitality. At the end of our war, Osman Ağa and some of his men were taken to Ankara. There he killed an opposition deputy, a very popular retired naval officer. That was his idea, and generally an old idea, of loyalty, and he felt that he deserved an official blessing for destroying opposition. Instead, a warrant was issued for his arrest, and he was killed while trying to resist.

My final stop for military observation at Konya filled me with admiration for the ingenuity revealed in the supply system used in an area cut off from the outside world. The workshops organized there by General Kâzim with incredibly limited means were far more ingenious than the remarkable German

successes with *ersatz* materials. Then I went to the southern provinces to join in celebrating their liberation from the French
occupation. The French had withdrawn and left us the bulk of
their ammunition and equipment, partly perhaps in pique at
the British dominance instead of the partnership envisioned in
the secret treaties to partition Turkey after the Sick Man's death.

I made my way back to Istanbul as quickly as possible to
convey to my readers my absolute trust in our complete victory
and the full success of our new national government. I could, in
all honesty, blazon the message that the old idea of the incapacity
of the Turks was a lie. As soon as the Turks had the chance,
they proved that they have every reason for self-respect and self-
confidence.

11: END OF

THE SULTANATE

THE TOWN of Akşehir is small, but has been famous in Turkey since the sixteenth century as the home town of Nasreddin Hoca, our most popular humorist and philosopher. Every Turk knows by heart his anecdotes which illuminate all situations in life. He put the experiences and foibles of past generations in a nutshell, and so wittily transmitted them to the future that they amount to a complete popular education.

As soon as I could do so after my arrival in Akşehir, I visited the tomb of Nasreddin Hoca. It was built according to his own instructions and is itself a remarkable expression of his ironical view of life. The tomb consists of a big gate with a tremendously large and elaborate lock, but there is no fence and nothing behind the gate. The tomb symbolizes the vanity of taking life too seriously.

I learned later that President Woodrow Wilson, who was a special admirer of Nasreddin Hoca, had heard of him from his friend Charles Crane, the former minister to China. Crane had somewhere heard and remembered the stories of Nasreddin Hoca and knew how to tell them to illustrate various situations.

This was in Paris after the war. Woodrow Wilson had committed the great error of coming personally to Paris and becoming a subordinate figure, instead of sitting in America, using American prestige to defend the sound principles which he had promulgated for the world, and achieving a peace worthy of the

121

name. There are malicious people who pretend that the course of world history was changed because an ambitious second wife wished to go to Paris.

In a moment of despair and self-realization, Wilson asked Charles Crane to tell the story of Nasreddin which best fitted the situation in Paris. This was the story Crane told: "On a bright night, with a full moon, Nasreddin was passing near a well. He looked down and saw that the moon was in the bottom of the well. 'I must save the poor moon,' he decided. He took a bucket and drew bucketful after bucketful of water. The poor moon still remained in the bottom. At last the bucket became stuck under a rock in the bottom of the well. Pulling hard, Nasreddin fell on his back and saw the moon in its full splendor in the sky. 'I have worked hard, but I have at last saved the moon!' he declared, satisfied with himself." Woodrow Wilson readily admitted that the story was a perfect representation of so-called peace efforts made in Paris.

The Inter-Allied occupation was still in force in Istanbul, but by the time I returned from my tour of Anatolia, the people's minds had at last come under the nationalists' sway. The occupation authorities no longer attempted to oppose this trend. Indeed, fraternization with nationalist Turks was not only permitted but eagerly encouraged.

There was still a Turkish government in Istanbul, nominally dependent on the Sultan, but it actually took orders from Ankara. The Grand Vizier, Tevfik Pasha, a man of eighty years, asked me to write and publish an interview with him in which I should use my knowledge of the spirit in Ankara to make "his" words echo that spirit. The tone of this interview was to indicate to Ankara that the Istanbul government was at its service, and to the outside world that basic unity in Turkey was perfect, while the apparent division between the Istanbul and Ankara governments was only temporary, the result of circumstances beyond the control of either side. I wrote this interview, and the Vizier accepted it without changing a word, thus committing himself to a bold position—doubly bold because his son was married to the Sultan's daughter, a family bond not to be lightly ignored in the palace circle's code. This actual abdication of power crowned Tevfik Pasha's long career, every part of which had remained strictly honest in spite of the general misrule by the old government.

Despair thereupon swept over those who had sided with the British against the nationalists, and they prepared to leave the country at the first alarm. Ali Kemal, the leading antinationalist journalist, continued to urge the British to stand firm against the nationalists. Some desperadoes caught Ali Kemal in a barbershop in the most crowded part of the city and took him to İzmit to be tried for treason. He was stoned to death by a mob there. This incident turned the antinationalist alarm into a panic.

And the last Sultan, Mehmed VI—what was he doing at this moment when fate so clearly put the stamp of doom on the Ottoman dynasty which had ruled Turkey for more than six centuries? The victory of the nationalists would mean the *coup de grace* for the Ottoman Sick Man. Sultan Mehmed VI, however, was completely apathetic in the face of the impending end of his dynasty. His interests were concentrated in his personal drama, a passion for the eighteen-year-old daughter of a gardener of the palace. Unable to add her to his harem because the girl, who was engaged to a young sea captain, resisted fiercely his passionate solicitations, the Sultan placed pressure on her family. Finally she had to yield, thus becoming the last wife of the last sultan, although this "honor" hardly appealed to her. So the final collapse of the Ottoman dynasty was staged amidst a scandalous side show. A lecherous old man of more than seventy had forgotten his throne, family, and country in pursuit of a young girl of eighteen; he had separated her from a young sea captain, had married her against her will. This indirectly contributed, at that moment, to the antidynastic drive by Ankara. It destroyed the last vestige of respect and attachment for the Ottoman Sick Man. It was the final act of a dynastic suicide. A British warship carried Mehmed VI and his bride to exile.

Years afterwards I became involved in this drama in a strange way. The young wife of the last Sultan returned to Turkey after his death in San Remo, Italy. She married the captain who had been patiently waiting for her all these years. They had two children and were living a secluded life, trying to keep in oblivion the first chapters of a sad, romantic life. One day, while I was at a dentist's office, I was informed that this woman was in the next room with her small son. Following my journalistic instincts, I made the dentist introduce me and help me to persuade her to give me the story of her life.

It was an amazing story of a poor girl who, against her will, had become the favorite wife of the last Sultan. She was favored in every way for years, even having a new palace built for her just as the old empire was crumbling. She was the most intimate eyewitness of the last days of Sultan Mehmed VI, of his flight after the victory of the nationalists and of his last year in Italy. There was a pathetic story of the scenes after his death—the electric current and water were cut off in the large house because bills had not been paid. There was not even money for the funeral, because the old man had been robbed by his favorites. The young woman, also, was robbed of everything. She returned home to start an existence full of privation. Then, she met her old fiancé and married him. Fate had chosen to play with her. After a dream—or nightmare—as a favorite in a palace, she had returned to her previous life just where it had been interrupted by the spectacular events which had dragged her away for some years. Was she happy now? Did she regret all those past splendors? Well, she had a grim feeling about fate, which had played with her so mercilessly.

No journalist could wish a serial with a more exciting appeal. We advertised it on a large scale. I wrote it as she told it to me and started to publish it in the form of a day-by-day diary by the young woman. However, the pleasure of this journalistic triumph was of short duration. One day my door at the newspaper office was burst open by a madman. He was her husband, the sea captain, now quite aged.

"You cease that publication immediately," he said, "or there will be a great many dead people. You are unearthing a tragedy which I did so much to bury. I was a poor captain. Only one girl existed for me. My path was crossed by the Sultan himself. He could marry any woman, but he chose to marry my girl. I had plans to kill him. I could not, but history more than killed him. The woman of my young dreams returned to me after being the subject of gossip for a whole country. She is now the mother of my two children. As the sad hero of such publicity, life is of no value to me. If another installment is published, I kill the woman, I kill my two children, I kill the dentist, I kill you, and then myself. Choose!"

We argued hours and hours, consuming many cups of coffee and packages of cigarettes. Finally we made an agreement that his wife's personal memoirs be discontinued immediately, but the story of the last days of Sultan Mehmed VI might be continued as a serial written by the newspaper. It was hardly the same thing, but I had really no choice.

Now let us return to the days when the Sultan's government still existed in phantom form, but the country, including Istanbul, was actually ruled by the new government in Ankara. During this period of government in two "capitals," many interesting Americans and Englishmen visited both cities in order to learn firsthand about the Sick Man's demise and the incredible young heir governing in Ankara. I would like to give a few sidelights on the personal and informal reactions of some of these visitors.

In Ankara I was on the lookout for the new Russian ambassador, Comrade Araloff, hoping for the first interview with him. In the city's only restaurant, there was a man wearing badly rumpled though good-quality clothes and several days' growth of beard who jibed very well with my preconception of a Russian diplomat. I approached him and asked, in French, if he was Comrade Araloff. I was startled to receive a reply in French with a nasal American accent. He turned out to be Julian W. Gillespie, the new American commercial attaché, just arrived after an eight-day trip by horse carriage. I managed to find a room for him in a newspaper building, little realizing the decisive role he was to play in my life later.

That evening, in the house of a member of parliament who had been in Malta with me, we gave Gillespie the *rakı* test, which he passed brilliantly. *Rakı* was very popular in the desolate Ankara of those days in spite of, or perhaps because of, the prohibition of its manufacture. Gossip had it that the shrewd director of police had a flourishing business in a secret distilling plant. An adventurous life had led Gillespie to Turkey. A Texan, brimming with pioneer spirit, he had enlisted in France after studying law in Texas, and had become a colonel in the new Polish Army after World War I. Some vagary of fortune shifted him to Turkey as representative of the United States' new Department of Commerce. The pioneer atmosphere in Turkey must have appealed to him, for he settled here. His three children were born here, and here he lived seventeen years, until his death in 1938. He was a popular and influential figure in Turkey through those years.

William Bullitt, former United States ambassador to Paris,

came to Turkey in the early 1920's, after completing a mission of investigation in Russia for President Woodrow Wilson. He rented an old house which had been built on the Asiatic shore of the Bosporus centuries ago by the family of the Grand Vizier, Köprülü Mustafa. (Today a descendant of the same family, Fuad Köprülü, is the Turkish Republic's minister of foreign affairs.) Mr. Bullitt devoted most of his time to writing a novel including both Turkish and American heroes, which he never completed. He took as a protégé a boy whom he noticed favorably among the neighborhood children playing in the streets, and who was a descendant of the Köprülü family. He sent the boy to the best private school in Turkey. As the years passed, the boy spent many vacations in whatever country Mr. Bullitt happened to be, and finally entered aviation in America. One day, he returned to the land of his birth as a licensed aviator, with letters of introduction from Mr. Bullitt, who had become the American ambassador to Moscow. This trained lad was Mr. Bullitt's gift to Turkey.

On one of the many times that I saw Mr. Bullitt in Turkey, he remarked, "I believe I shall open a world-wide subscription campaign to help the Turks to survive economically. They are the only people in the present reign of money who refuse to submit to its domination. They all try to pay each other's checks in restaurants, and one man may spend his entire salary for this honor. You cannot expect fellows with such contempt for money to survive in this age, but it is cheering for the world to have one species that scorns money, so let the world pay for this pleasure."

Recently, in America, I reminded Mr. Bullitt of this jocular suggestion, and he said that he had seriously attempted to raise money in America for Turkish relief organizations, explaining how the Turks had suffered as a result of World War I and their own War of Independence. "But," he said, "the anti-Turkish propaganda was so thick in the American atmosphere that all too few would admit that Turks, too, are human beings. What a change of sentiment you Turks have brought about since then!"

Lord Beaverbrook, owner of the *Daily Express,* came to investigate the other side of the anti-Turkish views which had guided Lloyd George's disastrous policy. I hastened to his hotel to offer some objective information. We lunched and dined, and talked together all afternoon and evening. He asked question after question about facts that no one in England had ever heard about. The impressions that he cabled to his paper from Turkey, he told me later in London, were so unpleasant for the Greeks that he was not allowed to land in Greece on his return trip.

An English Labor party member and former diplomat, George Young, who was *persona non grata* with his own government, came secretly to Turkey. While he was British chargé d'affaires in Lisbon, at the beginning of World War I, he had refused to obey orders that would have dragged Portugal into the war. One subject of our many long talks in Ankara was the democratic spirit and attitude of the new leaders in power in Turkey, men who were not spoiled by their victories.

"We must wait and see," he warned me. "Men are not blinded by power but by its external trappings. Let these men move into palaces and have a large entourage and many proselytes. They will enjoy their exalted and privileged position as men always do."

George Young's prophecy might have had an early test if the new government had moved to the old capital, Istanbul. But in the new capital, Ankara, the lack of palaces and indeed anything but minimum, hence generally equal, accommodations for all, and the vigor of the spirited idealism, warded off power-blindness, at least for some time and to some degree.

The visit of Professor Arnold Toynbee before the signing of peace had a very significant outcome. The chair of Byzantine history, which he occupied in London University, was endowed by the Greek government. Consequently, the Manchester *Guardian,* a liberal paper that was published in a city with a large Greek colony and that was taking an anti-Turkish position, chose him to go to Turkey as presumably a pro-Greek observer. Here, Professor Toynbee unearthed the full truth about Turkey, including the mistakes of the English and the Greeks. He reported this with courageous frankness. He did more. Upon learning that a massacre of Turks in Yalova by the indigenous Greeks was imminent, he went to Yalova and averted it by his presence. He helped the Turkish Red Crescent to remove the Turks from the danger zone.

The Manchester *Guardian* showed remarkable integrity in publishing his reports which ran counter to its own previous stand. This publicity cost Professor Toynbee the chair of Byzantine history, and he was without a position for some time; but he never expressed regret for this price he had to pay for truthful reporting. In the book that he subsequently wrote, entitled *The Western Question in Greece and Turkey,* he pointed out that massacres and such crimes were not practices peculiar to any one religious faith or nationality in the Near East. His honest appraisal of the situation in Turkey, published in an important British newspaper, was a bright ray of light breaking through the stormy clouds of anti-Turkish propaganda in the Western press.

In order to keep pace with the remarkable experiment in national regeneration in the interval between my visit to the nationalist lines and the Turkish general offensive in August, 1922, I repeatedly visited Ankara and also İzmit, the Anatolian listening post nearest to Istanbul and the outside world to which Mustafa Kemal could come safely. One day there, in İzmit, he said to me privately, "Don't go back to Istanbul with the other newspapermen. Stay in my headquarters. You will not be sorry."

He did not, however, disclose to me that this was my golden chance to be the only newspaperman to accompany him in the final offensive of our War of Independence. I begged off with the plea that I had just become engaged. My fiancée was a young girl who had already made a name in magazine writing.

"You are useless, then," Mustafa Kemal said. "The attention of any man thrilled by new family prospects will be divided between that and the national cause." Thirteen years later, when he met my wife, he admitted that I had a good excuse.

In Istanbul we had no idea when the offensive would start, but it happened on my wedding day, and the first attack was followed by startling success. The Greek front crumbled; and in the days necessary to reach İzmir by cavalry from Sakarya, the invasion army, including the commander in chief, was captured, and the Turks returned victoriously to İzmir. My wife and I, without a moment's hesitation, chose İzmir for our honeymoon, and we arrived three days after the reoccupation to find the city in flames.

Turkey had always had a large Greek and Armenian population. Although these resident Greeks, very few of whom had ever been in Greece, were technically Turkish citizens, they had aided the invading army from Greece in every possible way. In the panic of the fire, tens of thousands of these citizens, turned refugees, packed the docks and shore for miles. It was a rare and graphic spectacle of a terrible historic process, for it led to a huge population exchange. All Greeks disloyal to Turkey were told to consider their Turkish rights forfeited and were advised to emigrate to the country of their choice. For the Greeks, it meant the overnight loss of homes and sources of livelihood, it meant facing a new life in a parent country, actually foreign to them, as victims of a dream by an ambitious Greek statesman supported by Prime Minister Lloyd George of England. From the Turkish standpoint it was a tragic but necessary amputation of hostile elements in the population of Turkey, essential to peace and political health in the Near East. These people were to follow their personal loyalty to another country. A spontaneous Turkish order then, the emigration was ratified eventually in treaty terms for the formal Turkish-Greek exchange of population, supervised by an international commission.

The extent of the tragedy was recognized years afterwards when the Greek emigrants, who were culturally 100 per cent Turks, speaking only Turkish even in their church services, suffered homesickness for the land of their birth and the loss of prosperity enjoyed in underpopulated Turkey, while they lived from hand to mouth as refugees in overpopulated Greece. The immigrant Turks, though more easily absorbed economically in Turkey, belonged culturally to Greece, where their families had lived for generations. When we arrived in İzmir, an international organization was rushing emigrants onto ships hastily summoned to rescue them.

A queer sort of honeymoon began for us, coincident with the days of joy at the war's end for the Turkish population. Everywhere we heard, "Who could have thought in the gloom of foreign oppression that God had such joy in store for us?"

Moreover, it was our personal delight to discover a romance developing in Mustafa Kemal's headquarters, opposite the house found for us by two fellow exiles with me in Malta, now the governor and the military commander in İzmir. The Gazi's headquarters were in the large residence of a rich notable, Muammer Bey. His eldest daughter, Latife Hanım, ran the house. Though it was the most appropriate building for his purpose, Mustafa Kemal had first rejected it, saying, "I don't want family intimacy, especially with that girl dominating the house too much for my taste."

Fate took a hand. The second-choice house burned that night, and Mustafa Kemal was soon receiving a conglomeration of visitors on the terrace of Muammer Bey's house, overlooking his gorgeous garden. Nobody thought of protocol in those festive days, and anybody, native or foreign, who came with a man known to an aide-de-camp, was admitted. Latife Hanım attracted the admiration of all, for in addition to running the house skilfully and interpreting in various languages for foreign journalists, she was soon acting as interpreter and private secretary to the Gazi. Before long the great man forgot what he had told me in İzmit about the disadvantages of family ties during a national crisis and became engaged to Latife Hanım.

Soon after the Turkish victory, four warships, one each from England, France, Italy, and Greece, converged upon Mudanya harbor on the Marmara Sea, about forty miles from Istanbul, and the eyes of the world converged on a little waterfront house to which each country's armistice negotiators came, from their floating headquarters, to meet Colonel İsmet, commander of the victorious Turkish Army. Whereas the Allies had intended the 1918 Armistice of Mudros with Turkey to be a prelude to dismemberment, this new armistice in 1922, for Turkey's successful War of Independence, meant the end of the Greeks' and the Allied Powers' generations-old dreams of becoming the Sick Man's heirs. A real stumbling block in the negotiations was the Ankara government's insistence on the immediate removal of Allied occupation authorities and forces from Istanbul and the rest of European Turkey, whereas the Allies wished to retain their hold on that area as a trump card in eventual peace negotiations.

Journalists from practically every country scrambled for advance news tips from aides-de-camp and secretaries, who mostly scurried busily past the newspapermen. There was no telegraphic communication, so the correspondents had to use their ingenuity to find daily transportation to Istanbul and back to send dispatches. The night the crisis was reached, we heard, about midnight, that the decision for peace or more war was near. The break came at dawn. The Turks were to control Istanbul and Thrace (European Turkey), dressed not as soldiers but as gendarmes, as long as the Inter-Allied occupation continued, which was to be until a peace treaty was signed. Journalists present vied for souvenirs. I got the plain pen used by the Italian delegate. Then I got a lift on a French torpedo boat to Istanbul.

When a nationalist regiment in gendarme uniforms entered Istanbul, the Turkish population's welcome was overpowering. Demonstrations were organized to clear the air of grievances incurred during four years of chafing under the occupation; and, at the end of many decades of palace oppression, corruption, and injustice, the Turks celebrated at last the rebirth of the Turkish nation. For days and nights, half a million people deliriously enjoyed an unbelievable good dream after a long nightmare. General Refet, the Ankara government's representative in the reoccupation, promised no excesses if pressure by the Allied authorities did not provoke the public. The Allied police discreetly disappeared, and there were no excesses.

The Sultan's palace, however, was in deep mourning. All traitor Turks fled on British ships. That day, October 7, 1922, was when Sultan Mehmed VI joined the refugees and was taken to Malta on board a British war ship, the same transportation and the same destination imposed on us, his former victims, just a few months after my release from imprisonment on that island —a quick reversal of fate! Istanbul had joined the Ankara government on October 4, in spite of the Allied occupation. On November 2, 1922, the Grand National Assembly in Ankara declared the "personal sultanate" abolished and proclaimed the "Sultanate of the People."

12: END OF

THE KHALIFATE

THE NEXT ACT took place in Lausanne, Switzerland. There the Allied negotiators met İsmet Pasha, now a general and chief of the Turkish delegation from Ankara, to write a treaty of peace. The negotiations were long and harassing to the British delegation headed by Lord Curzon, a very obstinate negotiator who, however, met his match in the calmer-tempered İsmet Pasha.

From beginning to end of the national struggle, Mustafa Kemal and his government had adamantly rejected the peace treaty of Sèvres which the Sultan's representatives had signed. Mustafa Kemal, therefore, sent İsmet Pasha to Lausanne to secure entirely new terms, acceptable to the new Turkish government. Article by article, the Sèvres terms were whittled away under İsmet's imperturbable insistence, and new terms were presented. The final result was the Treaty of Lausanne, the only peace by mutual consent following World War I, and it bore good fruits, as is amply testified by the world-wide respect thereafter accorded to Turkey for her recovery at home and her voluntary co-operation with the Western powers.

I had foolishly refused the position of personal interpreter to İsmet Pasha because of my fanatical will to remain a 100 per cent journalist, free from official government duties. This post would have enabled me to follow the inside workings of the historical Lausanne conference, day by day. As it was, I spent only a few days in Lausanne, just long enough to sense the atmosphere in order to interpret better the reports from there.

Moreover, I had an important personal reason for remaining in Istanbul during the months of the conference. I had decided to establish a new daily paper, *Vatan* (*Fatherland*), with Ahmet Şükrü Esmer, my former fellow student in Columbia, and Enis Tahsin, the best news editor in Turkey, so I liquidated my partnership in the newspaper, *Vakit,* which had reached the second largest circulation in Turkey. Remarkably enough, *Vatan,* on its first day of publication, enjoyed an equal circulation. From that day to this, *Vatan*'s course has been inextricably interwoven with Turkey's fate. Happily, we had been able to hire the complete printing plant of a daily which had ceased publication after the national victory. That daily was the *Sabah,* on which I had started as a journalist in 1907 and of which I had become editor in 1916. In a few months our new paper was so firmly established in our at last happily governed country that I could leave Istanbul when invited to represent the Turkish press at a journalistic conference in Sweden.

After the Treaty of Lausanne was signed on July 24, 1923, it is sad but true that the honeymoon atmosphere in Turkey did not last very long. As soon as our invigorated nation felt the release from foreign pressure, its unity was endangered by personal dissensions bubbling to the surface. The vastly changed status of the Turkish nation lacked stability because remnants of the old imperial psychology still were strong. The Ottoman dynasty, since 1517, had combined the temporal power of the sultan of Turkey with the religious power of the khalif, a sort of pope or patriarch of all Islam. Each sultan, from then on, held both powers. The law abolishing the sultanate, passed by the Grand National Assembly in Ankara, vested temporal sovereignty in the Turkish people, but it allowed the eldest male member of the Ottoman dynasty to retain the title and dignity of khalif. Hence Sultan Mehmed VI's successor, Abdul Mecit, exercised religious authority, a situation which caused considerable uneasiness and animosity.

In Islam, the body of religious law, called the *Sheriat,* extended to many secular matters, such as inheritance and property rights. It became obvious that not only individuals but perhaps even other Muslim governments would make an issue of the extent of the khalif's authority in a secular state, or try to use some weak khalif as a pawn in their own interest. Many people knew of this conflict, but no decisive restriction of the khalifate seemed even thinkable. For centuries the dynasty's propaganda had instilled practically slavish acceptance of the importance and prestige of the khalif, who was used to sustain the aura of the earlier Ottoman glory. As this glory and power had waned in Christian parts of the Empire, it was often repeated with pride, if with dubious relation to fact, that the khalifate still gave Turkey mastery over three hundred million Muslims. Another idea widely circulated was that the Friday prayers would lose their validity if the khalif were to be deprived of administrative power. In the face of these convictions, who could discover a practical way out?

Well, Mustafa Kemal did. As a matter of fact, he had made up his mind very early, and the journalists were the first persons to be taken into his confidence on this subject. A journalist's ear has never heard a more startling challenge.

One day in January, 1924, the editors of seven Turkish dailies were asked to proceed immediately to İzmit to confer with Mustafa Kemal. The meeting took place in the large hall of the government building. Dr. Adnan, vice-president of the National Assembly, and his wife, former Corporal Halide Edib, were also present. Stenographers were ready to take notes. There was unusual solemnity as we gathered in the President's presence.

Mustafa Kemal asked each of us this question: "What do you think of the future of the khalifate?"

No one of us had thought more than vaguely about it. We gave various answers. We suggested that Istanbul should be made a center of enlightened learning for all Muslims which would attract tourists from Muslim countries. Someone spoke of a reformation in Islam. Mustafa Kemal listened patiently. At moments you could detect traces of an ironic smile on his face.

When we had poured forth all our wisdom, he told us bluntly: *"There is just one possible solution. The khalifate has to be abolished altogether."*

We felt as though we had been struck by lightning. Our brains stopped functioning. Somebody dared to think and speak of the abolition of the khalifate! It was like telling the Irish that the Vatican was to be outlawed. What about sacred traditions, centuries old? What about the resentment of the whole of Islam, and of the people of Turkey? How would all those influential religious dignitaries, *hocas* (teachers) and *imams* (prayer leaders and preachers), of thousands of mosques all over Turkey react to this revolutionary move? How could a young government just emerging from wars and revolts accept such far-reaching risks and court the dangers of revolt? This man, Mustafa Kemal, had proved up to now that he had superior vision, but had he not suddenly gone mad?

Mustafa Kemal waited a moment for the first dramatic effect. Then he continued: "I see from your looks that you have objections and doubts. I would like to hear them all. Don't hesitate; attack my idea, say that it is crazy, but give specific arguments for your opinions. We have to co-operate to bring about a far-reaching social revolution. It means crossing from the Middle Ages to modern life, from authority to reason. If everybody is not persuaded 100 per cent, if he does not feel the urge for this move, if he does not side with me with full enthusiasm, his co-operation is valueless."

We certainly had objections, enough to keep us there in discussion for thirty-six hours. Some were so obvious: "Would we not lose the sympathy of three hundred million Muslims?"

"What is there to prove the actual value of this sympathy?" Kemal asked, and replied: "We proclaimed a holy war, and hundreds of thousands of Muslims fought against us in the ranks of a Christian enemy. No mark of sympathy was ever shown by them. I don't say they would mind our risking our existence in order to fight for them, if their independence were at stake. But let them do that themselves, if they wish independence. We Turks must at last live our own lives."

"Would the abolition not mean a loss of prestige in foreign policy?"

"Prestige? We have been lost in a fool's dream. All the imperialistic powers would rejoice to have us retain the khalifate; they would pretend to be hearty friends. We would remain slaves of theocracy and deprive ourselves of all serious opportunity for modernization; and that would suit them well. Every imperialistic power has had a clear-cut policy of using religious illusions as opiates to maintain subject populations in ignorance and half-slavery. When we abolish the khalifate, watch the European papers which are most hostile to our existence. They will be very angry because we did so, because we shall be emancipating ourselves from bonds of theocracy and blind authority."

I must anticipate my story to say that this forecast came true. All friendly foreign papers commended Turkey for the courage of making, at one stroke, such a tremendous social revolution. All hostile ones, so keen for their countries to control our land and destiny, criticized us for deliberately depriving ourselves of the great "influence and prestige" with which the khalifate had endowed Turkey.

Our questions continued, one after another. Mustafa Kemal gave clear, convincing answers to every one. Still our minds needed time to travel from the depths of fixed stupidity and illusions to a clear view of facts. We were under the pressure of traditions, blindly accepted, and we had not his wide vision to see immediately beyond accepted limits.

The question which greatly perturbed me was how the religious classes would take the abolition. I carefully formulated a question on this, giving free play to my anxieties. Mustafa Kemal was far from sharing my alarmist views.

"There is a class of people in this country who act as brokers of influence," he said, "using religious fanaticism as their weapon. They go to the people and pretend that the government yields to their influence. Relying upon this pretended relationship, they exploit the people. Then they come to the government and pretend that the people follow them blindly. So they exploit the stupidity of the government. The fact is that we all have been parties to a game of blind assumptions. The educated classes in this country are not fanatic-minded, but pretend to be so in order to please the people who, as a whole, reflect the attitude of a domineering religious class. Actually, the large masses are far from having orthodox views, but they have felt that they must pretend to have them. In the midst of these pretenses we are losing our way, and we feel obliged to make a colorless compromise instead of following the requirements of pure reason. The moment we decide not to be fooled any longer the real situation will appear like a lovely view, unveiled by disappearing clouds. Dethronement of the religious demagogues will follow automatically and immediately."

This man certainly had different eyes from ours. He was the clearest example of emancipation from social stupidity one could hope to know. For him, every aspect appeared in its true light as part of a rational order.

But our doubts persisted. Another question was, "Why was the abolition of the khalifate not carried out at the same time as that of the sultanate?"

"When we abolished the sultanate," he explained, "the khalifate should have been abolished at the same moment; and all members of the old dynasty should have been ousted from the country for their criminal behavior. However, performance of this major operation seemed to be very complex and too severe a strain on our people, especially when peace had not yet been signed. So I divided it into two stages—suppression of the sultanate and then of the khalifate. To keep the old dynasty permanently in the country, adorned with the religious title of khalif, would mean the continuation of intrigue and unrest, obstructing any balanced development. Yet, the advantages of giving the nation a slower, hence better, chance for readjustment to extreme changes has seemed, up to now, to outweigh other considerations."

Even this long discussion did not bring to light the fact that Mustafa Kemal had prepared his major operation not in two, but in three, stages. He evidently passed over the third stage silently in his mind without revealing it just then because the time was not ripe, in his opinion, to disclose his project in its entirety. He would not risk losing the concentration of our effort on one stage at a time, a unification necessary for full success. Unaware of this, we asked at İzmit: "Are any more radical reforms to follow?"

"The abolition of the khalifate," our daring leader told us, "is a part of a general scheme to end every vestige of theocracy in our public affairs. Our laws and education will be free from religious domination. We shall be able to do new things because we think in a new way, and because scientific intelligence requires it. We shall no longer act this way or that merely because ancient rules and ignorant 'authorities' order it. Education and justice in Turkey will simultaneously become free to follow the requirements of the changing times."

This conversation, barely outlined here, but continued over many cups of Turkish coffee and hasty common meals, gave not one of us any feeling of fatigue. We were all conscious that the wheels of history were turning with an overwhelming speed in this very room. A society, medieval in its make-up and outlook in spite of superficial changes, was about to be forced, by absolutely unique methods, into the modern mold of the era of reason, and into a more balanced order than any society had been previously able to achieve. Throughout history, equally extreme changes had been made high-handedly by dictators; each change was enacted in great secrecy at first; then all publicity media were used to praise convincingly the *fait accompli*.

Mustafa Kemal did not want to dictate; he wished to persuade. The tactics we finally agreed to use were unique. We, in our newspapers, were to attack the government for not realizing the danger to the unity and stability of the country which the continuation of the khalifate constituted. We were to point out that the khalifate was obsolete from the standpoint of a modern Turkey, that the prestige attributed to it was a myth, and that the victory of the Turkish nation would not be complete without a concerted assault on the theocratic influences which blocked progress.

This plan was carried out in a marvelous spirit. We were astonished when we did not encounter the opposition and resistance anticipated. Following this concerted preparation by the press, the law to abolish the khalifate was passed on March 1, 1924; and two days later, laws for the secularization of courts and schools and the abolition of all theological seminaries (to be replaced by a theological faculty at the university) were passed as matters of course. Deportation of all members of the old imperial Ottoman dynasty caused general feelings of joy and relief.

In January, 1924, there had been no one in Turkey except Mustafa Kemal who thought the abolition of the khalifate a possibility. By March 4, 1924, every Turk was asking himself, "How was it that I did not discover for myself sooner that these theocratic institutions had become obsolete, and totally lacking in vitality? How could I mistake those gilded clouds for real convictions rooted in the minds of the people?"

A barrage of publicity was fired against the departing dynasty. A sort of magical spell which had protected the palace from being seen realistically suddenly vanished. Unrighteous acts, which had been tolerated as the time-honored privileges of the sultans, those trustees and owners of the Empire who also were self-styled followers and delegates of Muhammad, the Prophet, were now seen in their true light. Limitless polygamy, debauchery, and barbarous slavery stood revealed in all their real ugliness. Uncounted children had been born into that palace world of unrestricted sexual appetites. In some cases, an official marriage bond did not exist, or it was thought to be undesirable for the sake of the child; and abductions of children were everyday occurrences, without any regard for the mother. All the scandals and crimes which had been taking place, even in recent times, behind the palace walls were mercilessly divulged. The whole thing presented an abominable picture.

Then came the third stage. Even after the abolition of the khalifate, a reference had been left in the constitution to Islam as the "state religion" of Turkey. Elimination of this stipulation was the final stage in Mustafa Kemal's major operation to sever the theocratic grip on public life. When the khalifate was a thing of the past, this incongruity of a state religion was discussed in a press conference. I asked Mustafa Kemal, "Why have you left recognition of a state religion in the constitution so long after a regime based on free reason and full tolerance seems well established?"

"Why don't you attack me in your paper for not being radical and consistent in my acts?" he challenged me.

"I don't feel that it is a proper subject for discussion in a newspaper."

"The moment that you feel it is proper to make this a subject of public discussion, you may rest assured that the provision to which you rightly object will be taken out of our constitution."

As a matter of fact, this last stage of the operation was performed in the constitutional changes of April 15, 1928, so that a regime of secularism in Turkey became complete. In this fashion, the old theocratic authoritarian block to free progress was removed in three successive stages. Thus the people had time to understand and assimilate the meanings of the reforms their new government put into effect.

These sweeping reforms did not interfere in any way with religious devotion and the right to worship as one pleased. Religious practices could continue freely in the home, mosque, church, or synagogue, but could no longer exert dictatorial authority or insidious superstitious influence in the government, courts, and schools. Such tolerance rendered the Turkish religious revolution different from any kindred movement in history. Religious hypocrisy was attacked as mercilessly as the vanishing palace rule. Through well-planned and well-executed publicity, basically persuasive, one of the more radical and rapid reforms in social history found general acceptance as a matter of course, and public life continued without real shock. Finally, a special law was passed stipulating that any attempt to use religion as a political instrument would constitute high treason, religion being properly a source of altruism and love and not a weapon of selfish striving for power and influence.

143

13: NEW TESTS

OF LOYALTY

THE PERIOD of our national struggle, 1919–23, including our War of Independence, was one of free discussion. Mustafa Kemal tolerated bitter political criticisms and personal attacks. He did not use external dangers or internal crises as pretexts to silence critics. He realized by his own sensitivity to the forces involved that only persuasion and free consent could bring success in a struggle so difficult. In the Grand National Assembly itself, free discussion by the two blocs—one supporting the government, the other in opposition—did not mean divergence in purpose, but vigilance against abuses of power. The benefits of this freedom seemed to justify further liberty for discussion and persuasion.

Unfortunately this tolerance and fairness in the Assembly rapidly declined after the Treaty of Lausanne confirmed the success of the War of Independence. Those deserving the most credit drew deeper on the fund of public gratitude and tended to monopolize all credit. Personal passions and animosities gained ground at the expense of public benefit.

It seemed to me that a critical climax was reached the day that an interview with Mustafa Kemal appeared in the *Neue Freie Presse* of Vienna, Austria, to the effect that Turkey must have a regular republican form of government. This was a radical departure from the original conception of the Grand

National Assembly. Our Assembly of the people's representatives was not only a legislative but an executive body which delegated powers, under ministerial and other titles, to selected members of the Assembly who governed this or that aspect of public life, but always under Assembly control. No provision had been made, or deemed necessary, for other branches of the national government to balance the power of an executive Assembly. The regular republican system would add a president of the republic and presumably a cabinet to share and balance the responsibilities and powers of government.

I, along with others, had taken seriously the new regime's original idea that we did not need to imitate other countries, but must create a form of government fitted to our own requirements. Therefore, somebody had to persuade us that a change to a traditional republic would be better for our needs in peacetime. Instead, the whole thing struck like lightning. The Assembly, using all due constitutional gestures, "rubber stamped" the change a week or so after the appearance of the interview in the Austrian newspapers, and without any advance statement of the proposal in the Turkish press, the Republic of Turkey was officially declared on October 29, 1923, a date now celebrated annually as a national holiday.

There was nothing basically wrong about the idea itself, but the highhanded method employed was wrong. It was a conceited act by individuals, sure of their power, eager to assert it, and in a mood to enjoy it. Most of the Istanbul dailies took a vehement stand against the Ankara declaration. On the whole, my paper was the most moderately critical among the independent papers. Still wholeheartedly on the side of the new regime, I kept stressing unity and harmony, but I pointed out that such an important modification of original intent should have come through committee consideration and free discussions in the Assembly and the press. The degree of political passion in the air, however, compelled taking sides, and I could not entirely escape it.

Our dangers, at that turning point in our national destiny, seemed clearer to a Swedish historian, Professor Kolmodin, than to me. He had come to Turkey with a rare knowledge of our ancient poets acquired in the universities of Upsala and Berlin. Professor Kolmodin's object was to write a thesis on the seventeenth century sojourn in Turkey of the Swedish King, Charles XII, but he had stayed because of the fascination the amazing national struggle held for a historian. (He finally left Turkey to become a political adviser to the Negus of Abyssinia, and died in that country just before the Italo-Abyssinian War.)

His view of our situation, when the issue of the republic arose, was stated to me in repeated warnings. "You of the intellectual class in Turkey," he said, "are committing suicide by your rigid adherence to ideals. You have an opportunity, unprecedented in history, to follow virgin pathways, now that you are rid of the burden of the past. But if you are too rigid in ideals beyond the reach of any human society—to say nothing of a retarded nation deprived by wars of material satisfaction of its fundamental needs and desires—the dissensions you foment will weaken the regime. You will force it to become oppressive, hence undemocratic, in its desire to survive.

"If well-meaning idealists refuse to co-operate with Mustafa Kemal, more and more men with selfish aims will step into the vacuum they leave. All of you are shortsighted not to see the danger signs. What are you after, for instance, in this passionate discussion of the republic? Rule by an assembly, as you had during the War of Independence, could be only a revolutionary and transitional measure. A separation of powers, with a head of state, was a normal step and bound to come. Ushering it in by the legalistic discussions you propose could have dragged along for months and months and caused much trouble. Under the existing chances, a short cut was unavoidable."

Although Professor Kolmodin's views were accurately prophetic, the voice of wisdom is not of much avail when passions blur your vision and obscure the main issue. Circumstances compelled me to open my eyes. Dissension was becoming so intense that the smell of civil war was in the air.

An opposition party was in the making. I was cautiously sounded out on it by Dr. Adnan and by Rauf Orbay, a former prime minister and later ambassador to London. Rauf was a popular naval commander in the Balkan war because of his one-man campaign on the cruiser *Hamidiye* against the superior Greek fleet, and also for his participation in the War of Independence. But relieved of the pressure of foreign danger, he became a dissenter because he could not agree with some of the government's methods and did not share the politician's penchant for compromise. His personal popularity was increased by his enthusiastic impulsiveness and his ability to carry away those who listened to him. All discontented elements were eager to use him as their spokesman and besought him to step out as an opposition leader. My own intimate acquaintance with him in our imprisonment on Malta had made me like and respect him greatly.

He proposed to form a new political party to be called the "Republican Progressive party" and to contain all the big names in Turkish public life—with the exception of Mustafa Kemal, İsmet, and Fevzi Pashas, and Fethi Bey, who, up to then, had headed the executive council of the Assembly. Rauf Orbay named an imposing list of hero generals, former ministers, and former Union and Progress politicians who would join the new party.[1] I expressed fear that the Union and Progress politicians

[1] The names included General Kâzim Karabekir, who had been the outstanding figure in the first move in eastern Turkey for the defense of Anatolian

would dominate the party in spite of all the vigilance of even as public spirited a leader as Rauf Orbay.

"Events," I argued as Professor Kolmodin had warned me, "will develop counter to your ideal. Malcontents will fill your ranks and force you to turn the clock back in spite of your party's 'progressive' name."

Dr. Adnan fully agreed with me and declared he had no intention of joining the new party, but, eventually, his friends induced him to do so.

In spite of my esteem and affection for Rauf, and in spite of my own idealistic opposition to the undemocratic trend towards monopoly of power displayed in starting the Republic, I came out in my paper strongly against the idea of the new party. I likened it to our drink, *rakı,* which, in its pure state, looks perfectly harmless and clear, but is an intoxicant which turns cloudy when another substance such as water is added. The intentions of the new party, I maintained, appeared harmless and clear, but, in fact, the party would turn into a power-intoxicant upon the addition of political elements which would cloud its purpose. The outcome of all this controversy was a step for democracy in a wholly unanticipated direction.

The government, greatly alarmed, took vigorous action. It induced Generals Cevad and Cafer Tayyar to resign as deputies, stay out of the new party, and devote themselves to their military duties. They had to choose between the army and politics. The unusual and undemocratic practice of soldiers on active duty serving in the Grand National Assembly was ended.

The Progressive party came into existence with fewer reper-

---

rights and had led the eastern forces in the War of Independence; General Cevad, commander of the Diyarbekir region; General Cafer Tayyar, organizer of the defense of Thrace; General Ali Fuad, a hero of the early fighting in western Anatolia and, later, minister to Moscow for the Ankara government; and General Refet, former minister of war and former delegate for the Ankara government to Istanbul.

cussions than anticipated. But the infiltration of malcontents and the supremacy of the Union and Progress politicians were, all too soon, obvious. At this juncture, I published an open letter to Mustafa Kemal which drew from him a vigorous statement about political parties. In my letter I pointed out the Gazi's great services to the nation as a whole, and requested him, as a national leader, to crown his past achievements by taking a stand above partisan politics. I insisted that, in Turkey, political parties were only an imitation of foreign examples and unsuitable to our own national needs.

"We have at present," I wrote in substance, "no real differences of interest or of classes to divide us. We are a retarded people, and we have a common goal to reach as early as possible; that is simply the average level of life in the civilized world. This is not a party job; it is a national job. We should postpone the formation of dissenting parties to a later time when there may be rational bases for conflicting interests and ideas, and when the dissensions can be constructive. At present we should unite in a national coalition of various groups to concentrate all energies on the immediate common goal. The complete success of our first national pact against foreign appropriation of our rightful heritage should encourage us to make another national pact for the development of that heritage in our own hands under the same national leader."

The idea was sound, in view of the circumstances existing then. It appealed to citizens who could view the circumstances dispassionately. But, in general, passions had gone too far. The leaders on both sides were fighters. Mustafa Kemal enjoyed a fight under difficulties, and eagerly he accepted the challenges of all his opponents. To critics who took a nonpartisan stand, the Gazi replied: "I cannot be a neutral who does not take any side. With my ideals I am a side by myself. I mean to carry out my ideals for the country's good in spite of opposition and in

149

spite of lack of understanding. I need a party mechanism of my own to carry them out."

The party of his adherents which he thereupon founded was the "People's party of the Republic." It remained in absolute power for twenty-seven years, until the first free multiparty elections in Turkey, in 1950, overturned it with a landslide victory in Assembly seats for a new Democratic party, born in time for a pseudo-free election in 1946.

Mustafa Kemal had produced great social reforms with incredible rapidity by methods of persuasion. He had displayed great patience, tolerance, and foresight in using democratic methods in acute crises and in the face of extreme external and internal dangers. He was inclined to live up to these virtues and to avoid arbitrariness, but he was not able to maintain such a high standard at all times. It was a pity he did not adhere to a nonpartisan national principle for his own leadership or always examine dispassionately just grievances of his opponents. He certainly could have been that kind of leader if he had so chosen. Unfortunately, he too often succumbed to the temptation to win political battles against powerful opponents. He won his battle against organized party opposition, but it proved to be a costly victory which led to a plot against his life and his government. This plot was used as a pretext for the only purge in the history of republican Turkey. Punishment fell not only on those guilty of the plot, but on a number of men guilty only of determined opposition. Like any purge, it was unjust; it meant the death of some thirty men of strong personality and merit and caused many more people to go into voluntary exile for long years. That sort of thing was never repeated, and everything was done to repair its effects, including new laws to insure court trials. Mustafa Kemal, himself, deplored it bitterly in later years, but the purge remains on the general record of the regime.

A revolt broke out in March of 1925, in the southeastern

A conversation with Refik Koraltan, left, president of the Grand National Assembly.

The new Machinery Building of Vatan.

provinces of Turkey, which are inhabited largely by Kurds. Under the general mask of religious reaction against modernism, the revolt involved many deeper factors. One was the Kurdish separatist movement, fostered mainly outside of Turkey, which aimed to provoke the Kurds to revolt. Another was the resistance of the semi-feudal system to centralized government authority. Other factors were sheer misgovernment and local abuses. Also, active foreign interests, pretendedly British, thought the revolt an opportune time to destroy the independent progressive regime in Turkey.

Military forces quelled the actual revolt. Meanwhile, the Assembly passed a special law establishing two extraordinary "Tribunals of Independence" composed of selected members of the Assembly with power to impose and enforce capital punishment in disloyalty cases. The law had measures designed to create "stability" in the country and was to remain in effect for two years.

The problem of the press received special attention, and several papers were suspended. The editors of some of the more conservative papers were charged with "undermining the authority of the government and indirectly causing the revolt." They were called before the eastern Tribunal of Independence in the region of the revolt. Among the papers which had indulged in varying degrees of criticism, my paper, *Vatan,* alone was spared. We acquired the circulation of the suspended papers, thus more than doubling our own circulation. The jealousy this aroused in some of our competitors made the management of *Vatan* a delicate task.

The Progressive party was suppressed on the charge that its reactionary activities had been one cause of the revolt. A hint came to me that my paper would survive only if I wrote an editorial approving the suppression of the opposition party. I refused.

151

On August 2, 1925, the eastern Tribunal decided to suspend my paper. It asked that the remaining journalists critical of the regime be sent to Elaziz in eastern Turkey for trial, along with the journalists already there. This was a bitter dose for me. My life work, to which I had devoted myself with love and with patriotic and altruistic motives, was suddenly smashed. This was done under a progressive regime which I was proud to support, although I criticized some of its acts and methods.

Seven of us made the trip under police escort. We all felt embittered against our ungrateful profession which had inspired us to participate in the exciting birth of great events, and then led us into trouble at a moment of crisis. Our first impulse was to quit the profession.

We quickly made a surprising discovery. In spite of the crisis, in spite of the personal enemies we had made in Ankara, Mustafa Kemal's regime did not endorse terror. Losing perspective and allowing excessive severity was a rare governmental occurrence. The treatment we received was not that of men sent before an extraordinary court for "indirectly causing revolt." Our strange trip, under police escort, had all the earmarks of a pleasure trip carefully planned for a group of esteemed journalists to survey certain conditions in the country.

At Konya, we were amazed to find the governor and the high officials at the station to greet us as we passed through. In Adana, our first stopover, the offices of the director of police had been transformed into a temporary hotel with clean, comfortable beds. No hotel there at that time could offer as much comfort. We were served the choicest local dishes. The same treatment continued in every town. We met the governor of each province and discussed with him local conditions as if we were collecting material for a series of articles. We were free to go sight-seeing in each town, to buy souvenirs, and to send them back with cheerful letters to our families and friends, who were, in the meantime, terror stricken over our impending fate.

Communication with people on the train and in towns was not forbidden; on the contrary, it was almost encouraged. Thus, we were given a true picture of Turkey and became aware that Turkey as a whole did not present a uniform pattern with normal local deviations, but displayed discrepant stages of development in different sections. We saw an over-all picture of heterogeneity and retardation which called for maximum unity, harmony, and co-operation by us all.

We woke up to the fact that we editors had been basing our criticisms on mere assumptions. The government officials themselves already were aware of their shortcomings, but their hands were tied by certain primitive conditions in various parts of the country. The more we saw of the interior, the more clearly we recognized our share of responsibility for the existing crisis; we had failed to understand and explain to our readers the actual problems. This recognition of our errors and our new feeling of bitterness against journalism led us to an act, en route to our trial, which we regretted afterwards. We telegraphed to Ankara as follows:

"We fully recognize our errors in writing about the nation without realizing the true conditions in the interior of the country. We voluntarily give our pledge never to return to journalism, but to devote the rest of our lives to economic or cultural pursuits."

Fellow passengers of all classes did everything to comfort and console us. Among them was a witty landowner from Bihesni in the south central province of Malatya. Through affiliation with the somewhat Bohemian religious order of Bektashi dervishes, he had received a wider cultural outlook than his small-town environment would lead one to expect. The Bektashis have an Epicurean philosophy of life and represent the greatest deviation from orthodox religious practices. Their organization had been abolished along with all other religious orders when the khalifate was ended and the secular regime was established.

This Bektashi asked us if we would not trade our whole investment in education for a quiet country life free from such difficulties as we were in. In our mood it was a tempting suggestion. This wonderful fellow showed particular interest in my partner on the *Vatan,* Ahmed Şükrü Esmer, and myself, and cheerfully advised us not to condemn life because of our recent troubles, but to keep thinking of cheerful moments still in store for us. "It is true," he said, "that life is short and moments of respite and cheer are few. When they come, don't spoil them by thinking about troubles to follow." He claimed to be a friend sent to us by God when our own profession had engulfed us in worries. "Don't worry," he said. "I raise pistachio nuts on a large scale. I will ship my entire crop to you exclusively. I grow them; you sell them. Thus all three of us, by co-operation, will have means to ward off material woes." But we did not go into the pistachio business.

We went on to Diyarbekir, where we learned that the Tribunal of Independence had moved on to Elaziz to investigate the revolt in that area. This signified that Sheik Said and his chief adherents, who had been responsible for the large-scale revolt in the Diyarbekir region, had been hanged or sentenced to prison. We had a friendly chat with one of the members of the Tribunal who happened still to be there on our arrival. He suggested that we stay two or three days to rest and see that historic town—if we were not in a hurry to be tried by the court. We were not in a great hurry.

A National Assembly member from Diyarbekir offered us his whole house as long as we cared to stay. Hospitality there meant party after party for us. We found the local *rakı,* distilled from raisins and flavored with rose petals, had a romantic odor which intoxicated you even before the first sip.

Our reception in Elaziz was far different. A severe-looking officer and a few civilians attached to the court received us and took us to an abandoned church, then packed with Kurdish tribesmen.

"Can they stay here till tried?" the officer asked the civilians.

"No room," one answered curtly. "Try the other building."

That building was an inn converted into a prison. We saw two or three terror-stricken men in each room, waiting to be hanged any hour. We trudged in bewilderment from place to place, all of which were very filthy and evil smelling, like so many waiting rooms to death. Was this a joke, or would we really share the fate of the people we saw? If so, our prospects of survival could not be as high as our favored treatment en route had led us to believe. We caught a glimpse of our colleagues who had been sent there months ago. They were staggering under heavy burdens, under guard. They looked depressed. Finally, taken to an attractive villa with a large garden, we were put into a dark charcoal cellar. Our somber thoughts were suddenly interrupted by roars of laughter outside. Our grim approach turned out to be a hoax arranged by our colleagues in co-operation with members and officials of the Tribunal. The owner of the villa put it at our disposal. We settled down again, in comfort, for a round of parties—often with members of the "terrible Tribunal." For daily exercise, we were provided with spirited horses. For longer rides, the governor's car was always available. It was a political trial, the equal of which cannot be found in the annals of any other country. Our experience had been more like that of sons of a loving father who wanted them to see for themselves the other side of a picture of which they had been unfairly and ignorantly critical.

During the actual sessions of our trial, however, we had moments of real distress. I was in special trouble. Two personal letters from Rauf Orbay, the recent opposition leader, had been found in my seized papers. Rauf had asked me whether I considered it advisable for him to accept an offer for a lecture tour in America to be arranged by a Turk living there. I had replied, advising against it and casually mentioning a rumor of his marriage. In his second letter, denying the rumor, he had made a bitter allusion to misgovernment in Turkey. This correspondence was interpreted by one member of the tribunal as evidence that I had plotted with Rauf against the government. My published articles against Rauf's organization of his opposition party were my defense against this charge. But the member in question had a grudge against me because, in my paper, I had attacked and ridiculed a legislative proposal of his to restrain the press.

Seeming to say, "It is now my turn," this member took pleasure between court sessions in personally holding up to me a different gloomy prospect every day. Once he took revenge by telling me not to worry because death by hanging was the severest sentence that could be imposed on me. And, he explained, this would not be too painful—just one throbbing moment of suspense, and then it would be all over. It would mean less actual pain than having a tooth pulled. Another day, he said my fate might be permanent exile. He mentioned, also, that orders might be given for my father and brother to be brought to Elaziz. His was a mean method of torture. In contrast, the treatment by the president and other members of the Tribunal was most courteous and humane. In addition, we received telegrams from Prime Minister İsmet, expressing regret at our trial and his hope that we would be set free.

During the three weeks before our day of judgment, Ahmet Şükrü Esmer and I, who had enjoyed our student days together in America, found the town of Elaziz most interesting because it had been the only real center of Turkish emigration to America. Following the precedent of one prominent influential citizen, thousands of Turks from this province had gone to America and found work in the tanneries in Peabody and the wire factories in Worcester, Massachusetts, and also in plants in Providence, Rhode Island. Elaziz was the only town in Turkey with American-style barbershops and soda fountains. One-fourth of the population spoke English.

Then came our final day before the Tribunal supposedly established to inspire terror. Its verdict in our case was this: "The acts committed have been found not to constitute an offense in a legal sense. The publications of these journalists were harmful, but their intentions were not disloyal. The court dismisses the entire case against them."

On our return trip to Istanbul we discussed the situation among ourselves. We had to admit that this unique trial manifested again the cleverness of Mustafa Kemal and the government headed by Prime Minister İsmet. Instead of using the pretext of the revolt, to which we unwittingly might have contributed by our criticisms, to punish all the independent and opposition journalists severely, the Tribunal and government merely gave us a remarkable lesson. They compelled us to judge for ourselves, after firsthand observation, that the actual conditions in Turkey as a whole were different from those assumed by editors sitting in newspaper offices in the old Sick Man's capital. This amazing heir to his estate, the Turkish Republic, had to be understood in its towns and villages.

14 : AN EXCITING MEETING

WITH ATATÜRK

U SUALLY, coincidence has given me the best seat for important scenes in the Turkish drama. My voluntary pledge to forsake journalism led me behind the scenes where I could catch direct glimpses of our economic problems, Atatürk's methods, and the power of the Turkish press.

My untoward surrender of journalistic dreams dragged me into business life, the best vantage point from which to examine the process of economic reconstruction. First, however, the coincidence of again meeting Professor Shotwell of Columbia, in Istanbul, just after my partner and I had liquidated our *Vatan* printing plant at a fair profit, permitted me to continue for one year to serve my country with my pen. Professor Shotwell was looking for someone to write the Turkish volume for a series on the *Social and Economic History of the World War,* which he was editing for the Carnegie Endowment for International Peace. I was delighted to co-operate in this for my beloved and respected teacher and friend, and also to tell English-speaking readers Turkey's side of the story. This volume, *Turkey in the World War,* was published by Yale University Press in 1930.

Next, the commercial attaché of the American Embassy, my old friend, Julian Gillespie, appeared in the role of Providence for me. Over our *rakı* glasses in the Istanbul Club, he proposed that I start an importing business for which he could suggest American agencies. The next day, despite my total in-

experience in business, I was the Turkish agent for the Goodyear
Tire and Rubber Company. I should explain here that our young
Republic had very few experienced businessmen. Banking, importing, and exporting, indeed commerce and industry beyond
the small shop and handicraft stage, had been almost wholly in
the hands of Christian and Jewish minorities. But, now, many
of the Greeks and Armenians had been exchanged or had emi-
grated, so it was up to the Turks to go into all types of businesses.

I was relying on my brother, Rıfat, who had become the
best business manager in the Turkish press. Together we formed
a company and established a dealer organization all over Turkey, soon adding to our first line the Dodge Brothers, Cater-
pillar, Curtiss-Wright, Sperry, and other American agencies. I
specialized in government contracting. Between 1927 and 1929,
with abundant credit from American finance companies, we
doubled the amount of American exports to Turkey all by ourselves and tripled our capital.

Then the depression struck. Our boldness turned against
us. As Turkey lacked skilled workmen and foremen for mechanized industry, we had set up a subsidiary construction company to demonstrate the use of machinery in construction work.
This was a calamity. Our entire capital was sunk, and we had
outstanding debts of $250,000, for which our only collateral was
used cars and trucks, unsalable machinery, and spare parts.
Mr. Gillespie assumed the heavy moral responsibility of assuring
our creditors, the American factories and finance companies,
that we could be trusted to make good.

Existence for me then dragged from one draft or note
maturity to another and involved difficult renewals, trouble with
banks, and miraculous last-minute solutions. It took six gloomy
years of hard labor to clear off all our obligations. During those
years I learned that Turkish economy under the state capitalism
of our young government, which was burdened with a bureau-

cratic heritage originally copied from the French system, contained endless futile formalities designed, but alas ineffectually, to make every act of the government wholly faultless and safe. It was to take many years to relieve the country of even part of the time-wasting rules and formalities and the evasive shifting of responsibility from one person or bureau to another.

When our business was fully solvent once more and my business partners no longer needed me, coincidence again took a hand. On an evening like so many other evenings in Ankara, my wife and I were dining with friends in Karpitch's Restaurant. It was in January, 1936, exactly ten and one-half years since my retirement from journalism—and I had never been happy away from it. The friends with us were two American scientists, a Miss Jordan who was a micropaleontologist, a geologist whose name I do not recall, and Cevad Eyub Taşmen, one of my closest childhood friends and a Columbia classmate. Cevad had returned to Turkey to organize oil-drilling operations after twenty years as a field geologist in America. These were three of the many specialists that the Republic had summoned to help develop Turkey's natural resources.

Suddenly, Mustafa Kemal, whom the Grand National Assembly had recently voted to name Atatürk, entered the restaurant with some of his friends. They were seated at a table near us. This was the first time since before my trial in Elaziz that I had come face to face with him, and, not knowing whether he would be friendly, my first impulse was to leave, but that could not be done. Very soon a member of the National Assembly came from Atatürk's table to ask my wife to dance, and a young aide-de-camp suggested that it would be a good idea for me to ask one of the ladies at his table to dance. This much friendliness emboldened me to pay my respects to Atatürk. Thereupon, my wife and I were invited to sit at his table, one on each side of him. This was in the presence of hundreds of Turks and foreigners in the crowded restaurant.

I shall give some details of our long conversation which illustrate more intimately the personality of Mustafa Kemal than many volumes of biography.

His first abrupt question was: "Well, do you feel satisfied with your present occupation?"

Before I could say anything, my wife answered: "I am not satisfied. I married a newspaperman, and he has turned out to be a businessman. It is just like delivering goods which are not up to the sample. I certainly feel most dissatisfied with things as they are."

Atatürk turned toward me: "Would you like to go back to journalism?"

"I certainly would. I consider my years outside of journalism like condemnation to a long term at hard labor."

"Then listen to the story I have to tell you. If you give me the right answer, you can go back to your profession. Long years ago I had a beloved teacher at the military school in Salonika. He had a deep appreciation for any sort of merit. He noticed that I had earned good grades in all my courses and did not mind giving me a good mark in calligraphy, although my handwriting was almost illegible, just so that I could keep my standing at the head of the class. Years passed. During these years I rendered various services to my country and to the cause of peace. In the meantime, the son of my very appreciative teacher came face to face with me in politics and gave me a grade of zero for all my accomplishments. What have you to say about this?"

His parable was about my father who had been his teacher and my activity as an opposition journalist. My answer was: "I have to say that I am second to none when it comes to appreciation of your splendid accomplishments. They went beyond my boldest dreams. I esteemed them so highly that I wished everything to meet their standard. It may be that I was mistaken in some of my views, or had an impractical approach to the problems of the day, but my motives were always pure. I had no personal ambition; I was free from any outside influence and only wished the good of the country."

I was in deep emotion. My eyes were full of tears.

"I know this very well. Otherwise, I would not have addressed a word to you. Are you ready to make public what you just told me now?"

"I am ready."

"All right. Take down the suggestions I will dictate for a public statement."

Out of old habit I started to write in Arabic script. I must explain that the Arabic script, in which Turkish had always been written, had been abandoned by a law promulgated as one of the startling and daring reforms of Atatürk and had been replaced by Latin characters.

"What are those strange things you are writing from right to left?" came his question in a tone of dissatisfaction.

"Old shorthand," I said apologetically.

"Drop that," he ordered me, "and get used to the new Turkish alphabet for all occasions. If we don't break old habits at the expense of some pain and effort, the new cannot take root."

The sense of his dictation, which I took down in Latin characters, was this: "I have been barred from my profession for ten years. This number of years constitutes a short span in the life of a nation, but a long period in an individual's existence. Ten years ago I failed to readjust myself to the course opened by the 'forces of Nature.' It was not my fault, and it was not the fault of these forces. Immediate circumstances were to blame. After ten years' schooling in the field of experience, I feel fit to co-operate again with the man who answered, 'Yes, there is!' to the question of an old Turkish poet, 'Is there nobody to resurrect this country from its ruins?' "

Atatürk wished me to stand up and read the statement aloud. I tried. I could not. I was too excited. This happy occasion, which coincidence prepared for me, was too moving. It meant the end of a career of business slavery; it annulled my pledge to keep away from journalism and reopened for me the gates to activity in public life.

Atatürk noticed my excitement and said: "You are too excited to do it. Let your wife read aloud the statement."

When my wife read the statement aloud, the entire improvised audience in the restaurant cheered warmly. It was an act of goodwill and harmony, a sign of a wider freedom of discussion in the Turkish press.

Atatürk thanked my wife for carrying out his desire and added: "You are a clever Turkish girl and a brave one. Years ago, I gave your husband a chance to accompany me during the great offensive I was planning against the Greek army of invasion. He refused. His excuse was that he had become engaged. I criticized him and said that a man forming a family tie is lost to active effort for his nation. I am ready now to take back my criticism and to excuse him. A family tie with a clever girl like you is certainly an asset to a man. My own life would have been different if I had met the right sort of girl at the beginning. Unfortunately, I had bad luck.[1] I have, at this table, more than one man who has corrected the error of circumstances by entering into a second marriage. I have been amazed to see how their outlook and their tastes have changed as a result of the right sort of companionship. I could not do it. My own consolation is this:

[1] Atatürk's marriage had ended in divorce, perhaps the last divorce in Turkey under the Islamic law whereby a man needed merely to declare his own divorce in the presence of witnesses. The Republic adopted the Swiss civil law.

163

I am free of ties. After devoting all the necessary time and energy to my public work, I can live my own private life. I am not a slave to convention or protocol. The great calamity for a man in public service is in losing his sense of humor and his contact with the everyday life of millions of Turks; in becoming a product of an artificial hot house."

It was true. He always resisted fiercely the influences which tended to make him a half-god. When he was in the right mood, no one could be more sincere in giving expression to his most intimate feelings. This conversation took place several months before the question of the private life of King Edward VIII became a public issue in England. At the next table some Englishmen were sitting. Atatürk became interested in them and asked:

"How about your king? Does he like to live the life of the people? Does he enjoy feeling like one of them? Does he show interest in remaining in full control of his private life after performing satisfactorily and seriously his daily task?"

The Englishmen answered that King Edward VIII was certainly inclined to that sort of view about life, but convention was too strong to allow it. A short time after this conversation, King Edward VIII paid an incognito visit to Atatürk in the company of Mrs. Wallis Simpson. The two men felt greatly attracted to one another. It may be that the example of Atatürk had helped to bring to a boil the already bubbling desire of the King for independence in private life. He tried to carry out, in England, Atatürk's conception of public duties, but it hardly worked. He had to pay with his throne. When Atatürk heard the news, he made the following remark: "If I were in his place, I would proclaim a republic in England and announce my candidacy for the presidency."

The day following my lucky encounter with Atatürk, I announced my intention of publishing a weekly political paper under the name of *Kaynak* (*Source*) in the format of a daily paper. The unusual format did not appeal to the public. It would have been necessary to fight patiently for a long time to create a taste for my weekly. I did not feel inclined to wait patiently for years until *Kaynak* caught on, discovering, too, that I could not breathe outside of daily journalism. I succeeded in forming a company and in buying back from the Bank of Affairs (Iş Bankası) the printing plant I had sold to them years ago. This deal included the paper *Tan*, which was published there.

I had a delightful time for over two years as an editor of *Tan*, preaching definite principles of cleanliness and efficiency in public life and a "good neighbor" policy and collective security in foreign relations.

I soon had an opportunity to engage in a fierce one-man fight against a whole front of abuses and preferential dealings in the city administration of Istanbul. I began the campaign by publishing some facts about the secret sale of franchises for running buses in Istanbul, sales which took place through a certain man reputed to be the evil spirit of various other men in office. I challenged the "Governor and Mayor" of Istanbul (a joint title held by one man)[2] to make an inquiry and to offer the public an explanation.

Instead of doing this, the governor made the following statement to our reporters: "Ask Ahmed Emin for me how much he has been paid to write the article." Several city officials were present.

I immediately published this statement and invited the governor either to offer apologies and to state that he did it out of nervousness or to prove his words.

No answer came until the next day. Then, I received a for-

[2] In Istanbul and in Ankara, the national government appointed one man to the joint office of provincial governor and city mayor, while elsewhere the offices were separate, the mayor being elected and the governor appointed. A law to free Istanbul from tutelage by the central government and thus end this unusual situation has since been passed.

165

mal protest through a notary public, signed by a dental surgeon whose name I had never heard. He said in his protest: "You are asking the governor of Istanbul to give proof of your receiving money for writing your article about bus franchises. I will answer for him. I am the one who paid you the one thousand pounds you asked as a price to get me a bus license from the city. When you could not get the license, you wrote the article, attacking the city out of spite. I am not interested in your article. I wanted the license. As you were not able to deliver the goods, you must pay me back my thousand pounds."

A copy of the protest was addressed to the governor, and his assistant summoned newspaper representatives and formally handed them copies of it for publication. This was intended as a deadly assault on my character—as an attempt to prove that I was not disinterested. It was a plot organized too transparently, and it gave me the chance of a lifetime to use the power of the press as a weapon in a real fight.

The next day we had a full story on the identity of the dental surgeon, about his voluminous police record and his share in all sorts of doubtful deals. He was being pursued for various debts, one of them as low as five Turkish pounds; his furniture was seized by the treasury because he had not paid taxes amounting to a few pounds. Apparently he had not seen a thousand pounds together in all his life. We had great luck in establishing in detail how the plot was organized, how many people were approached with tempting offers to play the part finally accepted by the surgeon, and what sort of people acted as intermediaries. The plot was so badly trumped up that it became an amusing farce on the very day of its happening. At the same time, the entire population of Istanbul constituted itself a team of detectives to supply us with information. The people were delighted to read exposures of all the secret abuses in the city government.

A long list of libel suits was filed against us. The court proceedings were followed with great interest. The final verdict was: "Ahmed Emin Yalman is guilty of libel and has to be condemned to four years imprisonment and a fine, but as it has been proved that he acted out of disinterested motives of public service, and as he could not but defend himself against an outrageous plot to ruin his moral reputation, the entire punishment is canceled with no retroactive legal effects."

The instigators of the plot received prison terms of varying duration. After coming out of prison, they started lawsuits against each other, and the dentist admitted that, after being offered a chance of election to the city council and a compensation of one thousand pounds, he had actually received only a small advance sum and had used it to shut the mouths of false witnesses. As a matter of fact, all the witnesses brought by the dentist subsequently made statements against him and told how much money they had been offered to bear false testimony.

The result of our exposure of the scandal was the dismissal of the governor of Istanbul, a very powerful man. A lawsuit was filed against him by the Council of State, which is the government's supreme advisory council consisting of twenty-five persons of distinction, special knowledge, and experience, who are chosen by the Grand National Assembly for lifetime appointments. Not only the men involved in the Istanbul scandal, but all racketeers who did business by paralyzing the laws and buying privileges from government officials were stopped—at least for some time.

Coincidence granted me a great scoop, while I was still editor of *Tan,* in the form of a talk by Atatürk which could be taken as his political testament to the world. It was in March, 1938, just a few months before his death, and the year before World War II. After an official reception for the Romanian foreign minister, Mr. Antonescu, who was in Ankara with his wife and a group of Romanian journalists, Atatürk spoke informally to all the guests in the night club of the Ankara Palas Hotel. I took notes discreetly. I refused to hand them over to Atatürk's private secretary when reminded by him that publication of the President's private utterances was strictly forbidden. I replied that the government was free to take action against me in case I published my notes. The other Turkish journalists, taking no notes, laughed at me for doing so.

I thought the situation was one in which I could successfully trespass on forbidden ground, and my paper carried the full text and the details of the whole scene. It exploded like a bombshell. However, no action was taken against me, and the next day all the papers in Turkey copied my story. Here is the essence of Atatürk's talk:

"The first task of national leaders is to guide their governments so that the people have a happy attitude towards life. In my youth, I was curious about what philosophers thought of life. Some were gloomy, and said, 'Our temporary existence on earth has no place for gaiety and happiness.' I read other books by more sensible men. They said, 'The end is nothingness, so let us be happy while we live.' I side with these more sensible men, but with the following qualifications:

"Any human being who believes that the destinies of other human beings depends wholly upon him personally is a petty man, failing to grasp the most elementary facts. Every man is doomed to perish physically. The only way to stay happy while we live is to work, not for ourselves, but for those to come. Real contentment in life can be enjoyed only by those who work for the future generation's happiness and honor. A man with this ideal should never address to himself the question, 'Will the coming generation know that I have worked for them?'

"My personal pleasure in life is to raise public-spirited men. Other people like to raise flowers. The man raising flowers does not expect any gratitude or allegiance from his flowers. The leader raising men should expect none from the men he raises.

"Any man who makes himself the center of his own ambitions cannot claim merit for any public service that he renders because such service is only a medium to a personal end. It is folly for any man to imagine that his nation will cease to develop and progress as soon as he passes away.

"So far, I have spoken of a leader and his nation. But a wise leader and a wise nation cannot consider their own destinies separate from the destinies of other nations. It is our duty to our own future generations to attach the same value to the happiness of other nations as to our own. That leader who desires for his own nation something other than he desires for other nations is a shortsighted fool. All world events tend to prove that the destinies of us all are interdependent. We never can tell that our own security, stability, and peace may not some day be touched by an event which, at the moment, we believe to be far from us. The only wise way is to consider all humanity as a single body and all nations as members of that body. Any member who does not react to the pain felt by any other member of that one body must consider itself lacking in sensitivity and true vitality."

15: THE RECORD

OF ATATÜRK

ATATÜRK was ill—dangerously ill. What would happen? The outside world held the opinion that his achievements were purely personal, that there would be no continuity to new Turkey after his death. Many secret plans were being made in case internal disturbances afforded certain individuals opportunities which they hoped and expected would follow the loss of the great man. Patriotic Turks loved him for saving the country and making possible a new national existence, and they excused any error he might have committed. Although they had faith in the continuity of their national life, the danger of losing Atatürk filled them with deep anxiety in addition to their sorrow.

In spite of the general worry and keen interest, no bulletins on his condition were being published, on a pretense that he, himself, wanted no public announcements. Still, the lack of information gave rise to great uneasiness and to all sorts of wild rumors. People insisted that he was already dead, and some underhanded work was being prepared by interested politicians behind the scenes. I thought that such a situation was unbearable and that it might lead to unforeseen troubles, inasmuch as foreign interests were suspected of being behind the wild rumors. We needed complete clarity at this moment of destiny, and somebody had to voice this need. As nobody else seemed inclined to take the responsibility, I felt that, as a journalist, I had to do it.

170

The people of Turkey awoke on August 27, 1938, to read on the front page of *Tan* a well-displayed article about Atatürk's health, about the right of the Turkish nation to know the truth day by day, and stating the importance of staying alert and united in such days of trial. Under the circumstances this article sounded revolutionary. The government was deeply shocked, and, using the authority given by the Press Law for extreme cases, it decided to suspend my paper for three months. This was a deadly blow for a daily paper. Although my partners had seen the article before its publication and had approved it, they pretended in their contacts with cabinet members that they had not. In disgust, I immediately liquidated my position and retired from the paper.

For me to establish a new paper during this critical period was out of the question, so I retired to a mountain resort and devoted two months to writing a book on *The Dreams Which Came True*. It was a timely book. Although it was not addressed to the general public and could not have a big sale, it received wide attention.

About this time I received an offer from two capitalists, with brilliant business experience in newspaper administration, to establish a morning paper in which I would have one-third interest without investing any money. I accepted on the condition that I should have sole control of editorial policy. We discussed all the details, but then I hesitated. Would this be a desirable type of paper for me? Whatever our agreement was, the invested capital would someday become the dominant influence. I decided to be patient and seek to establish a paper over which I could have complete control.

Meanwhile, the anger of the prime minister and the cabinet members had faded away in the realization that they had been unjust. As compensation they offered to send me to New York in charge of a general publicity campaign in connection with

Turkey's participation in the New York World's Fair. I accepted.

I left Turkey in October, 1938, for America. The work at the World's Fair would keep me there for more than a year, so I took along my wife and my son. A student in the Preparatory school at Robert College in Istanbul, my son transferred to Lincoln School in New York to get experience in progressive education in America.

When we arrived in Milan, on our way to Paris, a railway conductor gave me the terrible news of the death of Atatürk.

Mustafa Kemal Atatürk dead! That such a man of inexhaustible vitality, creative power, iron will, and humane heart should cease to exist among those who lived sounded unbelievable. His long illness had prepared us for the end. Still, the actual news was a shock. We wept; all the Turks on the train wept; an entire nation wept for months. His was a farewell such as few men in history have received. The whole world stood in awe before the memory of this man who had established historic precedents by precise, clear thinking, by understanding, by pursuing seemingly impossible aims with endless courage and attaining them through sheer persuasion.

This book would be incomplete without a general picture of the achievements of this great man. Although the whole world has heard of Atatürk and admired his great work, the meaning and scope of his accomplishments have not been fully understood. They deserve to be more widely known because they constitute a remarkable experiment for any nation, demonstrating how seemingly impossible things can be achieved according to a plan; how possible it is to do away with prejudice, fanaticism, and conceit; and how decency in international politics can be a profitable course.

Atatürk had seen his nation almost dead, exhausted by continual military defeats, migrations, losses of territory, and the unbearable drain of a world war, and finally by a foreign occupation which had almost led to the dissection of Turkey into small pieces. Turkey was truly the "Sick Man." The obvious thing for any Turkish patriot had been to salvage from the ashes as much unity and autonomy as possible, and to try to revive even an instinct of survival in the Turkish nation. It was not so with Atatürk. He believed in the Turks, and he resolved to secure for his people their full heritage and re-endow them with the vitality of their early ancestors. For this bold man, the collapse of the edifice of the recent past was no reason to mourn; he could see in this seeming tragedy an opportunity to launch constructive innovations and reforms which would have been completely impossible under normal circumstances.

I have already described the manner in which he abolished the khalifate and the temporal authority of religion, opening wide the avenues of reason for the advance of science, education, and justice, hitherto saddled with religious dogma. He made secularism a going policy in Turkey, more so than in most advanced countries, leaving religion its proper function as a source of altruism and love, but preventing it from being used as an unfair and reactionary tool in politics.

Religion had hampered the freedom and equality of women by depriving them of opportunities for public activity. Atatürk gave them equal political rights with men and opened all professions and offices to them. The result was that Turkey swung, within a few years, from one extreme to the other. In Turkey today there is a larger proportion of women judges, lawyers, architects, engineers, chemists, and high-ranking government officials than anywhere else in the world. Usually people are surprised to learn that the assistant head of the aviation school run by the Turkish Air League, confined exclusively to military aviators during World War I, was for some time a woman pilot with an iron sense of discipline and duty.

After the reforms in religion and the status of women, a

173

sweeping change in personal attire, itself a symbol of the old, narrow life, was introduced. The Turks had adopted European dress for men about one hundred years earlier, but had kept the red fez as a sign of Ottoman distinction. The conservative mind clung to it as its last symbol of religious and political difference from the Christian West. Atatürk, on the contrary, thought that there should be no symbol of difference. The fez had to go.

Resistance rooted in habit and prejudice is always strong. No Muslim, and no man of any religion in government service, would have dared to wear a hat in Turkey, though he would do so as a matter of course when he left the country. If a Muslim Turk had worn a hat in old Turkey, public opinion would have taken it as an open divorce from both religious and national bonds, and would have resented it bitterly. Only to the *kalpak*, a brimless tall hat made of sheepskin, was any tolerance shown. Atatürk chose a remarkable way for eliminating the fez. He singled out Kastamonu, a town north of Ankara reputed to be the most conservative community in Turkey, as the place to inaugurate this phase of his program and arranged there a meeting with noted reactionaries of the town.

"I have brought you some nice presents," he told them, on arrival. "Look at them. They are called hats, a much more suitable headgear than the fez as protection against sun and rain."

The men were startled and terrified at the prospect of wearing hats. All of them said they could not accept the gifts. "But why?" asked Atatürk. They gave reasons easy to repudiate. Atatürk told them that the fez was of Venetian origin, that when Sultan Mahmud II had introduced it as a radical reform to do away with the turban, there had been a full revolution against that innovation in Bosnia, then a part of Turkey.

Contrary to expectations, the reactionaries were easily defeated in the discussion. One by one they had to admit that their opposition was based on prejudice. Then Atatürk said, "Let us separate into two groups; one favoring prejudice; the other, the dictates of free reason."

There was just one group. Everybody accepted the hat. When a group of pious conservatives led by Atatürk, all wearing hats, took a stroll through the main street of the town, people could not believe their eyes. Such was the case with the entire population in Turkey when they read an Anatolian News Agency dispatch in their papers the next day, saying that the conservative men of Kastamonu had accepted the hats given to them by Atatürk and had begun to wear them as more practical headgear. In all communities the radicals started to wear hats that very day. Others followed. Then a law was passed forbidding the wearing of the fez. Here and there the law met silent resistance, but there was no open manifestation of it. A reform thought impossible had taken place simply and smoothly.

"Now we need a new law to do the same thing with the veils of women," Atatürk was told by his political friends.

"Oh no," he said. "You can't catch me doing that. When religious prejudice and men's jealousy over their women's faces being seen in public are coupled in this problem, it becomes most difficult to cope with. No legislation about veils! There is a natural law which will take care of it more easily than any written law. It is called 'fashion.' "

He proved to be right again. Some women discarded the veil; others followed. Those in government service were obliged to discard it at work in the offices. After a short time only a limited number of veiled women could be seen in the streets. Nobody cared. It had ceased to be a public issue and a crucial factor of conservatism and prejudice.

The change in the alphabet was another sweeping reform by Atatürk. The complicated Arabic characters, so long used by the Turks, were one of the main causes of illiteracy. Adoption of the Latin alphabet had been a wish in the hearts of a few radicals, perhaps, but it was hardly a subject for public discussion. To change the alphabet would be a tremendously difficult and unpopular job. But Atatürk called a conference of writers and leading authorities to consider language problems. The majority approved the adoption of Latin characters.

"How long a period of transition do you foresee?" Atatürk asked them.

"About fifteen years," was the almost unanimous answer.

"No," said Atatürk. "It must be completed in six months."

The entire country became a school to teach the new alphabet. Evening classes were compulsory for men up to sixty and women up to fifty years old. Atatürk was one of the teachers. From partly Arabic and partly Latin, the newspapers went, in a few months, to entirely Latin characters. Circulation fell; the government had to subsidize some papers so that they might survive. The clever papers used many pictures and the new characters in very large type for some time. Then circulation began to rise and soon passed the old sales limits of papers in Arabic letters.

As a rule, Turks had no family names and were called by their given names. There were no surnames to denote a common family bond except in a few families in large cities—mostly families with historical backgrounds—and more frequently in small towns and villages. Even in such instances, the family name was not officially registered. To differentiate a man from others with the same given name, it was necessary to add detailed information about him, such as "son of," "native of," and so on. In military schools, where thousands of students enrolled each year, it was quite a problem for teachers to distinguish between hundreds of Mehmets, Ahmeds, Hasans, Mustafas, and İsmails in the same class. Ordinarily the name of the district or the town where a man lived was mentioned with his name. Some men were known by colorful nicknames.

THE RECORD OF ATATÜRK

A law passed in 1935 made it compulsory for every Turk to adopt and register a family name. Mustafa Kemal was given the name of Atatürk by the Grand National Assembly. Atatürk gave General İsmet the surname "İnönü" in honor of his victory in the battles of İnönü. Everyone used his imagination and wits in selecting his own name. I spent hours searching in a dictionary for a euphonious name without a poor meaning. "Yalman," meaning "the highest summit of a mountain," seemed to be all right. It sounded pretentious, but most people were taking pretentious names. As long as they could choose, they took the best.

During the period of these reforms, much had been achieved in the economic field through two five-year plans and by the creation of government banks as holding institutions for a number of separate industrial undertakings on a public-utility basis. A new generation of Turks interested in economics was reared, and the experiment was successful, at least in its honeymoon stage, while effort was concentrated on following the better practices of private business and avoiding red tape. Unfortunately, the new business techniques practiced in the government banks—the selection of men on the basis of fitness and efficiency, and the system of paying living wages and encouraging initiative and merit by prompt increases in salary and position—was not applied even to a small degree in the government bureaus. This lack of harmony in two different fields of government activity was one of the reasons why the progressive measures were shortlived.

In the government bureaus, the old red tape, the fear of making errors, the habit of delaying decisions by unnecessary consultations remained predominant, with the result that selection fell to unfit but obedient personnel rather than to employees of merit and ability. That is where the Turkish revolution failed in its first phase.

As early as 1924, we had a press conference with Atatürk

in İzmir. I asked him, "How about bureaucracy? Do you think you will be able to reform the bad and inefficient methods now used in governing this country?"

"Reform them?" was Atatürk's reply. "They are so bad that they cannot be reformed. We must tear down the entire system and build it over again on a rational, efficient basis."

This reconstruction was never done. And the bad and inefficient methods remained a source of weakness and waste in government which caused perpetual discontent among the people. The main fault was that the one-party system, so excellent on paper, did not allow the proper play of discussion and criticism. The Grand National Assembly was composed mostly of deputies nominated by the party's executive committee from among its own appointees already serving in lower government offices. Therefore, it acted as part of the established bureaucracy instead of putting a brake to it.

Atatürk saw the necessity for an opposition party. An attempt was made on two occasions to encourage another party, but the whole thing was done badly and halfheartedly. Atatürk insisted he was not neutral as the head-of-state, that he had to insure control by his own side. Under such circumstances, a free system could hardly be expected to have a chance.

Atatürk struggled fiercely not to become a dictator in spite of his personal power and prestige. The one purge, made under the pressure of a crisis which seriously threatened the regime, resulted in so much disgust and unpopularity that it was never repeated. On the contrary, all Turks living outside of Turkey were granted the right to re-enter their homeland, including the 150 men excepted from the general amnesty proclaimed after the Lausanne Treaty.

The new regime exhibited democracy in form, but with a stiff dose of personal power and inefficient bureaucracy. Fortunately most of the personal power was used in the public interest and within the framework of the laws as far as possible. Still, abuses and tolerance of self-interest in ardent political supporters were not absent, and the system of personal tutelage afforded little chance to investigate evils and determine the right course. Haphazard reforms, carried out as a result of personal whims, were responsible for terrifying wastes of energy. These were the reasons why I repeatedly opposed the regime in spite of being in full sympathy with its general aims.

The main contribution of Atatürk to the prosperity, progress, and survival of the Turkish nation is not confined to the sweeping reforms most widely publicized abroad. More fully, it consists of his liquidation of all tendencies toward irredentism, imperialism, militarism, and extreme nationalism in Turkey; in preaching the doctrine that all imperialism is a liability, that Turkey cannot afford adventures and appetites which would make her dependent on great powers for support based on political trading, that a policy of peace, harmony, and mutual respect should be pursued with all other countries, that the Turks should be busy for hundreds of years solely in developing their own homeland within the strict boundaries set by the National Pact, and that anything diverting attention from this task would be a national danger for Turkey.

A foreign policy based on the immutable principle of respecting engagements, which has been carried out with adroitness and decency, has not only made the Republic of Turkey a factor for stability in the world and caused her to gain prestige and respect, but has also proved that honesty in international relations is the only course which can yield good returns in the long run.

The remarkable feature of the whole thing is the fact that this respect for decency and this hatred of militarism was sponsored by one of the most successful and brilliant military masters in history. The world situation offered to Atatürk many occasions when he might have used his genius for personal adventure and glory, but he abstained from all that, preferring to create good-neighbor relations with Russia, Greece, Yugoslavia, Romania, Bulgaria, and the Middle Eastern Islamic neighbors.

His main fear was that he might become the blind dictator, a slave of flattery and conceit. That is one of the reasons why he went to night clubs, to keep in touch as an equal with all sorts of people, and why he did many things which he knew would make him unpopular. It is remarkable that the public in Turkey was not influenced by the gossip about the private life of Atatürk. Turkey did not approve of his private life, but found always that the good side outweighed the bad, so that the man, human in all his make-up, could afford unconventional behavior in his leisure hours.

In giving this general picture of Atatürk, I do not want to create the impression that he ushered in, overnight in single-handed fashion, a new regime in Turkey. The main spadework had been done by a score of public-spirited men for a century. As for the reforms pertaining to religion and the status of women, much pioneer work had been completed during World War I, as a result of the efforts of Ziya Gökalp. Atatürk took advantage of the work done along many lines by his predecessors, but made a new, important contribution: He put an end to the era of compromise and duality of secular and religious authority, so fatal to progress in Turkey, and he laid a firm foundation for future progress and development.

In respect to the continuity of the regime which he established in Turkey, there was considerable hesitancy in many minds, both inside and outside of the country. The following questions persistently occurred to those interested in the welfare of Turkey: Was not the whole thing a product solely of Atatürk's personal influence? Could it be expected to survive him? Would there not be a conflict for the succession between the leading figures in public life?

İsmet İnönü, Atatürk's closest co-worker and his prime minister for twelve years, was considered the fittest man to succeed to the presidency. But the fact that İsmet İnönü had fallen into disfavor in 1937, through various personal misunderstandings, seemed to complicate the succession greatly. Fortunately, both Celâl Bayar, who had succeeded İsmet İnönü as prime minister, and Field Marshal Fevzi Çakmak, chief of the general staff—the other two possible candidates for the presidency—showed remarkable self-abnegation. They both urged İsmet İnönü to become the next president. So everything stayed under harmonious, friendly control. The death of the first president of the Turkish Republic did not interfere at all with the continuity and stability of the regime.

16: CRUSADING

TURKISH JOURNALIST

A CRUSADING Turkish journalist in the second quarter
of the twentieth century was sure to find his opportunities, like
his troubles, fluctuating with those of his country and the world.
My assignment to the New York World's Fair shortly before
World War II led me into a new round of opportunities and
troubles: opportunities for fresh observations in America and
Europe in the war's early months, and the troubles of starting
an independent daily paper and keeping it alive in Istanbul during that war.

My New York Fair office was soon running smoothly with
the help of three bright Turkish girls who had studied, lectured,
and written much in the United States; and I again had free
time, so I participated in the Conference on Canadian-American
Relations arranged by Professor Shotwell. Through his courtesy
I received full membership privileges, the only outsider thus
favored. The conference reflected the general unrest and sense
of instability in 1939. Discussions of the world's destiny took up
more time at the conference than direct Canadian-American
relations. I joined in the discussions, offering from our Turkish
experience with the Great Powers a plea for relations based on
collective security.

The fact most interesting to me was that the isolationists
had no illusions about the risks involved in their own policy.
They knew that war was coming and that their country would

be dragged into it in the long run, but they seemed to lack the courage to assume the responsibility necessary to check aggression. Equally they lacked the initiative to try to remedy the smouldering animosities resulting from World War I by seeking new treaties based on *mutual* consent of the victor and defeated, according to the successful precedent of the Treaty of Lausanne.

An invitation to the Islamic Society attracted my attention one Sunday in August, after my wife and my son, Tunç, had returned to Istanbul, where he would enter Robert College. The society, I thought, might reflect only the whims of a few faddists, but the speaker that day delivered a message most congenial to me. Like the majority of Turkish intellectuals, I maintained that orthodox conceptions of religion were used to obstruct progress and becloud reason. The speaker, Miss Nilla Cram Cook, the author of *My Road to India,* gave me an unexpected view of religion and Islam. No religion, she said, should be held responsible for some men's abuses of it. Religion properly represented love, tolerance, charity, and a will to judge one's own acts honestly and to become a better person. She considered Islam the best road to such ethics.

"Nobody can dare to pretend," she said, "that he is a *good* Muslim, because Islam means a continual struggle to conform to ideal goodness. At moments when we come near to it we are almost good Muslims. Material appetites and other incentives cause us to drift away from the ideal at other moments, but that does not spell defeat. We are on the right path as long as we keep up the struggle for purity."

Her charming view of the function of religion, I thought, might render it possible to make good use of the religious channels in Turkey which had been dug by centuries of effort but were now choked by corruption. My eventual insistence on using religious channels to sustain integrity in personal and public relations once caused the suspension of my paper for forty-five days, but the story of that is to come. Miss Cook responded warmly to my plan for a non-commercial newspaper as a medium for certain ideals, although at the time, I had no place, no machines, no capital for it. Her optimism emboldened me to set about getting these.

Through an old and dear friend, Reginald Orcutt, a vice-president of Mergenthaler Linotype Company and author of *Merchant of Alphabets,* I secured from the company's president an approval for the purchase of three linotype machines for a small down payment and the balance within two years. With the naïveté of a child, in spite of previous adverse experiences, I invited Miss Cook to accompany me to the observation roof of the Empire State Building to indulge in starry dreams of the new paper. The sight-seers around us could hardly imagine that the future birth of a Turkish paper was being celebrated by the light of a full moon on the top of a New York skyscraper. Any peasant in Turkey, with his characteristic realism and humor, would have told me, "You have a horseshoe; if you find three more shoes and a donkey, you can ride your donkey." I was to discover, before leaving America, that not even one horseshoe was mine. I went to say good-bye and thanks to the president of the linotype company, whereupon he told me, "I am sorry, but war has intervened. We have had losses in Poland, and I am no longer authorized to make sales on credit."

When I left America, my optimism about creating a daily paper out of nothing—without commercial capital, and therefore without bowing to business domination, and without a board of trustees to check the paper regularly to see that it established fair nonpartisan standards and remained 100 per cent true to them—was not exactly at its peak, although Dean Ackerman of the Pulitzer School of Journalism and other American friends in journalism had said they would follow the experiment with sympathetic interest. Yet, I kept my dreamer's zeal because I felt sure that the Turkish people were in a mood to respond to such an effort, and I had the patience and persistence to fight hard for it.

On my way back to Turkey in January, 1940, I spent two weeks in Italy. Though that country's close neighbors, Germany and France, had been at war for four months, the Italians seemed absorbed in preparing for their 1942 Rome Fair and pointed to this as the best proof of their peaceful intentions. Unlike the temporary buildings of the New York World's Fair, the constructions of the Rome Fair were to remain as historical monuments at a cost which, added to the costs of great municipal improvements in Rome and the new cinema city, could have built a formidable number of planes, tanks, and guns.

More than a few Italians whispered into my sympathetic ear, "Mussolini wants to attire us in wolf's clothing, but we are lambs. Most of us are hard working, simple men who deeply love the fine arts and long for tranquility and stability. We cannot and do not want to be warriors."

Italy paid a huge price for Mussolini and his lust for conquest. Comparing fascist Italy in my mind with the gay, prosperous country I had visited in 1910, I felt that the new monuments might become tombstones. Some months later, when Mussolini's government sent its "warriors" to battle in the belief that the fall of France presented Italy with a chance which could come only once in perhaps five thousand years, I said to myself, "This is not the fault of the Italian people. They are simply Mussolini's first victims. Their future architects, instead of building monuments, will have to solve the problem of draining the political swamps which breed would-be Napoleons."

In Turkey, I promptly consulted friends with a sound knowledge of affairs and modified my prospectus for my ideal

185

paper accordingly. After thawing the previously frozen shares in my former company, I became the first investor in Vatan Publishing Company, Ltd. My wife, my father, my brother, and friends followed, but no investor of large amounts was admitted, and each one's character was carefully investigated. *Vatan,* the name of my former paper suspended in 1925, means "Fatherland" and was to serve the true interests of Turkey. Its charter stated that investment in it did not entitle anyone to influence the paper for self-interest or to depart from the standards agreed upon at the start.

To my amazement, within ten days, I accumulated a sum of 45,000 Turkish pounds (approximately $55,000 at the official exchange rate then), just under one-half the amount I needed to start. With this much capital to use, I went abroad to buy equipment. In Greece, I found a rotary press in perfect condition, and at a ridiculously low price, for quick disposal by the paper, *Ethnos,* which needed space for a new multicolor press. I spent six weeks in Paris and London, ordering more equipment and newsprint, and returned to Turkey to arrange the monetary exchange. Alas, the Germans' western offensive started just then, making commercial deliveries from Paris or London risky or impossible.

My trip, although wasteful of business time, gave me a glimpse of wartime England and France. I had seen these countries, on the eve of the war in 1938, divided into classes and parties, and even into coteries sympathetic to either Germany or Russia. I found, in 1940, that war had not fully united the people of either country. Excessive Maginot Line preparations gave them a false sense of security. The governments were at war; the nations were not.

After selecting a suitable building for *Vatan,* I returned to Greece where the red tape for the export license and clearing payments tied me up for weeks, but I managed to get my press on the last Romanian steamer leaving Greece before the war turned in that direction.

We announced that *Vatan* would appear on August 19, 1940. Meanwhile, I thought all the time of my heavy responsibility in taking all this risk with other people's money, solely on my moral credit. To be sure, other papers, newsdealers, and the readers seemed to be confident that, from its first number, *Vatan* would be *the* paper, dynamically alive and successful. Rival morning papers were greatly worried. I was both confident and worried—confident of recapturing my old readers and worried by obstacles and insecurity. There were fourteen other well-established dailies in Istanbul. I had found just enough news-print to last one month, and it was poor in quality and exorbitantly expensive. My two linotypes were only rented, and I lacked the good quality supplies for even a normal printing job. Moreover, we lived in daily expectation of bombs dropping on us. France had fallen. Great Britain seemed helpless for the time being; America was still isolationist; and Russia had made a pact with Germany. Turkey certainly would not allow Germany to cross her boundaries. Unterrified by France's appalling example, Turkey was preparing to face an armed attack.

Despite maximum insecurity, we engaged an excellent pressman for *Vatan*. The staff worked hard to prepare the first issue, but when the time came to go to press, no pressman! A rival paper, it seemed, had induced him to absent himself. Our press had to be run by the mechanics who had come from Greece to install it, but who had had no experience in operating it. When it started to roll, one cast, loosely attached to its cylinder, dropped suddenly and ruined another cylinder and some minor parts. This, too, might have been deliberate sabotage. Mechanics from other papers came after their day's work, full of curiosity because *Vatan* was not yet on the newsstands.

No newspaper in Turkey handles its own distribution.

Newsdealers estimate each day's sales prospects and place advance orders accordingly. They had brought us huge orders in excess of the circulation of any existing paper. But they went away empty handed. Mechanics, who came out of curiosity, stayed to help. Our new morning paper finally appeared along with the first editions of the evening papers, and it was hardly readable. Newsdealers and readers were openly and rightly disgusted. Every newspaper expert agreed that *Vatan* was a stillborn baby.

I spent the whole night pacing nervously in the pleasant garden of the residence which we had converted into a printing plant. Life did not seem worth living. Towards dawn, however, I resolved to make that stillborn baby come to life. Hardly any working capital was left, and there was a heavy deficit. Not much advertising was available especially for an "unsuccessful" paper. Production costs would be abnormally high for supplies necessarily purchased in small quantities day by day. I could have secured the necessary capital at once through political concessions or by placing the paper under commercial domination, but, for me, such a course would be moral suicide. The only solution was to line up new partners, though that, too, was a humiliating task. The invested capital rose gradually to 100,000 Turkish pounds without solving the basic problems of adequate mechanical equipment, good-quality supplies, and a competent staff. There was the problem of how to secure and shape a staff into a working team. Before publication, we could have drawn experienced men from every other paper. Now nobody cared to leave another paper to take a chance with us. Miss Cook had come all the way from New York as a correspondent for *Liberty* magazine, but also to write feature articles for *Vatan* which were expected to fascinate the reading public. But both her efforts and mine were lost in the badly made up and badly printed pages.

By traveling at every opportunity and keeping in direct

touch with events, I managed to keep cool enough about problems at the office to improve the quality of our publication while training young men for our staff. *Vatan's* objectivity on foreign affairs and its steadfast stand for domestic improvement began to win recognition. We adopted the motto, *"Doğruya doğru— iğriye iğri,"* meaning that we call "Right, right, and wrong, wrong." Circulation and advertising grew, the deficit shrank, and my mind became free again to turn to public affairs.

"Towards Clarity" was the general heading of a series of forty articles which I wrote. In them, I analyzed frankly and loyally the shortcomings in Turkish political life—the government's authoritarian tutelage in the guise of democracy, the selection of the unfit who sacrificed concrete projects to biased conventions about aims and methods, and the inaction resulting from fear of doing wrong or of taking responsibility. The series stimulated eager public interest; back numbers were in demand and passed from hand to hand. I continued the series with a critical discussion of the religious situation, a subject which had heretofore been taboo. But such a discussion had been my intention since my talks with Miss Cram in New York. At the end of this series, some government officials decided that I had gone too far. They had *Vatan* suspended for forty-five days! This was a terrible blow. Our revenues would cease, and most of our expenses would continue. But, after briefly yielding to despair, I decided once more not to give up.

Some papers had established the precedent of partial pay to employees during suspensions. I decided not to punish my co-workers for my follies, but to encourage them by continuing their full pay. How I managed to do it, I hardly know. I obtained from friends courtesy drafts; I explained the full situation to other friends in the banks, and they were willing to discount the drafts. Miraculous as it seems, we were able to reappear in a more vigorous form after keeping up full payments. We had not wasted the forty-five days; we had worked out improvements in the contents, arrangement, and display which made a better appeal to our readers.

The government's experiments in war economy were creating an extensive black market and all sorts of abuses. People were dissatisfied, so I began a frontal attack with a large array of concrete facts in a series of open letters addressed to Dr. Refik Saydam, then prime minister. Our efforts to attain a sound national economic policy to be carried out by honest men with business sense had the readers' approval. *Vatan,* from then on, acquired an increasingly distinctive personality, marked by bold integrity, through assuming that there were no restrictions in Turkey on constructive criticism and concrete discussion.

The death of Dr. Saydam brought in a new prime minister, Şükrü Saracoğlu, who immediately declared that he had an open mind and full confidence in the people. All wartime restrictions on the press were abolished, and decisions were left to the discretion of the press. New cabinet appointments indicated the selection of the fittest. The new war economy began to place the control of distribution in the hands of businessmen and local representatives of the people.

My stillborn paper was alive and sturdy enough in its policy and in public esteem for me to leave it in the hands of my co-workers while I accepted the invitation of the British and American governments to be one of five Turkish editors to take a close look at the war efforts in those two countries.

The change in England since 1940 was amazing. At a suicidal cost to themselves, the Germans unwittingly had forged a united English spirit in a nation of silent but cheerfully determined heroes. The English people seemed confident in a government which merited support for its efficiency and capacity to learn by experience. But a question that stayed in my mind was this: Would official Great Britain be able to take permanent advantage of this unity and regeneration? There I had my doubts.

I spent a full day in Oxford in free discussion of postwar possibilities with a Chatham House group assigned by the British Foreign Office to study such problems. It was headed by Professor Arnold Toynbee, whom I had met and held in high esteem. In some private publications, indirectly influenced by this circle, I had noted a tendency to ridicule the prospect of a new world and to foresee only the traditional balance of power between Great Britain and Russia. America was to be allowed in only as a benefactor on special occasions. While I greatly admired the war record of the British people and their leaders, it seemed to me that the official British scheme, resting plainly on imperialism, would revive and even encourage Russian imperialism—perhaps to provide the British Empire itself with an excuse to survive. The forces likely to oppose this scheme were scattered, unorganized, and partly subdued by the necessary wartime discipline.

We reached America in October, 1942, to complete our survey of the Allied effort. We visited Ottawa and toured every part of the United States. We met President Roosevelt, Vice-president Henry Wallace, Secretary of State Cordell Hull, Undersecretary of State Sumner Welles, and leading senators and representatives. We saw D-Day in the making and were amazed at the seriousness of the American war effort in the production of material and the mass training of men.

My high optimism about the Allies even during the gloomiest moments of the war had been ascribed by Germans and pro-Germans to subsidies for *Vatan* from English and American sources. This was wholly erroneous. Yet I was glad to be able to write with fresh conviction from personal observations as follows: "When the Germans lost the air battle for London, their 'blitz' was transformed then and there into a struggle based on endurance and resources. The extremely efficient handling of production and training problems in America leaves not the slightest doubt that the power of the Germans and the Japanese is doomed to complete annihilation."

Quite different were my impressions of the postwar prospect. In spite of adverse experiences after the last war, America again had lent its resources without a guarantee of payment at least in moral settlements. The borrowers were free to make their own terms and might even resent the generosity when the time for gratitude arose. Everybody we met in America agreed that the future would require a new structure of world relationships, but actual steps towards it seemed to be clear to almost no one.

In my alarm and distress I wrote an article, "Shall We Be Able to Defeat Stupidity This Time?" I explained that stupidity, with a capital *S,* had been the chief factor in making history in the past, and unless the atmosphere changed *during* the war, future prospects were gloomy. The *New World* published this article along with a testimonial, signed by Professor John Dewey, who had encouraged me to submit it, saying that it expressed the most sensible view he had read since the war began. Writing this article gave me the satisfaction of knowing that at least I had done my modest share as one human being to give a timely warning.

I continued to write article after article in the same vein in my own paper. Always I insisted that a lack of agreement on definite moral principles between England and America would create a vacuum, and that Russia, after her astounding military successes, would tend to fill any vacuum unless a proper moral brake was provided to protect her against herself. My tone indicated a readiness to see the best in Russia and an expectation of Russian leadership for collective security. The Russians received my articles in a friendly spirit, saying that, "although critical of Russia, they came from the heart."

Hüseyin Cahit Yalçın, the editor of *Tanin,* and I left America by plane ahead of the other Turkish editors and a few days after the Allied landing in Algiers. On our way to British Guiana, our plane caught fire. We endured two hours between life and death, an agonizing period in which to make a balance sheet of your life and take mental farewell of your loved ones. Our lives were spared by the miracle of a safe landing in Haiti with one side of the landing gear entirely gone. Flying on, by way of Brazil, Ascension, Africa, Egypt, Palestine, and Syria, we reached Turkey in December.

The day I arrived in Istanbul, eager to start a long serial narrative of my experiences, I received the startling news that *Vatan* was suspended for ninety days. I could not believe my ears; I thought it was a joke.

It was a joke—but a bad one—on me, caused by Charlie Chaplin, though he never knew it. The great comedian had spoken via short wave on the Turkish Hour from New York, and had told a Nasreddin Hoca story about men and donkeys, giving it a twist that portrayed Hitler and Mussolini as asses. *Vatan* had carried on its front page the story and a large picture of Chaplin caricaturing Hitler. This drew an immediate and vehement protest from Franz von Papen, the German ambassador to Turkey. The story and picture technically violated a clause in the Turkish Press Law forbidding journalists to offend heads of foreign states. But three months' suspension, again without revenue and the whole staff and costs to pay, seemed beyond endurance.

I rushed to Ankara to argue that this was too much punishment for a mere joke. The government officials asked me, "Don't you know that Hitler is mad? Is it right to provoke a madman when he has large armed forces close to our frontier and is asking himself whether he made a mistake in not attacking Turkey before the offensive he has just started in Russia? You deserve ninety days punishment for your thoughtlessness."

"But," I protested, "it was not *my* thoughtlessness. I had not yet set foot inside my office after a long trip abroad. The night editor wanted a picture of Charlie Chaplin to go with the story of his broadcast from New York, and this one of him in the Hitler role happened to be in the files."

All the official would say was, "It's just too bad, but it's too late to change the picture or the penalty."

I decided then to publish my travel notes in book-page form every other day and to sell them through newsdealers. I chose the title, *50,000 Kilometers in the Air*. Extensive publicity, which brought the sale of twenty thousand copies, made it one of the best-sellers in Turkish and carried us through the suspension without any deficit. *Vatan* resumed publication before the pages for the third volume were on the stands, so we published the remaining instalments in *Vatan,* setting them in book-page measure—four pages a day—to be cut out and bound in covers which we furnished. Many buyers of the travel notes, who had not been readers of *Vatan,* became subscribers. The sudden jump in circulation and revenue after the suspension made the paper so prosperous that I changed the limited company capitalized at 100,000 Turkish pounds into a corporation at 150,000 pounds, which assumed all assets and debts of the old company.

A circulation of twenty thousand, even without much advertising, in issues of four pages four days a week and six pages three days a week, at the equivalent of five cents a copy spelled prosperity. This price was set by agreement of newspaper owners in order to enable the papers with smaller circulation to survive. Our circulation of twenty thousand meant at least one hundred thousand readers, because thousands of coffeehouses subscribed for their patrons' benefit. Furthermore, each copy passed from hand to hand and then was mailed to out-of-town relatives and friends. Finally, newsdealers have a despicable practice of "renting" papers to readers for the dealer's personal profit. These are later returned to the publisher as "unsold" copies. Thus many people read each copy.

After this episode, we remained free of debt and grave financial worries. Reaching this turning point was a great relief to me after two years of constant worry and trouble. I was the one who had not been paid regularly, although I had to keep the façade of unaltered standards of living and entertaining in order to keep *Vatan*'s situation healthy in appearance. Bringing true health to that stillborn paper had meant no vacations or time off during the desperate struggle for its existence. My wife had been very brave. Through her faith in final success, she had co-operated by writing for the paper and by discreetly adding money to the family budget. I learned later that she used for this purpose some of the property she had inherited from her mother.

For me, the newspaper was a trust. If I had felt compelled to make political or commercial concessions, I would have preferred to engage in commerce without any pretense of devotion to the public interest. Happily—and miraculously—it was possible without compromise to devote the paper consistently to the defense of ideals and high principles. Yet I, myself, am at a loss now to understand how I kept my cheerful fighting spirit without the slightest concession to an easier way out of *Vatan*'s troubles. The reader may think that I overwork the word "miracle" in this book, but the things that happened in Turkey and to this journalist in sharing Turkey's destiny never cease, in retrospect, to seem miraculous.

I am far from being superstitious, but a funny coincidence of dates almost makes me so. The first suspension of *Vatan* was on Pearl Harbor Day, December 7, 1941, and the second on

December 7, 1942. Leo Hochstetter, chief news editor of the American Office of War Information in Istanbul, laughingly advised me to stay in bed on December 7, 1943, and do nothing. I was not laughing when that December 7 came around, but I was in bed with a severe case of diphtheria. As for December 7, 1944, *Vatan* was again under suspension, as I shall relate later. In common with Americans, I do not consider December 7 a happy day.

17: MY DREAM

FOR TURKEY

An ENCOURAGING report on world affairs was what Turkey needed most in 1942, at the start of the third decade of her brave experiment as a peace-loving modern republic. Yet my reports on observations abroad that year were militarily optimistic and morally gloomy.

I wrote that if Hitler had sent me to England, Canada, and the United States to prepare a report for him, I would recommend his early surrender, because he did not have a chance in a million against the incredible proportions of the Allied war effort and because both Germany's and Japan's powers were doomed to annihilation. But, I pointed out, victory in war should be a prelude to a new world with a higher morality. There was no sign of such a world in sight. The Allied countries' traditional political and psychological roots went deep enough to make it impossible for them to abandon their course of national self-interest, or to surrender any sovereignty to a world federation with the sole function of safeguarding international peace and justice.

My stand for Turkey was as follows: We are allies of Great Britain in this war and, indirectly, allies of the United States of America and Soviet Russia. We are definitely against aggression and fascism. Although we are nonbelligerents, we are keeping one million men under arms to resist the Germans in case they attack this strategic passage from Europe to Asia and the Mediterranean Sea. Thus we are protecting the flanks of the Russian armies in southern Russia and of the Allied armies in Africa and the Near East. In a defensive war we can always give a good account of ourselves. For offensive action we are not mechanically equipped or trained. We can make our best contribution without actual fighting, because we would only be a liability to our allies if they had to divert matériel and forces from other fronts to support us.

I concluded with very deep feeling: War sacrifices by a nation which has not the slightest aspiration or greed for territory or for domination outside of its own home boundaries will not be endured by the people unless those sacrifices are clearly for the sake of a better, safer world. As such a prospect does not now exist, we had better keep our resources in men and equipment intact in anticipation of an unsafe and unsettled world where each nation will still have to rely on itself for survival.

When the war was nearing its end in 1944, a press campaign in England and a violent Moscow radio crusade in Turkish tried to intimidate Turkey and to force her into active belligerence. Turkey was called "a pretended adherent to the cause of democracy," and was accused of rendering hardly any service to the common cause, although allied by treaty to Great Britain. Turkey, it was hinted, would not be invited to the peace conference if she persisted in nonbelligerence.

Such unjust and opportunistic propaganda from London and Moscow revolted me. In *Vatan,* I had opposed our government on nearly every domestic issue and criticized its lack of conviction, initiative, and courage in foreign policy, even while I supported the general direction of that policy. But I unhesitatingly led a restrained but determined countercampaign against this distorted foreign propaganda against our government. My weapon, as so often before, was a long array of facts.

President Celâl Bayar of the Turkish Republic follows classwork in a coeducational school in Karabuk.

*Democracy in Turkey: A meeting organized
by the Democratic party
near the Fatih Mosque in Istanbul.*

The mausoleum erected by the grateful Turkish people for Atatürk.

I quoted Winston Churchill's declaration to our group of Turkish editors in 1942, that Turkey had been almost the only unshakable ally of England in her darkest days of trial and could be relied on to do right. Again, at the Adana meeting of Allied and Turkish statesmen in 1943, Mr. Churchill had said to the Turks, "What? You have not yet been supplied with Spitfire planes? We cannot expect an ally to fight without proper weapons. Therefore, I do not ask of you a definite commitment to fight. I know that you will do the right thing when you consider yourselves strong enough."

But now, still without sending a single Spitfire or other adequate equipment, England expected us to enter the war. We were not even told in what theater of operations or by what action we were to enter.

In America in 1942, President Roosevelt had assured our group of editors that Turkey's firm diplomatic guardianship of the passage between Europe and Asia was a tremendous service to the Allied cause, and he had promised economic co-operation with Turkey. Cordell Hull said Turkey was the country most dependably fulfilling commitments. He said he watched Turkey as "the reliable barometer of the true trend of events."

As for Russia, we had the word first from Sir Stafford Cripps, former British ambassador to Moscow, that Stalin had told him that the Turks had "acted very correctly as guardians of the Dardanelles during the Germans' Stalingrad campaign." The Soviet dictator, Sir Stafford said, had further declared that since the Bulgarians had "acted badly" towards Russia, one harbor on the Black Sea would be sufficient for them to keep, and the other Bulgarian harbor with some of its hinterland must be added to Turkey to improve Turkey's position as guardian of the Straits. Stalin had repeated these statements in the presence of Mr. Anthony Eden. Moreover, Stalin had communicated them in a memorandum to the Turkish ambassador in Moscow and directly to the Turkish government by the Russian ambassador in Ankara.

Great Britain and Soviet Russia were free to change their opinions about Turkish policy in other phases of the war, but they had no right to go back on their own opinions emphatically expressed about the Stalingrad and El Alamein phase in 1942, when Turkey's reliability and diplomatic contribution, backed by the full mobilization of her manpower, had had decisive value. Blanket condemnations of Turkey in 1944 seemed discreditably opportunistic. I wrote articles about the two kinds of British: the British in England, open-minded, objective, fair, courteous, one of the most perfect products of civilization; and the British whose lives, maybe for generations, were spent outside of England—the Empire British—conventional, narrow, opportunistic, believing that arrogance could always uphold prestige.

Concrete criticism of Turkey's nonbelligerence by the foreign press in 1944 was to the effect that, although the British could not then state openly the specific co-operation expected from Turkey, the plan was for joint action in the Balkans to enable America and England to occupy the Balkan states and save those unfortunate people from becoming Russian satellites. This assertion cannot be supported by facts. To begin with, there was no agreement about a Balkan campaign between the United States and Great Britain. Secondly, even if such a joint action had taken place, resulting in the British-American occupation of the Balkan countries before Russia was ready to move in, there is absolutely no assurance that, in recognition of the Russian "zone of influence," the British and Americans would not have subsequently withdrawn their forces in Russia's favor. Russian pressure was so strong that the Western powers hesitated to act when the Romanians and Bulgarians were anxious to come to terms with them rather than with the Russians. A close study of the situation is sure to prove that the Western powers could have insured their own influence in Bulgaria and Romania with the full consent and co-operation of both these nations if they had displayed, at the right time, a determined policy based on clear principles.

My campaign against unjust propaganda continued in the following vein: "It is to Turkey's credit that she has held the Germans back by diplomacy and by her people's sacrifices for full mobilization. Turkey, without any territorial ambitions, cannot be expected to provoke a German attack upon herself or, unequipped for offensive warfare, to take suicidal offensive action in a Balkan campaign. If a plan for a new peace on sound principles could be clearly set forth as the aim of victory, the Turks, who are deeply interested in collective security, might well be induced to fight for it. Unfortunately no sign of it is in sight. If the prospect is only a new round of power politics, Turkey must hoard, intact, her resources for survival. If the peace conference is to be a real peace parley, we shall be insistently invited to participate as a reliable core of stability in the Balkans and Middle East. If the peace conference, as now seems likely, turns out to be merely another 'Big Power' contest for self-advantages, then a failure to invite us would be, for us, more a blessing than a threat."

My published views on Russia can be summarized briefly: "The Russians, since World War I, have broken away from many evil traditions and have created new hopes. Consequently their wartime allies look to them to continue to merit confidence and esteem. If the Russians forsake collective security and such high moral aims because of past grudges, and if they cannot resist a chance to strike back, the best hopes of humanity will be betrayed, and a world full of hatred, strife, and intrigue, far worse than before the war, will be ushered in. At a peace conference with clearly defined moral goals, Russia cannot afford to be unjust, inconsistent, and opportunistic."

These opinions won public approval so fully that the government paper in Ankara, *Ulus,* in spite of the government's general disapproval of my writings, and to the great surprise of the public and myself, republished word for word under my name one of my most vehement articles. The unity of Turkey, from my point of view, was more than justified during the early postwar period of appeasement and defeatism in the Western countries. When the West provided no firm moral brake, the Turkish nation's avowed will to resist, with its intact and strong defensive army, any aggressor against Turkey was the only positive check to Russian aggression.

Istanbul and Ankara have been and still are exceptionally good observation posts for world events. And through my trips to France, England, and America at various stages of the war, and also by maintaining as close contact as possible with the Russians, I have been in a peculiarly favorable position to judge the scene as a whole. The way things were shaping was filling me more and more with apprehension and alarm. There were no signs, other than mere words, to herald the advent of a new era. On the contrary, all signs pointed to an overwhelming victory by the Allies and then a peace lost by sheer, old-fashioned, capital-*S* Stupidity.

I felt sure that all peoples were ripe for a superstate in the form of a world federation with the function of security through police and judicial powers. Too, I felt sure the people everywhere were ready to sacrifice some of the prerogatives of national sovereignty to gain an era of interdependence and co-operation, rather than continue absolute independence in rival self-interest and narrow national conceit. The fighting governments were doomed to focus their interests and attentions mainly on vengeance and the maximum share of the spoils, especially in "zones of influence," and could not be relied on to take the initiative of working for a genuinely new world order. Still, somebody ought to take the initiative.

I decided in my mind that this was the natural task for Turkey—making history for the good of humanity and for her own benefit. Turkey was already a seasoned traveler on paths leading to a new world—with her past record of religious tolerance, her recent record of liquidating an empire, sticking to engagements, expelling from her heart all irredentism and lust of conquest, making real friends with neighbors and other powers, and converting into a museum the Muslim mosque, but former Christian church, of St. Sophia as a common symbol of harmony and tolerance. In addition, Turkey was one of the few Eastern countries which took secularism seriously in making religion a private affair and in basing citizenship on political loyalty, rather than on race or religion. Although it cannot be said that this conception of citizenship was applied with complete success in Turkey, it *was* successful, especially in contrast with the all-too-vividly remembered situation during the foreign occupation of Turkey following World War I, when minorities had not behaved generally as loyal citizens.

I repeatedly urged that Turkey assume the initiative in the cause of idealism. I pointed out that it was also a matter of self-preservation for us. A young republic, heir to long experience with futile power politics, we badly needed a world based on justice and security, which it was our duty towards ourselves to try to promote. We could not afford to indulge in a race of armaments at the cost which mechanization has made necessary for modern warfare. Whatever we could do for ourselves in that direction, in a world of Big Power rivalry, and at the expense of much-needed equipment for our normal peacetime existence, would not be enough, for we would still need the protection of a large power. We would have to pay for this protection in obedience, servitude, and dependence, while attracting the enmity of other powerful countries.

To be able to come out as a flag-bearer of a new order of equity and honesty, we had to improve our own system of government and apply more completely the principle of equality of opportunity for all citizens. We had to become a living model for neighboring states and the stabilizing factor so much needed in that area. Our past friendship with Russia, our present alliance with Great Britain, our cordial relations with America, and the importance of our geographical position added effective weight for such a role. Many small nations, temporarily occupied or disabled, insisted that Turkey was their natural spokesman. Unfortunately, such a positive and lively role did not appeal to the Turkish government. They considered it safer to cling to a passive attitude in a troubled world. I did not despair; I kept on fighting in the hope that there might be a change which would make a dynamic attitude the line of least resistance.

Then I had one of the greatest shocks of my life. The government, misled on the one side by financial difficulties, on the other by a misconception of "social justice," established a capital tax on wealth called *Varlık Vergisi*. It was true that huge amounts of illicit money had accumulated during the war in the hands of a few at the expense of the general public and in disregard of the spirit of our laws. It was also true that much of this money was in the hands of minorities and foreigners, who predominated in certain commercial fields. Many of these people, not entrusted to share in the defense of the country in armed military service, were not proving themselves loyal citizens. Pressed by the costs of keeping a million men under arms, the government was obliged to establish a capital levy; and it was entitled to do so, especially after leading commercial circles displayed a reluctance to share the nation's financial burden. Many businessmen even refused to subscribe to government bonds which bore a high interest rate.

The *Varlık* was announced and carried out under such conditions that, while it did bring in some revenue, it was highly detrimental to the government's moral and material credit both at home and abroad. To begin with, the tax law prescribed no scale. Local commissions could use their judgment in making assessments. Then, there was no right of complaint or appeal. If the commission thought you had one million and chose to assess you for eight hundred thousand, while in reality you had only five hundred thousand, you were still indebted for three hundred thousand after paying all you had, and you could also be exiled for nonpayment of the rest.

Data for *Varlık* assessments were gathered in unusually well-guarded secrecy. A good job had been done in establishing files on the sources of wealth of a long list of individuals, and considering the almost limitless possibilities of bribes, relatively little corruption was involved. Still, the data were inadequate, and discriminations of a political or religious character were often made, so that much injustice resulted. Above all, the scheme disregarded constitutional guarantees and was in open contradiction to fundamental principles of the regime. When exceptions, based on rights guaranteed in various conventions and treaties, were made for foreign residents as a result of complaints from their embassies and legations, Turkish victims of the tax openly resented less favorable treatment in their own country than foreign residents received. This was particularly bitter to the Turkish mind because it recalled the days when the capitulations existed and foreigners' privileges were above native laws and regulations.

The tax was enforced in an atmosphere of terror which made open criticism impossible. I could only venture some indirect hints; and I tried to show the good sides of the tax in private discussions with foreign friends, who were furiously indignant. In the long run, the arbitrary application of the tax levy, the injustices, and the loss of moral and material credit at home and abroad left me no choice. I began to attack the whole scheme more and more boldly. By then, the government also had seen its error and had started to ease the burden. First, the tax on salaried people was abolished, so the honest ones who had paid were in effect penalized, in contrast to those who had not paid and whose debt was now entirely wiped out. Then, the whole tax was abolished, and all remaining indebtedness arising from it was erased, resulting in a further injustice to those who had paid and benefiting only those who had refused to pay.

It was good that the government recognized the error of such tactics, but the wrong had already been done. The whole scheme had been suicidal, especially to the world prestige which Turkey needed in order to play an important international role. I was overcome by the realization that the bad effects of the widely publicized *Varlık* had destroyed Turkey's opportunity to assume the role on the world stage of defender of high human principles. The long record of equity which had won such high prestige for the Republic of Turkey, and had rendered most of its former Armenian, Greek, Jewish, and other minority citizens, now scattered all over the world, proud of and even sentimentally attached to their mother country, had been foolishly destroyed overnight by a single blunder.

I was convinced that Turkey should frankly and loyally admit her error, repair at least the most flagrant cases of injustice, and so become again fit for the role of defender of principles. Rightly or wrongly, seeing this matter closely related to the future of humanity and to the survival of my own country, I could not remain silent. I decided to go to extremes: I would try to shock both the government and the public into a clean sweep of cumulative faults. I began to publish strongly worded articles, full of facts, discussing the vital role Turkey could play in a world of democracy; but also pointing out the fact that she was being prevented from playing such a role by the unfortunate tax and its aftereffects, by a one-party system which, though good on paper, failed in reality, by using democratic forms as a show-window display and maintaining an arbitrary, slow, and inefficient bureaucracy and personal government sustained by the selection of the unfit and the blindly obedient.

To be just, I must admit that I was dwelling on the deviations from a very idealistic goal. Otherwise, the administration compared very well indeed with any in the south or the east of Europe. It was progressive along many lines; it concentrated wisely on education. The judiciary remained strong, reliable, and independent. I, myself, had come out from dozens of suits against me with a perfect record of acquittals. I must also admit that the government, for a one-party system, had shown remarkable tolerance of criticism and had warned me in a friendly way not to go too far. In general, government circles showed me affection and esteem and fully appreciated the fact that I was sincere, that I could be depended upon to admit publicly my error if I was rash and superficial in arriving at a conclusion. I always gladly gave full credit to the government for its good acts; I traveled throughout the country to discover them and to stay in touch with the people, particularly the peasants. I made a specialty of visiting village institutes, which are an admirable and original Turkish experiment in rural education, potentially useful in other countries, and I wrote a book about them titled *A Trip to the Turkey of Tomorrow*.

Another field of original Turkish pioneering was in prison reforms. Turkey has made headway during the last ten years with a prison island used as a social sanatorium, and has engaged in a most successful experiment in prisons with open doors. I kept in close touch with such institutions and gave the government full credit for its achievements in this field.

On the other hand, I was convinced that a much better state of affairs could be achieved in Turkey. Prompt attempts at radical reforms would make the people, who had become very critical, more contented and united. Moreover, by then, the Allied victory compelled an immediate adjustment to the spirit of democracy for the sake of co-operation with Western powers and for the sake of a decisive share in saving high principles from perishing again in the period of revenge and fatigue which follows war.

The government waited until the series of articles was completed. Then I was notified that *Vatan* had been suspended by decision of the cabinet. No time limit was indicated; not even the expression "indefinite period" was used. Complete suppression was illegal, and the authorities admitted it was an error. I found, however, that the error had been intentionally committed to satisfy the conservative members of the National Assembly. One of them told me on the street, one day, that I deserved to be lynched.

The prime minister stated that he hated to suspend a paper, but that he had warned me. He added that the period of suspension would be long this time, in view of my obstinacy in persistently vigorous attacks against the established order, and in view of the deep resentment and anger of some members of the Assembly.

All this happened when *Vatan* enjoyed the second largest circulation among Istanbul papers, was third largest in the country, and was very prosperous. Even my closest friends and supporters criticized me, saying I had no right to take such risks in an enterprise which represented other people's investments, that my vehement attacks had produced no apparent effect, whereas the continued activity of the paper could have been very beneficial. They also thought it was better to act in the Stephen Decatur spirit of "my country, right or wrong," and not to publicize unfavorable conditions so much.

I answered, "The government can establish censorship and take the consequences of doing so; or it can, on its own responsibility, give definite orders not to touch this or that subject. As long as the government does neither, it is my responsibility as a citizen to express any sincere opinion I have for the good of the country. If business considerations dominate a paper, it would be hypocrisy to pretend to be a journalist in the service of the public. I do not believe in the idea of right or wrong, my country first. Every country has its shortcomings, and it is to the credit of any country to be able to criticize itself freely, because that is the most reliable promise of a better future."

Happily, *Vatan*'s investors supported me. I did not hear a single word of blame from any of them. They also allowed the accumulated profits to be used to pay in full the salaries of forty-five men working on the paper. Just the same, another December 7 found me out of business again!

18: MISCARRIAGE

IN SAN FRANCISCO

A NEW WORLD united on freedoms—at least on the four of them proposed by Roosevelt and Churchill in the Atlantic Charter—and dedicated to the peaceful settlement of international disputes was taking form in words. Nations united in World War II were to carry on as united nations for peace. But what was back of the words? What was the moral and political environment in which this verbal embryo must acquire body and organs for healthy birth and growth?

The best way for me to find these answers and tell others, and also the best thing to do during a suspension of my paper for no predictable limit, was to travel abroad again and write more notes to sell in daily installments. I chose England first, in order to study the early stages of the tremendous changes which its imperial system was bound to undergo.

I reached there alive only by a strange twist of fate. At Gibraltar, because of serious engine trouble on our seaplane, our group of twenty-one passengers was to be transferred to a land plane. But a French child with sudden fever caused a family of four to cancel their flight on another seaplane. I was assigned to one of the vacated seats, objecting strenuously because the land plane was due in England five hours sooner. The local military authorities, however, insisted. So off over the water I went, thereby saving my life, for the land plane carrying seventeen of my former fellow passengers crashed in the Pyrenees Mountains, and all aboard were killed.

This visit to England was memorable for the number of political, literary, and social leaders I was privileged to meet. A conversation in the office of the Manchester *Guardian,* which was for me a shrine of liberalism, resulted in the publication in the *Guardian* of a long letter I wrote on the responsibilities of liberalism. This letter, I later learned with gratification, was the original incentive for the formation of the Liberal International, of which I shall write in another chapter. Days spent in the circle of the Duchess of Atholl, who had just established the Free Europe League for an open British policy in Europe, led me to write several articles along the same line. These appeared in the *Observer,* the *News Chronicle,* and other English publications. Their favorable reception illustrated the English people's tolerance of criticism in their homeland even during a war. I also especially enjoyed a day at Oxford with Sir William Beveridge, whose famous Beveridge Plan and ideals of national morality I greatly admired. But here are my main observations during a stay of more than six weeks:

I found that Mr. Winston Churchill, whom I venerated as an almost superhuman being, eternally young and vigorous in his outlook, had not escaped the common lot of most men in exalted position. Because some of his views had proved to be strikingly correct, he felt that other views dear to himself and his political set were entitled to acceptance, also. He did not seem aware then that he was losing his hold on the British people.

I found England, generally, in a state of revolt and self-criticism, but happily it was a revolt of moral sense against opportunism. Common remarks were, "We are really a small nation, and we must act honestly as one of the small nations. We cannot retain prestige and influence by opportunism and arrogance because we no longer have the physical power to back up that sort of approach. America has acquired control of the sea and the air, and Russia controls the land. We can expect to survive only in a world where law, order, and justice, not physical force and arbitrary power, prevail."

Many British leftists seemed no longer to believe blindly in everything Russian, but were becoming judiciously critical. The main problem was plainly how to understand Russia, to inspire the Russian people with confidence in the West, and to establish mutual respect without the spirit of appeasement then being displayed by the United States. The Russians were sure to fall into the conceit and greed which accompany the sense of power born of remarkable military success. They would be unable to develop their own brake to check their new power. The only effective brake would be a close agreement between the United States and England to uphold strong and clear moral principles in international relations. Canada, Australia, New Zealand, and all small nations would join such a moral front, and Russia would follow suit because it could not afford to appear as the only black sheep. At least, this was what I believed and hoped at that period.

Unfortunately, even the preliminary factors for such an Anglo-American agreement on moral principles to be upheld in international relations seemed to be lacking. As an outsider, I found myself impelled to a sort of missionary work, explaining to both English and American friends each other's virtues, and how they could complement each other to the great benefit of humanity. I held up, as an example, Canada, which can be considered their common offspring, and which is far superior to either of them in many respects. It seemed to me that my voluntary campaign was duplicating the efforts of *Union Now,* by my dear old friend, Clarence Streit.

I sorrowed over the appalling lack of information and understanding which I discovered between the two great Western powers. Rivalry and envy produced an entirely artificial barrier of differences. In discussing the whole problem with an

Englishman who seemed to me very broad minded, I said, "Do you remember the days of June, 1940? Mr. Churchill rushed to Bordeaux and proposed to the French the establishment of a new Anglo-French state with common citizenship. The pressure of present circumstances may not seem as great, but the need for really radical steps is as great as it was then. Cannot Americans and Englishmen relegate the American Revolution to the past and unite federally? If union could be even considered for the English and French in 1940, it should be more practical to consider it in 1944 for the United States and Great Britain, with the co-operation of Canada, Australia, and New Zealand, which already constitute natural bonds between the two nations."

"Oh, no," he replied sharply, "it is impossible; the French are closer to the English than the Americans are. The common language alone does not mean anything."

I argued and argued with friends of both nations, and had the satisfaction of convincing many that a lack of harmony between the two great English-speaking nations would be humanity's greatest source of danger in the postwar period. It may be worthwhile to mention here a prophecy made by Trotsky, a very close observer of historical trends, that "the latter part of the twentieth century will witness a revival of the British Empire—with the capital in Washington." What form Anglo-American co-operation takes is immaterial. Closer union is unavoidable, and the present misunderstandings and conflicts of ideas have to be interpreted as the pains of a new birth rather than signs of a parting of the ways.

A short stay in France, which was undergoing an unusually severe winter without proper heat, food, or clothing, gave me new respect for the French people who know how to suffer with dignity. With farsighted leadership, France could easily fill the role of standard-bearer for a world of security and justice, the only role which can give her world prestige and domestic harmony. But in 1945, she was in a state of lethargy, camouflaging old political factions as resistance groups with different names. If France did not assume her proper role, her only alternative would be to get what she could from more power politics, with no real power in herself; and I gained the impression that she would choose that alternative, to her own detriment and that of the world at large.

In Italy, for only a stopover at Naples, I renewed my conviction that the excellent Italian people deserve a much better fate than they have had in the past. Incidentally, I was shocked at a sign in the general washroom of the American Airport, "No Admittance to Italians." What deep hatred so few words can engender in a proud historic people! Why degrade them because unwholesome conditions after World War I created a Mussolini?

By a lucky chance, I met my friend, C. L. Sulzberger of the *New York Times,* in Egypt. He volunteered to hop on the plane with me for a day in Ankara, and to exchange observations on the way concerning the Yalta Conference about to be held. Bad flying weather delayed us in Syria for twenty-four hours, so I hunted up old acquaintances. I came away with the impression that the old Eastern question had been reactivated. On the pretext of "protecting" the people's interests, every Big Power was again competing for influence and the selection of officials favorable to itself in Syria and neighboring small countries. While the French and English vied openly for domination, Russia seemed to be competing also, exerting her influence on the Arab Orthodox Christians, the discontented intellectuals, and the class of people constituted by the poor.

No good news of any end to *Vatan*'s suspension awaited me in Ankara. However, our business manager, Nuri Turen, had found temporary jobs for the linotypers and printers, so that the mechanical staff's wages were no problem. I set to work on my *Reports from the World,* which, when bound, amounted to two volumes. This took care of the rest of our expenses.

Fortunately, a delegation of the Association of American Editors arrived in Turkey about then, on their good-will tour to stress freedom of the press and free flow of information between countries. I had met the delegation of three, including Dean Ackerman, in London, and they knew my plight. In their conversations with the prime minister, other government officials, and press representatives in Turkey, they persistently dwelt on what a bad practice it is to suspend a paper by government edict without a hearing in a court of justice. Their views made a deep impression. The government had already begun to realize that its legal right to suspend a paper—a right intended for application only in extreme cases in a national security crisis—had been greatly abused. Moreover, by then, Democracy had won the war; and Turkey, "entering" the war at the last minute, on the advice of the United States and England, had been invited to the United Nations Conference in San Francisco.

The time seemed ripe to ask for permission to resume publication of *Vatan.* Our request, conjointly entered with two other suspended papers, was immediately granted, and the prime minister added his assurance that there would never again be an arbitrary suspension of papers in Turkey. I faced the shareholders of *Vatan* in their annual meeting on March 25, happy to tell them that their paper, which had reappeared two days previously after six months of suspension, was enjoying a most enthusiastic reception by readers and greatly improved relations with the government. Then I could not resist the temptation to accompany the Turkish delegation to the San Francisco United Nations Conference to obtain for my readers firsthand reports on the founding of a new world.

The curtain rose in the Opera House at San Francisco; the

show began. Before the four pillars representing the Four Free-doms, the whole world bowed in hope that delivery from fear and barbarism was to come true. It was generally expected that the representatives of forty-nine nations would set to work with noble zeal to erect indestructible moral barricades against the demons of war. They would meet each other cordially and act as trustees and servants of the ideals of equity, honesty, and se-curity; they would forget greed and self-interest and be mindful of the interdependence of human destinies, thus enjoying the pride and dignity of human beings above all racial, religious, or even national barriers to unity of purpose.

The show was staged in one of the most stimulating environ-ments in the world, amidst the people of San Francisco and California who seemed to exemplify the best kind of public-spirited citizenship. Everything seemed favorable. Then, gradu-ally, the true state of affairs came to light. The masks fell from these "angels of peace," and the old demons of war reappeared.

Collective security? Morality and decency in international relations? Freedom and the right of self-determination? The principle that "sovereign rights and self-government would be restored to those who had been forcibly deprived of them"? Where were all these noble ideals? Very few conferees seemed to remember that these cherished principles were not quotations from authors, that they were not mere promises of statesmen. Millions of young lives had been sacrificed to make them come true. They were sacred pledges no statesman had a right to sur-render or compromise.

Yet, these basic principles seemed to be sacrificed—every one of them—with an unbelievable cynicism and hypocrisy. There was hardly any serious reaction or protest from any source. Was that because the people did not yet know what was happening? Had the truth been obscured by technical and legalistic language? Had human society become so fatigued by war that it was unable to resist evil and stand for decency?

It was an appalling spectacle. A charter for humanity was presented to the representatives of forty-nine nations with no unmistakable moral basis, no clear and specific purpose, no relevance to existing facts and trends. These representatives, who had been invited to meet in order to discuss and to decide, were told behind a smoke screen of noble words: "You can talk, but you cannot decide. You must accept dictation of the Dumbarton Oaks plan by supreme order of the Big Four. This may be the death sentence of your independence, but we expect you to countersign it."

Why? The answer was that agreement between the Big Four could be maintained only if the dictated terms were accepted. And the small states asked themselves this time, "Big Four agreement on what? On the abandonment of moral principles? Or on the temporary tutelage of small nations under trusteeship of the Big Four, who will expend the necessary physical force to run things until the sacred pledges have been fulfilled?" The agreement extended only to the point of keeping secret a basic disagreement—one that appeared impossible to bridge with the existing mentality, attitude, and methods of approach.

In reality, the most dreadful setback in history was experienced in San Francisco. Humanity was drifting backwards, not to the Versailles days, not to the Vienna Congress, not even to the Peace of Westphalia following the Thirty Years War, which at least established some degree of tolerance and good will. It was a step back to the Dark Ages of the right of might and arbitrary dictation to underlings.

The Big Powers (happily a remnant of honesty would not permit the use of the word "Great") had the monopoly of industrial systems and of the extensive resources necessary for the mass production of airplanes and tanks. This fact was to be the guiding principle of the coming world. The medium and small powers had no choice but to seek the protection of a big power and to enter into a strictly feudal sort of relationship—service and obedience—the price for protection. An imperialistic feudal system cannot be depended upon to keep engagements, and the armament race could be expected to continue in the world divided into zones of influence, with constant fifth column maneuvers and intrigues in the rival zones, with "peace" only a latent stage of war.

If big powers cannot resist the temptation to bully little nations and bend them to their will, then these little nations should become "big" by binding themselves into federations for their own mutual protection against the political lust of the giants. Such federations could be created overnight in Scandinavia, in the Danube, in the Balkans, in the Middle East, and in the Mediterranean if the small nations were in control of their own destinies. However, attempts at such federations are discouraged, unless promoted by a big power for its own advantage, because it is easier to crush the spirit of independence of the small countries, one by one. The whole attitude towards them disregards the fact that the most advanced stages of civilization have been developed in little countries like Sweden, Norway, Switzerland, Denmark, and Finland, free of the poison of greed for power. Surely these small countries, in and by themselves, can never be regarded as a threat to the peace of the world. In spite of that, the United Nations charter provides security measures only in case the *small* nations are involved in conflict.

As for the large nations which really are likely to be in conflict, the final avenue to peaceful settlement is closed by vetoes. The only method of redress will still be war. The charter does not even attempt to conceal its impotence to provide any other final redress. It seems to accept imperialism as a natural right and does not even pretend to guarantee a hearing for complaints of the people in colonial or other dominated areas. For each complaint, a vote must be taken on whether or not to hear and judge it. As to the scope of the trusteeship scheme, it is geographically very limited, and stipulations about trusteeships apply only to a small proportion of the dominated people.

The fact is that the old attitude of appeasement prevailed in San Francisco. The meek excuse was that appeasement was unavoidable, that any resistance meant another war, which had to be avoided at all costs. Had we not heard the same argument often in the periods prior to the two world wars? Was it not found to be the direct cause of the second war?

People continue to ask, "What else could have been done?" It was simple. The United States, which had entered this war as an advocate of firm ethical principles, which were used as justification for the huge burdens imposed upon its people, should have remained faithful to the principles of the Atlantic Charter and to the moral spirit of her own constitution, without feeling free to make compromises to imperialism. In that case, the small states would have readily joined her. A powerful section of public opinion in England was also ripe and ready for it. Such a move would not have been a threat against Russia. On the contrary, it would have given the Russians the guarantee of sincerity so necessary in establishing permanent relations with them.

There are people who say, "The Russians are not sincere; they are fanatical doctrinaires; they cannot feel an obligation to act ethically towards people whom they consider to be infidels. They live under a system of state absolutism—a system which cannot live side by side with one which upholds the freedom and dignity of the individual. Russia and the free nations are bound to clash. Why not settle the matter right now?" Those who think in this manner are themselves dangerous fanatics.

It is absurd to think that peace can be achieved by a new war. My own contention has been, all along, that unity among the nations which cherish liberty would constitute a moral brake powerful enough to stop Russia. The despotic dictatorship in Russia does not tolerate public discussion and cannot create an internal brake. Humanity must come to the rescue of the Soviets to perform this function. Time after time, the Soviets prove by their propaganda that they value greatly the outside opinion. In spite of their divorce from basic moral values and their attachment to materialism, the bulk of their internal propaganda rests on a type of idealism which they must make appear superior to that of the capitalistic states, which are portrayed as victims of complete moral degeneration. They cannot afford to be singled out as the only black sheep by the rest of the world.

I put these ideas into a report from San Francisco addressed to Ralph McGill, editor of the *Atlanta Constitution* and one of three representatives of the Society of American Editors who made a world survey on freedom of the press and free flow of information between countries. Some parts of this report were published in various American papers. The report itself was widely circulated and discussed among newspapermen gathered in San Francisco. In a private discussion of about twenty-five newspapermen at a dinner party, it was read and debated; I had the support of all those present—but one.

While in San Francisco, I kept cabling to *Vatan* my protests against the proceedings of the conference as a betrayal of the most cherished hopes of humanity. In the meantime, a new movement for effective democracy had started in Turkey, right in the bosom of the single party which had dictatorial power. I preferred to rush back home without waiting for the actual signing of the charter. I simply could not afford to miss the new movement in Turkey, and I wanted to contribute my own share to it.

19: STRUGGLE

FOR DEMOCRACY

Tʜᴇ ᴡʜᴇᴇʟ of destiny was whirling fast, and a reversal
of Turkey's and the world's fortunes was becoming apparent.
On leaving San Francisco, I felt that the world was suffering
from a fresh attack of its inherited disease of power politics; and
on arrival in Turkey, I quickly sensed new symptoms of good
health there.

Outwardly very little had changed. The single party still
seemed to hold absolute sway. It even triumphantly pretended
that it alone deserved the people's gratitude for keeping Turkey
out of the war and its attendant misery. Nevertheless, discontent
and impatience for progress had crept into the heart of the ruling party itself. This discontent and impatience led to an ardent
effort for more democracy, while the rest of the world, under
Soviet pressure, was sacrificing democracy to power. The inside
story of our democratic efforts is barely known outside of Turkey, and, as it is something new in history, the story is worth
telling.

Choosing Victory Day for the Allies as an auspicious date,
four members of the single party, the People's party of the Republic, presented a motion in the Grand National Assembly
which sounded very modest and conservative, but which soon
acquired historic significance. The motion proposed simply that
the guarantees of rights and liberties embodied in the Turkish
constitution be applied, and that, thereby, freedom of the press

be safeguarded from arbitrary control by the cabinet. The motion bore significant weight from the character and personality of its proposers. One of them was Celâl Bayar, a former prime minister, a close friend and co-worker of Atatürk, and the leader of the silent opposition within the party. Another was Professor Fuad Köprülü, a historian of world repute. The third, Adnan Menderes, a young cotton cultivator from Aydın, was a graduate of the American College in İzmir and had studied law at Ankara University while a member of the National Assembly. The fourth, Refik Koraltan, a former provincial governor, was also a law graduate and a brilliant orator.

The reaction of the government and the single party's executive committee, which were really identical, was outspoken bitterness and anger, followed by every possible move to suppress the new spirit of revolt. The four pioneers, however, refused to be intimidated. They used the ratification of the San Francisco Charter by the Turkish Grand National Assembly as the occasion to renew their insistence on the actual and immediate application of the democratic principles in the constitution— a move difficult to ignore because of Turkey's international pledge in signing the United Nations Charter. Single-party extremists called this blasphemy against national sovereignty; and Şükrü Saracoğlu, the prime minister, spoke publicly of "malicious voices of discord" within the party.

I immediately and vigorously campaigned against the "fake democracy on paper under the single-party tutelage" and in support of the new pioneer movement. I used tactics considered most daring under conditions existing then, for I criticized appointments of unfit but obedient personnel, the prevalence of favoritism, and the single party's misuse of government machinery for its own benefit. Hired pens of the party's flatterers mobilized against me in editorials, columns, cartoons, and false reports. It reminded me of an earlier distortion of the parting advice that Professor Giddings had given us when we graduated from Columbia. He had said, "If it is absolutely necessary to fool, fool other people, but never fool yourselves." I had quoted this in Turkey during a hot discussion in the press, and the humorous weeklies had avidly distorted it into, "Never put faith in what that fellow, Ahmed Emin, says; his American professor told him to fool others."

This time I avoided personal controversies and went my way. I brought to light facts, lest hysterical misstatements by others bias the younger generation, which could not understand events leading up to current issues because the single-party dictatorship had imposed such tight controls on public information.

The main charge against me was that, during our national struggle, 1919–23, I had supported the idea of an American mandate over Turkey and was, therefore, an enemy of Turkish independence. It was easy to produce evidence that I had opposed the mandate idea and that what I had done was to advocate close co-operation with America in order to inspire American investors' confidence in our credit. The public realized then, as it does now, that the failure to take this advantage caused a tremendous waste of time, money, and effort in developing Turkey's resources.

Two of the leaders of the democratic movement, Professor Köprülü and Adnan Menderes, still members of the People's party, wrote signed articles for *Vatan* boldly attacking the totalitarian mentality and practices of their own party. The "loyal" members of the party met in secret and decided to expel these two as "contributors to the opposition paper, *Vatan*." Dramatic action followed. Refik Koraltan, the third signer of the historic motion for democracy in practice, contributed to *Vatan* a detailed justification for the two men who had been expelled and a bitter attack on the "loyal" members for their intolerant, short-sighted, and suicidal decision. He dared the loyalists to expel him also. This they did, after a second stormy secret session, on the grounds that his statement in *Vatan* contravened party discipline.

The remaining signer of the motion, Celâl Bayar, thereupon resigned his seat in the Grand National Assembly, thus leaving no doubt of the solidarity of the proposers of the constitutional motion. On the other hand, the three expelled from the party chose to retain the seats in the Assembly to which they were entitled by election; and two more deputies, Dr. Cemal Tunca and Emin Sazak, joined them in opposition to the 460 other deputies. This small group cheerfully withstood the totalitarian pressure.

The People's party hardly deserved its name any more. Its source of power was no longer the will and consent of the people, but the "authority" of the government passing orders down a hierarchial line. By honorary titles, Atatürk, the first president of the Republic and the party, had become its "eternal chief," and İsmet İnönü, the second president, its "unchangeable chief." Any opposition to the party's will had become "sacrilege, directed against the survival of the Republic and the nation." The party controlled jealously all nongovernmental organizations, itself nominating the officers of the chamber of commerce, charitable societies, and even the few scientific societies.

As a gesture of the democracy which Atatürk had verbally encouraged and towards which he had pointed the way, the executive committee of the People's party nominated, in the Grand National Assembly, an official and most obedient "opposition," called the Independent Group. Annually it nominated new "independents" without even consulting its nominees' wishes. They attended People's party meetings without voting privileges and tried to behave like an opposition party. This was perfectly controlled "window dressing" for a regime which followed some democratic forms but, in practice, always managed unanimous elections.

The six dissenters met to establish a genuine opposition to the giant single party. I co-operated with them fully, although I was determined, as an independent journalist, not to join any party. In my freedom to call "right, right, and wrong, wrong," I felt justified in supporting this movement to end the wrong of single-party absolutism. Many obstacles other than the furious pressure from the People's party made our task hard.

Leftist elements, under remote control from Moscow, immediately mobilized to gain control of the new opposition party. Although not numerous, they had choice adherents among intellectuals dissatisfied with their own lot or with the conservative aspects of national life. This situation was extremely delicate just then, when Russia was claiming vast sections of eastern Turkey in the name of the Armenian and Georgian Socialist Soviet Republics, renewing her old efforts to gain control of the Dardanelles, and seemingly moving to introduce her own puppet government in Turkey as she had introduced it in the neighboring Balkan states.

Even a pinkish tinge could have meant early death to the opposition movement in Turkey, for the public, although most discontented with single-party administration, was wide awake to the Russian danger. Consequently, the progovernment newspapers tried their best to smear red on the new opposition party and the independent press. They tried, for example, to spread the impression that the patriotic *Vatan* was in league with the pinkish *Tan* in opposing the government. Since I was fully aware of Russian tactics, I repeatedly denied a *Tan–Vatan* axis, while the opposition party asserted its own patriotism on every possible occasion.

Taking advantage of the unstable atmosphere created by violent public controversy, the reddish leftists started a weekly paper, *Görüşler* (*Views*). In the first number, December 1, 1945, without any authority to do so, they named as their contributors all the prime movers of the opposition. This weekly sounded very patriotic—to Moscow! Being linked in any way with a weekly which carried so much "red" material—for instance, a pro-Russian poem on German aggression against Russia—was a disgrace to anybody. All of us involved by name or implication protested emphatically day after day.

Public indignation reached the bursting point when an openly red daily paper, *Yeni Dünya* (*New World*), appeared. A large group of students, on December 4, attacked and demolished the offices of *Yeni Dünya* and also of *Tan,* where *Görüşler* was published, and then attacked several bookstores which were reported to sell red literature. We knew that agents of vested interests dependent on the totalitarian regime might take advantage of the day or two of terror in Istanbul to destroy *Vatan*'s plant. I felt that my best course was to walk to my office, alone, through the streets crowded with demonstrators. Soon after I reached the office, a gendarme detachment and ample police forces arrived to protect our plant. Our dilemma was to make clear our conviction that public protest against red agitation was right, but that violent suppression was wrong. We made our criticism as clear as we could and recommended that only legal methods should be used to suppress red activity.

After obviating the red and pink dangers, the infant opposition party was exposed to a fascist threat from circles which tried to inject into its program a corporate system and a high degree of chauvinism. Signs of danger came also from certain men, formerly in Atatürk's personal entourage, who saw in a new party a danger to the political heritage from Atatürk. If they had had their way, "what Atatürk said or did" would have become a fetish, and a group of interpreters of Atatürk's intentions would have formed a sort of priesthood, detrimental to the growth of Turkish democracy. Happily this danger was averted.

However, a further complication arose when the People's party's defense against Russian pressure and territorial demands exacted blind obedience to the national chief, namely, their party president. The new party had to convert this dictated unity into unity by persuasion and consent. All this political upheaval in a country on the Soviet border worried the Western powers, but they soon were satisfied that Turkey was going through a fundamentally healthy transition.

A peculiar problem for the new party, akin to the problem of one and the same man holding jointly the presidency of the Republic and of the party in power, was the fact that the People's party had written into the constitution its own principles, symbolized by the "six arrows" of its party emblem. The arrows stood for republicanism, secularism, nationalism, etatism (state ownership and control of essential industries and resources), populism (government for the people), and revolutionism (radical rather than gradual changes). These principles were somewhat self-contradictory and restrictive for a truly liberal party. Still, by subtle reinterpretation, it was possible to get around this constitutional problem. The new opposition, soon known as the Democratic party, declared its ideals of the state as a servant of the people, of advanced conceptions of citizenship, and other basic principles of Western democracy.

Public acclaim of the new party caused mixed feelings in officialdom. Although agreeing that an opposition party was desirable, the government objected to party activity outside of the Grand National Assembly and complained that the Democrats were dragging politics down into the street by going out even to villages to organize branches. In some regions, Democratic organizers were repeatedly forced to quit, so bolder men had to be found to carry the flag of the opposition. Fresh hints of subsidies from Moscow for the Democrats were systematically promulgated. But pressure was resisted by the freedom that the press was able to exercise in reporting and discussing these political moves.

When the wind blew stronger and stronger from the Democratic quarter, the People's party (usually referred to in the Western press as the Republican party) determined to seize the initiative in being democratic—at least in appearing so. At an extraordinary convention of this old single party, President İnönü voluntarily surrendered his title of "unchangeable chief." This meant abdication from the *Führer* or personal-leader style of government. The convention also changed the election of deputies from the electoral system, in force since the original Ottoman constitution in 1876, to direct election by popular vote.

But a shrewd maneuver betrayed this show of democracy. Although President İnönü, in opening the Grand National Assembly on November 1, 1945, had said there would be no elections until that Assembly completed its normal term in the fall of 1947, the People's party convention, meeting in April, 1946, voted for immediate elections. Over the Democratic party's protests that this deprived it of time to organize and campaign, the People's party announced municipal elections to be held immediately and to be followed by national ones on July 21, 1946.

While *Vatan* led the independent newspapers in fighting hard against single-party dictation of elections, the Democratic party boycotted the municipal elections. A very minor new party, the Party of the Nation, won a few municipal posts. Boycotting the national as well as the municipal elections would leave the People's party free to continue its usual election tactics, and would also deprive the Democrats of Assembly seats from which to make their views public. Worse yet, a Democratic boycott would leave a political vacuum into which agitators, including red agents, would be drawn to lead the growing popular discontent. The Democratic party was not willing to assume

228

this risk. The party moderates persuaded the extremists that, in spite of inequitable election conditions, participation would be the lesser evil.

The election that July was anything but fair. The People's party, exercising full government authority, admitted opposition and independent observers to the polling centers, but did not allow them to check final tallies or to receive certified copies of results. Consequently, many tallies were falsified, but it was very difficult to provide formal proof of this. Nevertheless, the Democratic party obtained 62 Assembly seats against 396 for the People's party. Seven seats went to independent candidates, including Marshal Fevzi Çakmak, a much beloved national hero and chief of the general staff, who supported the Democrats after being put on the retired list against his will. However, he did not join their party; nor did Dr. Adnan-Adıvar, who, with his wife, Halide Edib, had been self-exiled in Paris during the single-party reign.

The Democrats were in a quandary, whether to refuse seats in an unconstitutionally elected Assembly or to accept the seats and use the Assembly as the sounding board for its demands for real democracy. It was a hard choice, but the new party deputies finally took their seats under protest. The Democrats' complaints about election abuses, even when documented, received no consideration at all by the People's party majority. National tension increased.

The new cabinet of ministers from the majority People's party came to power on August 7, 1946, under Prime Minister Recep Peker, who represented the most totalitarian faction. Immediately the Press Law and the Penal Code were revised "to protect the safety of the state," so that under martial law the Istanbul newspapers were ordered not to mention election abuses any more. The Democratic party firmly but tactfully refused to compromise. Independent newspapers, standing only for right and liberty, began to gain the readers that the government journals were rapidly losing.

I was personally exposed, day by day, to a war of nerves. I had to spend much of my time in law courts because the cabinet started every possible action against *Vatan*. Fortunately, Turkish justice proved incorruptible even under political pressure, and every suit ended in my honorable acquittal. Recovering the vigorous enthusiasm of my early youth in the zest of this movement, I took delight in being the object of continuous attacks by the government and its press, because these showed that my hits against abuses were direct and effective.

Trips to all parts of Turkey kept me in close touch with the people, particularly the peasants. They were a marvelous source of inspiration, for they represented my ideal of citizenship. Where did Turkish peasants get their democratic training? I learned that these people had been concealing a remarkable resistance to oppression under their outer resignation to fate. Suffering under arbitrary rule must be the best training for democracy! As soon as the peasants recognized an outlet for their complaints through an honest press and an organized opposition party, they emerged to claim their rights and liberty and to assert their human dignity. Illiterate as they were, they heard the news read aloud and got someone to write their letters to the press. I received about one hundred letters a day, mostly from peasants expecting a magic cure for their grievances through publicity. Our circulation soared to eighty thousand, a new figure for Turkey, and an enormous readership when each copy is read by, or read to, an average of twenty persons.

For diversion from political tension I often sought the company of a lawyer of Greek family, Theologos Gulbaloğlu, who had already devoted fifteen years of his life and his entire personal fortune to the conservation of pine trees on the romantic island of Heybeli, one of the Princes' Islands near Istanbul in

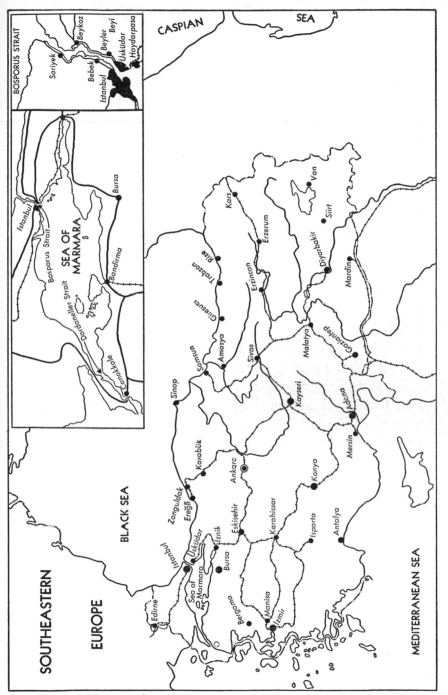

Modern Turkey

SOUTHEASTERN
EUROPE

BLACK SEA

MEDITERRANEAN SEA

CASPIAN SEA

Edirne
Istanbul
Üsküdar
Sea of Marmara
Bursa
İznik
Bergama
Manisa
İzmir
Eskişehir
Karahissar
Isparta
Antalya
Konya
Zonguldak
Ereğli
Karabük
Ankara
Sinop
Samsun
Amasya
Giresun
Trabzon
Rize
Sivas
Kayseri
Adana
Mersin
Malatya
Gaziantep
Erzincan
Erzurum
Kars
Diyarbakır
Mardin
Siirt
Van

Sea of Marmara inset
Istanbul
Bosporus Strait
Dardanelles Strait
Çanakkale
SEA OF MARMARA
Bandirma
Bursa

Bosporus Strait inset
BOSPORUS STRAIT
Sariyek
Bebek
Istanbul
Beykoz
Beyler Beyi
Üsküdar
Haydarpasa

the Sea of Marmara. He employed four trained men to care for old trees and plant new ones on Heybeli, while the pine forests on the three neighboring islands were decaying. Having a personal interest because I live on one of these islands in the summers, I contributed publicity for his demonstrations, and so together we ended the illicit sale of forest lands and harmful deforestation.

Pine-forest conservation on the islands had been a favorite theme of the Istanbul press for two generations. The government had frittered away much money and labor in futile measures to save the forests. But this man alone was doing the job for love of the trees. He would say, "All these forests are mine morally because I raised them and care for them. I am happy with these millions of 'children.'" I felt morally a co-owner with my Greek friend, because I, too, knew how to love the forests. I did the major part of my work in the summer under these trees, deciding each morning which part of the hilly forest would yield the best inspiration for the subject in mind that day. Whenever I had doubts about the relative efficiency of private and state enterprise, my friend and his forests were adequate evidence for me that the unhampered flow of personal interest and energy spells success provided the government also performs its functions honestly.

Turkey's future security and independence could best be assured in a democratic world of sovereign and equal states. For a fresh perspective on this prospect, I had taken time from our internal struggle for democracy to attend the United Nations Assembly's first session in London. The only cheer I found there was in the spirited effort of Ernest Bevin of England and his seeming delight in shocking the Russians. I saw, however, no real evidence that the United Nations was ready or able to open the avenue to a brighter destiny for humanity, so I left the session early to go to Nürnberg for the Allied trial of German war leaders.

There I did not find justice objective enough to punish *all* war criminals on either side, because only those on the defeated side were to be judged, and the victors were the judges. Yet it seemed to be a good beginning towards a much-needed new legal procedure. I was encouraged by finding a Russian representative, Professor Trainin, to be one of the, I am sure, hundreds of thousands of Russians capable of scientific, critical thinking, who are, alas, still unable to influence the course of events.

It was thrilling to see a large group of arrogant and barbarous Nazis on trial. My attention turned especially to Franz von Papen, "the old fox," a striking example of a split personality, who had done all he could as ambassador to Turkey to drag us into the Nazi orbit. It is to the credit of the Turkish nation to have foiled his clever scheming, especially after Russia joined Germany in the war.

The Allies' postwar policy in Germany seemed to me an appalling example of human stupidity. Then was the time and opportunity to liquidate German militarism forever and to pose as the Germans' savior from Nazi despotism, and so prepare Germany for a true welcome into the family of peace-loving nations. Instead, I saw atrocity propaganda being overplayed in a way to humiliate an entire nation, including those who had opposed nazism. To expect a whole nation, the innocent with the guilty, to admit guilt and depravity is to force its people to defiance and swaggering. The process of de-Nazification as I watched it seemed like potential re-Nazification. Divesting persons of their place in society for merely registering in the party for self-defense left them with nothing more to lose; they could not but become a disorderly element. I found the entire policy based on vengeful retaliation, more suitable to a nation like Russia, unready for lasting peace.

Little cause for greater cheerfulness appeared either at the

Paris Peace Conference or in England in September of 1946. French political confusion was distressing. And in England, I found a startling number of the sound middle class ready to emigrate for fear that the new socialist government was approaching an authoritarianism comparable to religious persecution. Sweden also provided disappointment because the socialist regime, originally broadly liberal but now in the hands of narrow doctrinaires, seemed set on a program of nationalization, although its citizens had passed the highest test of individual and social responsibility.

The Council of World Affairs and *Time* magazine invited me to address an international forum in Cleveland on the Middle East's view of "What the World Expects from America." (Others among the twenty-five speakers who discussed this subject were Eelco N. van Kleefens, Alcide de Gasperi, V. K. Wellington Koo, Jan G. Masaryk, Carlos P. Romulo, Oswaldo Aranha, Arthur H. Vandenberg, James V. Forrestal, James E. Carey, and Francis Cardinal Spellman.) I saw it as a marvelous opportunity to present to a world audience views formed in Turkey, which, in its position on the boundary of Russia, has been for generations the severest testing ground of power politics. A central thought for the address came to me from an unexpected source—Karl Marx.

En route to America I happened to see in Paris the eight volumes of Marx's dispatches to the old New York *Tribune,* for which he had been the London correspondent. They dealt mainly with the danger which Russian Byzantinism constituted for "the guardian of liberty," namely Western civilization. Only the unity of the Western world, "including America, that young exponent of Western civilization," he felt, could stop the voraciousness of Russia. Marx said that, confronted by unity in the West, the Russian bear would draw in its paws, while otherwise it would stretch out its claws. He also prophesied that disunity in the West would lead to an even more dreadful form of Russian Byzantinism.

Strangely enough, this came true when the Russians chose Marxism to cloak their ancient imperialism. Their reactionary tyrants seem to have usurped Marx's ideas, essentially those in support of liberty and applicable only to early nineteenth century conditions, to camouflage their own despotism and aggression. Since this fully applies also to present day Muscovite policy, I maintained at Cleveland that all peace-loving nations should unite and tolerate no departures from moral principles to gain pseudo agreement with Russia. Yet, I said, the doors should always be open and arms outstretched to receive the Russians if they decided to play ball fairly with the rest of the world. As often on other occasions, I insisted that Russia's despotic system, lacking an internal brake, should be supplied with an external one.

After the forum and while lecturing on the radio and at various colleges and gatherings, I was thrilled to find that America had gone a long way since the San Francisco Conference towards facing facts realistically and towards a truly bipartisan national policy. Alas, British policy had taken the opposite turn. The Labor party, embarrassed by its own rebels after coming to power, was placing its ideological survival above the national need to co-operate with the United States for a new world order. The brightest hope I saw was the Liberal International, organized by liberals from nineteen countries in Oxford, England, in April, 1947, to counter the Communist International. Its "Liberal Manifesto" stood squarely for private initiative, free competition, and, in contrast to nineteenth century *laissez faire,* public and private acceptance of responsibility for social justice.

At home again, I could report only that Turkey's new health and vigor were in bright contrast to the political sickness that seemed to be spreading in the West. I organized a Turkish chapter of the Liberal International, called the "Society for the Diffusion of Ideas of Liberty," a nonpolitical group mostly of prominent professors, lawyers, doctors, engineers, and journalists. The public turned to it hopefully because the complete failure of state socialism after fifteen years of trial had turned the people against wasteful bureaucratic control of the nation's economy. The public also welcomed American aid against possible Russian aggression and especially to fortify liberal economic trends in our domestic affairs. The Truman Doctrine recognized that the vigorous Republic of Turkey was ready and able to operate on a give-and-take basis, and was a stable bridgehead next to the "iron curtain" in the Middle East. My pet idea, which had exposed me to continuous attack for a quarter of a century, was coming true—a Washington-Ankara cornerstone for a sound structure for peace. The stand I took in *Vatan* was that the United States of America, undertaking a heavy postwar task without adequate support elsewhere for her basic ideals, needed Turkey's sympathetic partnership; and that, since our survival and development next door to Russia must depend on collective security, our duty was to support the United States, despite lethargy, unrest, and lack of understanding in the rest of the world.

Credit should go to the Twentieth Century Fund for underwriting, prior to the United States government's plan to aid Turkey, an investigation which was published under the title, *Turkey, An Economic Appraisal*. Even the preliminary reports by the investigators, headed by an exceptionally able and honest man, Dr. Max Thornburg, attracted immense interest among Turks because of their new self-critical attitude. I found Dr. Thornburg always most sympathetic to our liberal campaign. Another visit to Sweden and Denmark, in search of campaign ammunition against Turkey's wasteful state industrialization, reconvinced me that planned economy is a poor alternative to free competition. For example, Denmark's famous state dairy industry's efficiency and low operation costs suffered when government importation of essential fodder was snarled in the red tape of exchange with foreign nations afflicted by postwar paralysis.

My membership in the executive committee of the Liberal International increased the frequency of my visits to England, where I followed personal reactions to the liquidation of the pompous empire so dear to so many generations of Englishmen. Adjustment to the fact seemed to me remarkably slow and aimless, with an unfair and unreasoning tendency to blame America. I had been an inside observer of the liquidation of the Ottoman Empire, and I must say that we Turks, led by Mustafa Kemal Atatürk, have done a much better job of bold, cheerful, and prompt adjustment to new conditions.

Again in Germany, I stood aghast at the worsening situation. The Allied authorities seemed little perturbed by dangers which stood out sharply for me, because I had experienced the effects of Inter-Allied occupation errors in Turkey between 1919 and 1923. The semicolonial treatment, especially the distance, kept between foreign masters and natives (except only the female native), the shortages, and the sense of futility, since the Germans could not determine their own future, were breeding underground revolt. Many Germans even believed that in a Soviet world their place would be in the ruling class.

My conclusion was that the only solution lay in an Anglo-American union and a Swiss-type federation of France and Germany until the ground could be adequately prepared for a "United States of Europe" and eventually a world state with limited functions. A French-German federation would relieve the French of their obsessive fear, unfortunately justified, of new German invasions, and would end their impossible idea of achieving security by crushing Germany. Moreover, it would be a desperately needed bulwark against Pan-Slavic domination of Europe and potentially of the whole world. The prolonged test in Switzerland has proved that French and Germans can govern together; one side contributing liberty, the other stability. The Schumann Plan of French-German union for the Ruhr brought the first sign of hope for this federation. Karl Marx rightly complained a century ago of the diplomats' stupidity in thinking always in terms of the *status quo*. In facing the threat to peace and security from the East, the essential measure is to shorten the time necessary for minds to "travel" from reliance on the *status quo* to comprehension and adoption of practical innovations. This ability to discard the old and accept the new saved Turkey, and it could save the world.

20 : DEMOCRACY

WINS IN TURKEY

ONLY FOUR years after the Turks' struggle for democracy began, the world was astounded to hear that the Republic of Turkey, which it had been complacently calling a dictatorship, had peaceably defeated the single-party "dictatorship" at the polls. Turkey's 1950 election was probably the first instance in history when absolute power yielded, without violence, to the will of the people freely expressed by secret ballots which were honestly tallied.

When the new Democratic party took seats in the Grand National Assembly, as the result of the 1946 election, the totalitarian faction of the People's party tried hard to preserve its own absolute control. While the old party had a crushing majority over the new one, its totalitarians could find no way to crush discussion by progressive and moderate members of their own party. Moreover, they could not escape public demands for their party to explain and justify its acts to the people. These insurmountable limitations made it impossible for the extremists to create the blind confusion in which rule by terror is possible.

The Democratic party's tiny minority in the Assembly unrelentingly pressed its protests that government officials arbitrarily discriminated against the Democrats' local branches and its nominees in by-elections. The new party dramatized its protests by boycotting the numerous by-elections which took place in June, at the same time loudly demanding application of the improvements in the election law which had been enacted by the Assembly but not put into practice. General tension stayed at a high pitch, and the issues of constitutional rights and fair elections were kept in sharp focus.

President İnönü saw fit to intervene personally for the public interest. He arranged a series of conferences between Prime Minister Recep Peker and the opposition leaders for an airing of both sides' grievances. Some of the conferences were held in the President's presence. No agreements were reached. But each side made speeches informing the public of its stand and publicly answered charges of the other side. Finally, President İnönü, himself, issued a solemn declaration on July 12, 1947, which may be considered the beginning of Western-type democracy in practice in Turkey.

The President's first announcement was his own withdrawal from partisan politics. He surrendered his presidential duties in the People's party to an executive vice-president and became only titular head of the party. He stated that, thereafter, as President of the Republic, he would serve as nonpartisan arbiter, solely in the interest of the nation as a whole. Next, after listening to the discussions between the government and the opposition, he declared that he had found that the cabinet's charges of revolutionary activity by the Democratic party did not correspond to the facts, but he had found that the Democrats' charges of oppression by government officials had some foundation in fact, although their claims were somewhat exaggerated. In conclusion, he maintained that both parties were entitled to equal treatment and to the enjoyment of equal opportunities in every respect.

The President's position, publicly stated, brought new tolerance into the political atmosphere. Pressure to destroy the opposition did not cease, but it was modified. The public was jubilant. On the other hand, the extremists in the People's party could not restrain their bitterness. They secretly charged İnönü with betraying the People's party in favor of the Democrats. But the President's own personality seemed to experience a rebirth; he gave the impression of being a totally new man.

İsmet İnönü, ever since he was first recognized as one of the most gifted staff officers of the Turkish Army after the Young Turk revolution of 1908, had ascended the heights of personal prestige—through the stages of victorious commander in the War of Independence, successful negotiator at Lausanne, cabinet member, prime minister under Atatürk for twelve years, and finally second president of Turkey. An interesting side light on İsmet İnönü's influence comes from the fact that when he resigned as prime minister in 1937, at the age of fifty-three, he chose to devote his leisure to learning English. For more than a year he concentrated on English lessons each morning and worked on translation in the afternoons. He was soon able to read easily English books and periodicals. Opening this avenue of direct contact with the English-speaking world became highly important in shaping history, for it may be considered a vital factor in Turkey's firm stand at the side of her Anglo-American allies in war and world affairs during İsmet İnönü's term in the office of president, and thereafter.

When the democratic movement really got under way in Turkey, President İnönü could not immediately free himself from the firm grip of single-party authoritarianism. He tried by extensive traveling in his country to make contacts with all sorts of people, but he was walled in by the barriers inevitably erected around a chief with practically unlimited personal power. He moved in an aura of profuse flattery. Men around him warned all who were to meet him that they must tell him only pleasant things and avoid criticism, "because the President is in poor health, and the truth might upset him." Year after year, a conspiracy of silence had cut him off from the true state of affairs in his country. Consequently, for considerable time, he exercised an increasingly negative influence. But he refused to go beyond the point of no return in the negative direction. When his party's extremists would urge him to allow full repressive measures against the opposition, he would say, "No backward moves. We must do our best to use tolerance."

Finally, when actual developments in Turkey fully opened his eyes to the political maturity of the Turkish people and their readiness to shape their own destiny, İsmet İnönü quickly emancipated himself from the old political shackles and boldly issued his now historic July 12 declaration. His new personal orientation towards real democracy gave a tremendous stimulus to the democratic movement. The change in the national outlook soon brought a change in the men forming the President's close circle.

The press, reflecting the public's bitter antagonism to the totalitarian cabinet, pointed out that it would be suicidal for the People's party to approach its important convention with such men still in power. As long as governmental authority remained in their hands, they could pick delegates favorable to them and so control the convention. Whatever temporary camouflage they might throw over their totalitarianism would not lessen their moves to restore the People's party dictatorship. These extremists were plainly losing favor with President İnönü. Over their stout protests, the President received me in a long, off-the-record interview. I had his personal assurance that he wished to devote the rest of his life to establishing mutual respect and confidence between the political parties.

The President's new nonpartisan role put the extremists on the defensive and compelled them to call a meeting of the legislative group—the Assembly deputies of their party—before the Assembly's adjournment for two months, in order to enforce discipline and unity among themselves and tighten their grip on their party. Their natural choice for leader was Prime Minister Recep Peker. Loudly acclaimed by his partisans as the next national chief, Peker made a speech painting himself as a believer in authority but not totalitarianism. He used violent language to denounce the "revolutionary character" of the Democratic party, and asked his party—tactfully, he thought—to take an open vote, not of personal confidence in him, but of party solidarity against opposition. To the great surprise of Peker's faction and the country, the ensuing discussion suddenly brought to their feet young and idealistic party members in open revolt against the old guard. They declared themselves ready to face the risk of the People's party's defeat in an honest democracy and to reject the absolute power that the party exercised by illicit government controls.

When the party policy vote was taken, 35 members stood out against 303, who voted as the cabinet wished. The protest vote would have been higher if the habit of unanimous, "rubber-stamp" voting had not prevented other members from asserting their own convictions by a show of hands. The extremists threatened that deputies who voted against them could not expect re-election unless Recep Peker was empowered to reorganize the party. They also covertly circulated word that President İnönü had issued his July 12 declaration only to please the Western powers and still approved of his party's old policy.

Secret though this meeting had been, all the details were learned and published by opposition papers, with the names of the thirty-five dissenters, who were thereupon greeted as "heroes of democracy." Since the thirty-five represented the true value and quality inherent in the People's party, the split was both important and promising. The totalitarian stronghold had been shaken to its foundation, and more adherents joined the growing national bloc which was fighting for sincere democracy.

The now infuriated extremists arranged for a second vote by the People's party deputies. The dissenters, encouraged by public support, were more successful this time. The extremists' majority fell from 303 to 194. Forty-seven voted against the extremists, and nearly one hundred abstained from voting. In spite of its numerical majority of votes, the die-hard cabinet was forced to resign. It needs hardly to be said that the entire country felt a sense of relief.

The new cabinet, under Hasan Saka, could not be considered ideal since it contained some old hands, but its orientation seemed favorable to the spirit of the July 12 proclamation and to the revolt successfully started by the broad-minded younger men in the People's party. Several members of the "rebel" group were taken into the cabinet and brought to it an atmosphere never previously noticed in public life in Turkey.

The third party, the Party of the Nation, which had won a few municipal offices in 1946, now publicly accused the leaders of the Democratic party of entering into a secret agreement with İsmet İnönü to betray the democratic movement and to secure personal advantages and appointments for themselves. The third party's true aim seemed to be to capture the leadership in democracy from the Democratic party's leaders, who had initiated the opposition and led it through the first critical and risky stages. It was very apparent, too, in Soviet radio broadcasts to Turkey that Moscow had much too close an interest in the conflict. It tried to incite Turkish peasants and workers to rid the country of leaders who "were obstructing the free flow of expression in the people's democracy." It kept naming, as enemies of the people, all the moderate leaders who steadfastly stood against violence and open revolt.

The result of so much agitation, internal and external, was that the moderates in the Democratic party, in order to disprove the charge of a secret agreement with the People's party, continued to boycott all by-elections and avoided all contact with officials of the government and the People's party. Up to that moment I had co-operated 100 per cent with the opposition leaders and had shared all their activities. But I objected to this attitude and insisted that, in Turkey, a midway course was the only means of inspiring in the People's party enough confidence in a biparty system to induce it to accept the risk of an honest, clean election.

The Democratic party's own extremists, at their convention in July, 1949, compelled the adoption of a resolution of "disobedience," in which they upheld the "right" of citizens to resist all public servants who interfered unconstitutionally with the free expression of the will of the nation in a lawful election.

In the new cabinet, the most progressive elements in the People's party were in control. The new prime minister was Şemseddin Günaltay, a professor of history and a patriotic statesman. Most members of his cabinet were enlightened patriots untarnished by the party's past sin of dictatorship. They believed in democracy and were ready to accept every risk of a change of party as a result of a general election, and they offered to accept all the radical changes in the electoral law demanded by the Democratic party. They stated that the opposition was entitled to ask for guarantees which would prevent a repetition of the abuses of the 1946 election, provided that the opposition would, in turn, guarantee the future rights of the People's party in case that party lost the election.

The Democratic leaders finally recognized the need to reassure those who were in actual possession of the executive machinery and the police force, else those in power would not stake their future on the outcome of a free election. A meeting of the provincial delegates of the Democratic party reinterpreted the so-called "resolution of disobedience," and announced the following stand: "Any attempt to expose the responsibilities for past mistakes of the administration may lead to chaos and loss of recent gains. We believe in order and reciprocity as party policy. Even if the party in power resorts again to unlawful practices in the elections, we shall abstain from violence, because in view of external dangers, we believe that national security must remain our first consideration. If the government uses unlawful practices in the election, we shall simply retire from the election and leave the responsibility on them; we shall respect public order."

This statement, published on January 8, 1950, had a magic effect. The government called in a group of law professors to prepare a new electoral law after examining the systems of all the democratic countries. It was an admirable law in most respects, but was handicapped by an obvious feeling of insecurity in the party in power. It proceeded through discussion to final adoption by both parties.

The election—the eighth national election, but the first truly democratic one—was to take place on May 14. All parties campaigned freely. They had equal time on the radio. Even the Party of the Nation's use of religious fanaticism for political propaganda, though prohibited by the Law of Secularism, was tolerated. Some people believed that the Party of the Nation would carry many electoral districts by these tactics. Violence resulted during the election in some sections of the country where feelings were still bitter against the modernism ushered in by Atatürk.

Results of the election of May 14, 1950, astounded the Turks as well as the outside world. The election was entirely fair and orderly. The average participation was 75 per cent of the registered voters. The Democratic party won 55 per cent of the total vote. This, however, gave that party 434 seats, an 84 per cent majority in the Assembly, because the large electoral districts (27 seats for the Istanbul districts) went Democratic. Many voters who did not like the Democratic candidates, but believed in an effective opposition, had voted for them. Others had cast

246

French Foreign Minister Georges Bidault (left) and
French Premier Joseph Laniel are received by
Turkish Premier Adnan Menderes (right) at Ankara in 1953.

Photograph by Edward Clark, Courtesy *Life* Magazine

Ahmed Emin Yalman at the Cleveland Forum.

opposition votes to counteract possible cheating in the count by those in power, and because they wished a change after having the same party in office for twenty-seven years. The People's party received 43 per cent of the total votes, but only 51 seats, for the reasons already given.

It was most startling and edifying that the Party of the Nation, in spite of its appeal to fanaticism, won only one seat. And its single victorious candidate was not a fanatic, but a professor of astronomy, educated in France, and of a family popular and respected in his district.

The world witnessed, in amazement, the peaceful abdication by an old, established totalitarian party which had absolute control before the election. All the parties in Turkey, including those defeated, celebrated it as a victory for the Turkish nation and a successful test of political maturity. On May 22, the Democratic party took over the government. Its leader, Celâl Bayar, was elected president of the Republic, and its first cabinet was formed by Adnan Menderes, the youngest of the four leaders who had organized the party and led it to victory.

I had refused offers from several electoral districts to enter my name as an independent candidate for deputy in the Assembly. My reason was my promise to my readers, as a guarantee of my sincerity in objective criticism, never to aspire to personal political power, never to accept political office, but to live and die a journalist in the service of the public. I had succeeded in re-equipping *Vatan* with a modern plant and the most up-to-date devices of any paper in Turkey. I still had plenty of energy and enthusiasm to carry on my idealistic crusade in Turkish journalism. I received no personal political advantage or profit from the Democrats' election victory, yet I felt all the cheer and contentment of a man who witnesses a most happy culmination to a long career. I was ready for relaxation, gradually easing my work into younger hands. With the serenity of this prospect, I started to write this story of Turkey's life and mine. I intended to bring it to this point as a happy end. But before I finished writing it, events proved that my estimate of the future was quite mistaken. More exciting adventures and tribulations were in store than I had ever undergone before in my eventful professional life.

It is true that I experienced bitter disappointment after the new party was in power, and I had to criticize those with whom I had worked for democracy in Turkey. However, their failures seemed an unavoidable part of a critical transition period. Just how "critical" was not fully appreciated until the new administration was halfway through its first four-year term—when Fate made me the agent of revelation through a plot to assassinate me. Troublesome symptoms of serious disturbances were manifest soon after the 1950 election, but as long as the symptoms appeared to be purely local, the new government felt safe in only mild preventive measures.

Those rebellious elements in Turkish communities which were accustomed to taking advantage of religious fanaticism in order to strengthen their influence as local bosses had been silenced under the single-party regime. With the advent of democracy and liberty in Turkey, certain fanatic elements undertook a revival of excessive religious zeal, to invoke again the Islamic laws of the *sheriat* and to foment hatred against the secular regime. Weekly papers advocating these religious goals sprang up like mushrooms. In the early heat of the Democratic struggle against single-party rule, fanatic influence had been limited. For the first time, Turkey was experiencing the complete fraternization and mingling of the enlightened citizens, the peasants, and the working men. The uneducated masses, in the pleasure of these first contacts as equal citizens, listened readily to the opinion of the political leaders. Occasional manifestations of a reactionary and fanatic character were easily nullified.

Unfortunately, the Party of the Nation in the 1950 election campaign had used religious fanaticism as its main weapon to gain votes. Some individual candidates of the People's party, which had promoted and maintained the secular regime, had not disdained to use the same weapon in order to gain seats for themselves and to keep their party in power. Even certain candidates of the Democratic party had followed suit.

The first change of power in Turkey by means of popular vote caused great common rejoicing because it was a nationwide victory of a constitutional nature. But soon those who had been in power for twenty-seven years, and at first had bowed out most gracefully in defeat, felt the bitterness of losing control. On the other hand, the Democratic party became eager to maintain its new power through its overwhelming ratio of six to one in the National Assembly. Naturally it felt itself threatened from every side. In this nervous atmosphere, a race was run to enlist the support of fanatic elements, which are always quick to seize easy opportunities offered to them. The democratic rule and the secular regime for which generations of enlightened patriots had fought and suffered through 150 years appeared to me to be in real danger.

I took the lead in attacking both the entire reactionary camp and the people in the government with whom I had closely co-operated for years in the struggle for democracy, but who were now neglecting their duty of enforcing the laws to protect the secular regime against reaction. Other papers followed in a more subdued tone. My chief allies were that great majority of university students who proved faithful to Atatürk's famous message to youth, a sort of political testament. This message appointed the youth of Turkey to be the trustees of the rational and secular reforms, and it gave to them the task of fighting for the Republic and its fundamental ideals, however heavy the odds against them might be.

The agents of Moscow were using every sort of intrigue and device to undermine public authority in Turkey and spread dissent. In Turkey as well as other Muslim countries, red agents saw the advantage of assuming the roles of reactionary and ultranationalistic agitators. Organized as a result of Communist infiltration, these movements used secret material and clandestine moral support typical of the Moscow technique, and they appeared to be led from a common, secret center. These movements included:

Büyük Doğu (Great East) party. This party was a racket to derive money from every side for a professional gambler by the name of Necib Fazıl Kısakürek, who posed as a revivalist and had a widespread party organization and a daily paper, also called *Büyük Doğu.*

Islam Demokrat (Moslem Democrat) party. This group was led by a retired army captain, Cevad Rıfat Atilhan, a former Nazi agent closely associated with the Mufti, Haj Amin el-Husseini, of Jerusalem.

Nurculuk (Divine Light) partisans. The leader was an old agitator for Kurdish separatism who became known first by the name of Saidi Kurdi, when he was one of the promoters of a reactionary counterrevolution against the Young Turks in 1909. He changed his name to Saidi Nursi to make people forget his former identity.

Milliyetciler Derneği (Association of Nationalists). This society, with eighty branches, was made up of chauvinists, Pan-Turkists, and Pan-Turanists. Neglecting their ultranationalistic principles, they concentrated on reactionary religious aims and set themselves the task of destroying the general veneration which Atatürk enjoyed as the leader of the struggle for national independence and the promoter of secular reforms.

Scattered groups of reactionaries camouflaged under various names, or working underground.

I became "Enemy No. 1" of all these organizations and the target of their venomous personal attacks aimed at destroying my power to convince the public and at slaying me morally in the eyes of the readers. At the same time, I was bitterly attacked by the government press, which claimed that my anxieties about the reactionary movement, and my insistence that it was mere camouflage for a subversive communistic movement, were unfounded or greatly exaggerated. Once more, Turkey's fate and mine were inextricably interwoven.

21 : THE PLOT

AGAINST MY LIFE

A BEAUTY CONTEST in *Vatan* was the trifling and innocent affair which supplied the reactionaries with new weapons
against me. The promoters of the Miss Universe contest of 1952,
sponsored by Pan-American Airways and the Universal-Inter-
national film company, offered to place *Vatan* in charge of the
contest in Turkey. When we heard that the promoters had hesitated to extend the contest to Turkey because of the reactionary
pressure, we accepted the offer out of sheer pique to prove that
any hesitancy in Turkey was needless. The European Beauty
Contest had been carried on by another Istanbul paper for
twenty-five years without meeting opposition. Surely, I thought,
a world contest would not be received any differently.

The reactionaries, however, seeking ammunition to use
against me, seized upon this contest. They misrepresented it as
an attempt to lead Turkish girls into prostitution and to sell
them to "American Jews." The daily, *Büyük Doğu,* published
protest letters from all parts of Turkey, vying with each other
in the use of poisonous phrases. Many threatening letters poured
into our office. The daily and weekly reactionary papers repeatedly printed open provocations to young fanatics to kill me and
to destroy our printing plant.

I did not answer any of the poisonous press attacks, but I
continued my vigorous campaign against the entire reactionary
camp. I was unperturbed because I felt hopeful that the eco-

nomic metamorphosis in the country, stimulated mainly by American financial and technical help, would counterbalance the weight of reaction. As a matter of fact, a new road and harbor system, the bursting arrival of the machine age in our agriculture, extension of credit facilities, encouragement of personal initiative, development of water systems, and other factors had changed the entire face of the country. Individuals, groups, and whole provinces were carried away by the craze for bettering their fate, doing new things, and obtaining a larger share than others of the opportunities newly available. The fatalism, inherent in the age of stagnation and helplessness, seemed to have disappeared altogether.

I hoped that reaction could not survive in this dynamic atmosphere of vigorous, clear-sighted pioneering. So I decided to travel throughout the country, with a team composed of three reporters and a photographer, to make a firsthand study of local developments. We intended, in order to spread detailed information about transformed Turkey, to issue one or more provincial supplements about each of the sixty-three (subsequently sixty-four) provinces.

In spite of the concentrated personal attacks by the reactionary press, representing me as a traitor, unbeliever, American agent, or Communist, I was received with the most gratifying enthusiasm, cordiality, and even excessive hospitality everywhere we went. Our weekly provincial supplements, given away with our Wednesday issues, proved a great success. We have now reprinted and bound them in two volumes in order to meet the continued demand.

Not the slightest unfriendly incident occurred until we arrived in Malatya, the forty-ninth province on our tour. This place had a special interest for me. Colonel Nedim Zapci, a native of Malatya and for many years a very popular member of the parliament from there, is my brother-in-law. Consequently, I felt quite at home there with all my relatives-in-law showing me great hospitality.

Malatya, furthermore, is the home town and parliamentary seat of İsmet İnönü, the leader of the People's party, and is the stronghold of that party. The city administration is in the People's party's hands. Interparty relations there had been and still were rather strained. Nevertheless, our group was received very well by both the opposition and the Democratic party, by both the "outs" and the "ins." Our first two days of activity passed smoothly without any unfriendly incidents. On the afternoon of the second day, Prime Minister Adnan Menderes arrived in Malatya to visit, for the first time, the stronghold of the opposition and to address the annual local convention of his own party. My presence in Malatya at the same time was a mere coincidence.

Troublemakers who expected this visit to be the occasion of an open clash between the two parties, and therefore anticipated serious disturbances, were disappointed. The local opposition leaders went to the airport to receive the head of the government. The latter made a long visit to their office and discussed with them all their grievances about the partisan acts of the national government's local appointees. The dinner, given by the mayor for the Prime Minister, turned into a manifestation of Turkish national solidarity. Both sides, in their speeches, stressed the point that political parties were mere tools for the accomplishment of national ends, that party feelings should never overshadow national feelings, and that the majority party and the opposition complemented each other as the executive power and the balance wheel, respectively, of democracy.

I must note here that a promising moderation of friction had already appeared in Turkish public life months earlier. The conflict between the government and the independent press had been resolved. An issue about the distribution of government advertising, which could make or break papers financially, had been settled on the basis that equal amounts should be allocated to all legitimate papers, including opposition, independent, and progovernment papers without any discrimination because of different viewpoints. The Prime Minister had invited a representative group of five editors to accompany him on his official visit to London in October, 1952, as advisers.

Since I am an editor who stands always for moderation, tolerance, and mutual confidence in interparty relations to safeguard democracy, I felt really happy over the spirit of understanding manifested by Turkey's two main parties in a city like Malatya, where the opposition was strongest. I asked the Prime Minister's permission to leave the table to send to my paper the good news and my editorial comment upon it. When leaving the dinner, accompanied by a young member of our staff, I was entirely unaware that my movements were followed by a group of plotters against my life. At the telephone exchange I finished my part of the call, and leaving my colleague there to finish his, I started in the direction of my hotel on the opposite side of a spacious square. It was a little before midnight.

As I stepped out of the door, I suddenly had the sensation of being showered with pebbles. I had heard no noise; nobody was in sight. Having had no previous experience of being shot at, everything seemed to me rather uncanny. My first thought was that some boys were throwing pebbles at each other from hidden places, so I stretched out my hand and cried: "Stop that nonsense." Then I somehow felt that I was in danger and ran toward my hotel. I suddenly became aware that my right hand was full of blood, and something warm was dripping from my abdomen and legs. Noticing a group of men at the hotel entrance, I cried, "Doctor! Taxi!" They made no response. Judging, therefore, that they must be associates of my unknown assailants, I started to run in the opposite direction, only to fall to the ground, unconscious.

255

I came to my senses as some people were putting me into a car. During the drive I had only occasional flashes of consciousness. At the hospital I was surrounded by doctors and nurses. I heard a doctor murmur, "You can hardly feel the pulse. He is in a coma." I made no effort to speak; I felt too indifferent to everything. What I heard seemed to me to concern another person. I was actually at the threshold of the grave from loss of blood and from shock. Then a series of miracles saved my life.

First, the town of Malatya has a national hospital, and national hospitals usually are better equipped than provincial and city hospitals. It had a head surgeon of a caliber rarely encountered in any part of Turkey outside of the three or four large cities. To find such a man as Dr. Selaheddin Baş in a relatively small town was the greatest of luck. He immediately decided that my chief danger was from shock.

By another miraculous chance, a sample of a new injection against shock and the effects of loss of blood had been received from a medical firm in Germany just two days before. The administration of this new drug, together with injections to strengthen my heart, brought prompt general improvement. I could then be operated upon.

It was discovered that five bullets, fired at me from two sides, had penetrated. (Two others caused scratches too superficial to count.) One bullet pierced the middle of my right hand; one my middle finger on the same hand, detaching the nail; one, each, my right and left upper leg. The Xrays of the abdomen showed two holes, which created the impression that two bullets might be inside. When the abdomen was opened, it became apparent that one bullet had made both holes as it passed through the outer part of the abdomen. So I was told that my life could be considered out of danger.

The bullets which entered the legs seemed to have followed courses of maximum length. There was so much internal bleeding that the actual effect could not be detected at that moment. Later it was discovered that each bullet had followed, in its long course, such a friendly route that no bone was broken, no nerve center damaged, and no main artery touched. I spent more than three hours on the operating table and had to undergo several operations and endless injections.

Meanwhile, Adnan Menderes with Edhem Menderes, minister of the interior, and Dr. Hayri Üstündağ, minister of health, came to see me repeatedly to receive news about the progress of the operations. The Prime Minister told me that two leading medical experts, the Minister of Justice, and the Director General of Security had all left Ankara for Malatya by special plane, and that another special plane was bringing my wife and son from Istanbul.

The Prime Minister did not sleep that night. He led the search to detect the plotters. The coincidence of his presence in Malatya when the crime occurred, his close contact there with terrorists' secret plotting, and the shock he felt on the night of the crime influenced deeply the determined course he took thereafter against reactionary activities and in favor of moderate interparty relations. A bicycle found in the neighborhood of the telephone exchange led to the discovery of the plotters. The actual assassin was a *lycée* student by the name of Hüseyin Üzmez, the son of a poor working woman, a gifted but unbalanced and overzealous boy who was a member of several religious-chauvinistic underground organizations. Expelled from his school, he was paid regularly by "believers" to study in another school in a neighboring town. Documents found in his house led to the arrest of his immediate associates and then of the racketeers who led various underground reactionary associations and had planned and organized the plot.

A general uproar was caused in Turkey by the news of this attempt on my life. The feeling ran deep. With one or two exceptions, all the papers gave the biggest possible display to the news and published fiery editorials against reaction. Thousands of telegrams poured in daily from members of the cabinet, governors, mayors, Turkish ambassadors abroad, leaders of various parties, boards of provincial organizations of the same parties, and all sorts of associations and individuals. Celâl Bayar, president of the Republic, visited our office in Istanbul to express his indignation against the crime. Hundreds of telegrams were received from foreign countries and from foreign diplomatic representatives in Ankara.

I was deeply touched by an affectionate letter from Professor Arnold Toynbee, in which he said, "I feel so happy that your life has been spared. Not only your country but the whole world needs you. It will be benefited greatly by the continuation of your perseverant struggle."

On the morning after the crime, I felt like dictating an editorial, but the doctors and my wife would not allow it. I did it the next day, however, and continued to dictate editorials every day after that.

On the second day I asked to meet the young man who shot me. He was brought to my room in the hospital under strong escort. He was a tall, good-looking boy with lots of poise and self-possession. I addressed him in these words:

"Hüseyin, you pretend to be a good believer. As such, you must know that God is the only acceptable judge in moral matters. You usurped his prerogatives and felt entitled to judge my acts, to condemn them, and to execute a sentence of death against me. Would it not have been the right thing to give me a hearing before you carried out the sentence?"

"It would, and I felt so," he said, "but I could not approach you."

"Why?" I asked, "I am traveling through the entire country to meet people. I am accessible to anyone."

"I know," he answered, "but the difficulty did not come from you. It came from my own people. They would have murdered me the minute I approached you."

Then followed a long discussion of many issues which had been raised in reactionary papers. As Hüseyin had a good mind, he could not honestly refute my arguments, and he indicated agreement on every point. Finally he said:

"I am glad that I have had this opportunity to meet you and talk with you. But it will mean additional torture for me in my prison. I have already been feeling sorry that I have become a villain in the eyes of the general public, who are ready to raise a monument to you as a martyr to a cause. Now that I know you personally, I feel esteem and affection for you, and this feeling will cause me more suffering in prison than anything else."

The nurse noticed that the talk was causing me a possibly dangerous degree of excitement. My pulse had risen to 120. She put an end to the dramatic talk. I was really sorry for this gifted boy of nineteen, whose widowed mother had worked hard in factories in order to give him an education.

Before the young man's visit with me, my son had had a conversation with him and had found him arrogant and boastful. After his visit with me, my wife went to see him in the prison, without knowing that we had had a talk. She found the youth deeply sunk in thought, showing no interest in visitors. As soon, however, as he learned her identity, he rose immediately and respectfully. She said to him: "Hüseyin, I am a mother and share the sorrow and disappointment your mother must have at this moment. Why did you do it? Why waste your young life, your future as a promising boy? Why cause your mother so much suffering?"

"I feel sorry, very, very sorry," he told her. "If it could be undone, I would be so happy. But it just happened. It can't be changed now."

259

On the fifth day after the shooting, I was allowed to walk around in the room. This proved that my legs, in spite of the outward signs of heavy internal bleeding, were in good working order. In general, my body reacted wonderfully. On the seventh day, I was flown to Istanbul.

A triumphal reception awaited me at the airport. Representatives of the government, city, university, parties, trade unions, professional organizations, and students' organizations were present with innumerable bouquets of flowers. Many messages of sympathy were delivered. Then the daily routine of the paper seized me again.

I not only went ahead with work on the paper, but I had to address students' meetings and receive sympathizers of all sorts. The burden soon threatened my endurance. My family and friends compelled me to go to Switzerland for fuller convalescence. I spent a week there in the famous City Hospital of Basel. When Dr. Rudolph Nissen, the world-famous surgeon, examined me, he showed extreme surprise, and said, "It seems that God intended to perform a miracle, and he fully succeeded. Each of the five bullets followed a seemingly predestined friendly course, damaging no vital parts. At sixty-four, your body reacted like that of a man of forty." I left the hospital with the regenerated vigor and determination of a man reborn to life. Then I traveled for two weeks.

As my first activity, I wrote an editorial in German for the *Neue Zürcher Zeitung* under the title, "This Is a Hot War." My theme was the following:

We are mistaken in calling the state of actual war with the Iron Curtain world a cold one. It is a very hot one indeed. Firearms are still used in a limited way, but Moscow has chosen to use other weapons of a character enabling it to undermine the security and order in other parts of the world without incurring any risks itself. No counter-weapons have been devised against the armament that Moscow uses. The initiative is in the Soviet rulers' hands. They are free to choose the means, the field, and the time in a struggle of this sort." I then explained the character of the battle in progress in Turkey against the forces of evil organized by Moscow, which used the camouflage of religious reaction and national chauvinism just as it was doing in other Muslim countries. I outlined the circumstances which made me the first actual victim of those forces, and briefly narrated my narrow escape from death. The article created wide interest in both Switzerland and Germany. It was copied fully by several German papers and, in part, by some American papers.

I have had no feeling of vengeance against the plotters. My person was incidental in their plotting. The beauty contest in *Vatan* was a mere pretext to kill some crusader of the modernization movement in the new secular Republic, which had deprived them of their old "authority" of sheer dogma and superstition. The reactionaries wanted to undo the patient work of several generations to save Turkey from downfall and stagnation and to make it progressive and dynamic. It is up to the courts to deal with such offenses and to discourage Moscow from again using terroristic methods and reactionary agents in Turkey.

Those who made the attempt against my life were tried in the First Criminal Court of Ankara on August 3, 1953, on the charge of resorting to underground terroristic methods to overthrow the progressive secular regime in Turkey. The public prosecutor asked the death sentence against fourteen of them. Unfortunately, Hüseyin Üzmez, under the pressure by his fellow criminals, gave up his role of a meek lad, sorry for his crime. The verdict of the court was: "Hüseyin Üzmez, twenty years of imprisonment." But beyond the apprehension of these few criminals were graver problems to which the government was awakened by this violent affair.

22 : REASONS

FOR CONFIDENCE

The plot against me in Malatya resulted in almost a metamorphosis in public life. It awakened the entire country to the dangers of fanaticism and its unhealthy brew of religious bigotry and Moscow propaganda. The political parties now veered away from their past tendency to vie for power by any means, good or bad. Nonpartisan solidarity against any reversion to the use of religion for political ends was accepted as a supreme necessity, especially because of Moscow's political exploitation of religious fanaticism.

Choosing a liberal, modern step toward solidarity, Prime Minister Menderes inaugurated a monthly press conference with fifteen editors, representing the progovernment, opposition, and independent press. The invitations were personal, and the discussions were confidential, each editor, at his own discretion, using the material to promote good will and understanding. In these conferences, the Prime Minister reviewed current problems, with assistance, when necessary, from competent government officials. The editors were consulted on solutions for acute problems.

Turkey had a peculiar need for such conferences because the Turkish constitution provides the government with no system of checks and balances. The constitution is a haphazard one, hastily drawn during the War of Independence. As noted in Chapter XIII, the executive as well as the legislative power was placed in the Grand National Assembly. Only members of the Assembly can fill the offices of president of the Republic and cabinet ministries, and they retain their seats and votes in the Assembly. The inevitable result is that the president, elected by the Assembly from its own membership, is dominated by the Assembly, or else becomes a dictator either by dominating his party and through it the Assembly majority or by side-stepping the constitution. A dictator-president can rule with the efficiency of undivided authority, whereas a dominant Assembly inefficiently wastes time and energy with the not always unified five hundred "executives." Changing the constitution is difficult because the Assembly cannot be easily persuaded to surrender its present advantages.

Under these circumstances the monthly press conferences with the Prime Minister constituted a "Press Council" or "Press Cabinet," exercising unseen checks and balances by clarifying many vague issues and helping to re-establish good relations between political parties after conflicts. The conferences have also led to definite rules and common criteria of moral values for the conduct of the political game.

Foreign observers expressed dismay at the Assembly's unanimous adoption of a Press Law in March, 1954, penalizing, with imprisonment up to three years and heavy fines of thousands of dollars, anyone who, through the press or radio, insults another's honor or dignity, invades his private and family life or threatens to do so, harms the political honor of the state, or creates alarm in public opinion. The law increases the penalty if the person insulted is in an official position. Offenders are to be automatically prosecuted even without formal complaint by the person allegedly insulted. Drastic as this law sounds, the facts are that its terms were discussed by the press council in five long meetings in the presence of the Prime Minister, the Secretary of Justice, and Justice Department experts. Some opposition editors took full part in the discussion, and the government accepted some changes proposed by the press. Since this law went into effect, the best answer to its critics has been the opposition papers, which, with almost unbelievable license, continue to publish material seemingly aimed at discrediting the present government as an enemy "illegally usurping power," and, furthermore, at sabotaging Turkish-American relations. The law, however, keeps this from degenerating into personal libel, blackmail, and intentional spreading of false news. The press council has become more and more the vigilant umpire for the public in checking and balancing the government's powers.

Encouraged by this press council success, some of the editors organized a League of National Solidarity to provide an even better balance between the government and public interest. All policymakers on daily paper staffs—editors in chief, editorial writers, news editors, and columnists—met at the Press Club. The purpose of the League, unanimously approved at the meeting, is to safeguard against reaction the progress already achieved in Turkey, to keep the way free for further progress, to educate the public accordingly, to insist on complete disassociation of religion from politics, secular education, and lawmaking, and to give religion perfect freedom in the spiritual and ethical sphere. The journalists present chose, by secret ballot, a remarkably representative committee,[1] which, in turn, invited thirty-eight institutions and societies to send representatives to a general meeting.

Representatives came from universities, student and other

[1] The committee members were all editors: Hüseyin Cahid Yalçın of *Ulus,* the organ of the main opposition paper, the People's party; Mümtaz Faik Fenik of *Zafer,* organ of the party in power, the Democratic party; Falih Rıfkı Atay of *Dünya,* an opposition paper; Nadir Nadi of the independent *Cumhuriyet;* Ali Naci Karacan of the progovernment *Milliyet;* and myself, of the independent *Vatan.*

youth organizations; trade unions; and associations of war veterans, women, lawyers, doctors, engineers, chemists, teachers, and journalists; and also from societies with cultural and social aims. The League, as finally formed, is a confederation of non-political organizations, patriotic in aim and scientific in spirit and method.[2] Our League of Solidarity is an excellent example of public benefit inaugurated by the will and co-operation of newspaper editors. For me, its interests fitted in well with my activity in the International Press Institute, for the initiation of which I had been one of fifteen world journalists invited to America in October, 1950.

The League of Solidarity, from the first, created in Turkey a moral climate which, for some time, has checked extreme tendencies that, as so often before in Turkey's history, revive dogma-ridden dictatorial power. The presence of the powerful Textile Workers Federal Union is a check against class hatred. Destructive partisanship, chauvinism, unlawful influences in public administration and justice, and, above all, the heavy hands of reaction and communism all feel the strong restraints of the League's influence.

This moral climate enabled the Grand National Assembly to pass a law making the use of religious fanaticism for political ends a major offense, punishable by one to five years' imprisonment. This law, it is believed, destroys Moscow's chance to use in Turkey its favorite tactic of infiltration—a religious or racist camouflage which it has used so much in the Middle East and is using in virulent form today. Depriving fanatic circles of political means for silencing religious conceptions which are the

[2] The only individual memberships were held by five journalists from the original committee of initiative, and were for a three-year term. Organizations with statutes not permitting full membership in our League are allowed to have representatives participate in discussions, but without vote. Financing is by endowments and donations.

least bit unorthodox or broader than the strictest orthodoxy is the best guarantee of full religious freedom in Turkey.

The abortive attempt to kill me in Malatya did not end efforts to block my crusade for the ideals by which Atatürk had led us to victory in our national struggle. Incurable reactionaries and camouflaged Communists continue to attack my reputation in the hope of undermining my capacity for public persuasion. One morning paper, the only reactionary sheet among the fifty dailies in Turkey, issued a special sixteen-page supplement against me in 1953, and distributed 160,000 copies. This supplement pretended to expose me as a traitor, an agent of America, and an enemy of religion. Its authors were not at all handicapped by respect for the truth; their writing painted my long journalistic career a hue in direct contrast to the true color well known to the reading public.

We managed to get several copies of the supplement before the day of distribution; and, on that day, we published on the front page of *Vatan* a picture of the supplement's front page, advising our readers to buy it in order to see how far misrepresentation and lies can go. Then, we proceeded to the counteroffensive. We issued a special supplement to *Vatan*, giving the public the true picture of Atatürk's reforms, the right meaning of secularism, and the real nature of Moscow's strategy for undermining Turkey. That strategy, we explained, depends on direct and indirect co-operation with Turkish reactionaries, chauvinists, and others dependent for their selfish purposes upon pulling the country backward instead of forward. Nowhere in our supplement did we mention the daily paper which had attacked me.

The attacks my paper had to meet clearly indicated that certain underground groups were on the lookout for occasions and ways to undermine national unity in Turkey. In retrospect we can trace the course of such attempts, which, happily, were controlled in the long run by the public's constant awareness that Moscow had a hand in all subversion. It seems worth while for the sake of readers long used to democratic government to explain in some detail Turkey's novel experience with super-imposing democracy on a political foundation of absolutism and retarded economy, while under continual pressure from Russian expansionism. The situation is a strange one to the great Western democracies, but may be repeated many times in the small states in the Near and Far East now striving for independent self-government, although without the Turks' mature experience with government.

The sensibly patriotic factions in the two major parties seemed to grasp the fact that the surest protection against the weapons of red Muscovite imperialism was political unity and restrained party rivalry. Prime Minister Menderes occasionally met with the People's party leader, former President İnönü, to discuss public problems. In April, 1952, on the eve of the annual convention of the People's party, so long the only party but now the opposition, Democrat Prime Minister Menderes made a most conciliatory speech offering co-operation in national problems. İnönü, speaking for the People's party, in opening its convention, responded broadmindedly and sympathetically. Menderes sent a most cordial telegram of congratulation to the convention.

In spite of this high keynote, the reactionary and blind superpatriots controlled the convention. Still, this did not lead to uncontrollable extremes. A very aggressive Association of Nationalists (*Milliyetciler Derneği*), which fomented religious reaction and xenophobia especially directed against the West, was dissolved as subversive by court order under the law against using religion for political ends. Then, when reactionaries in the People's party wanted to bid for the disbanded ultranationalists' support by attacking the government, İnönü stopped them by asserting: "The People's party is a progressive and patriotic guardian of Atatürk's secular reforms. We cannot attack from the rear another progressive party while it, too, is fighting reaction."

Later, during this general tightening of controls on subversive uses of religion, the Party of the Nation (*Millet Partisi*), by then the third largest party, claiming a million members, was abandoned by its founder, Hikmet Bayur, and its progressive members, because reactionaries had taken over. The government thereupon disbanded that party, as it had the Association of Nationalists. This time, however, the chauvinists in the People's party thought they saw a chance to wreck the Democratic party by shouting loudly, "Our turn to be dissolved will be next," while secretly negotiating for a coalition with the members of the previously disbanded organizations. This attitude drew bitter attacks not only from the progovernment and independent papers, but from all the progressive papers that, like *Dünya,* were for the People's party. Any attempt at coalition with elements penalized for subversion smacked too much of opportunistic betrayal of the Republic's progressive aims and a grave disregard for external dangers. But the attempted coalition struck a snag: a quarrel developed over the division of the Assembly seats that the coalition might win. The dissolved Party of the Nation demanded one-half of them, and the People's party offered fewer. So, in the third year after Turkey's first truly free election had swept the new Democratic party into power, the forces of reaction against Atatürk's program, despite its proven success, were struggling even inside his own party to turn the clock back.

Adherents of the former Party of the Nation soon reorganized under the name of the Republican party of the Nation and adjusted its rules to comply with the law against political use of religion. The coalition having failed, it and the People's party launched parallel campaigns against the government. They gave the government no credit for its outstanding achievements in foreign affairs and basic domestic economy, but played up its shortcomings, especially pointing out the high cost of living and laws projected to encourage foreign investment in Turkey and foreign exploitation of Turkey's barely tapped oil resources.

The government was vulnerable at this stage of transition from old to new economic policies. In order to revolutionize the stagnant Turkish economy, which is based largely on agriculture, and to promote production and consumption simultaneously, the new government had taken daring measures to raise, overnight, the farmers' standard of living. It heavily subsidized some farm products and freed them from direct taxation; it granted large credits through the Agricultural Bank, a public institution established in 1863; and it inaugurated mechanized and modernized methods of farming.

Such pump-priming to increase production and accumulate working capital in the farmers' hands was made possible by American aid, but native means have continued it on a large scale. The immediate benefits were so thrilling that the nation-wide thirst for better equipment and better living opened flood gates for imports, which soon exceeded exports. Payments to foreign firms were more and more delayed. The black-market value of the Turkish lira dropped to one-half its legal value because businessmen imported various goods through black-market channels after import licenses had to be refused, and also because an eagerness to travel abroad became a contagious passion and used up much needed exchange.

Turkey's foreign exchange resources became too strained to pay for the imports of both equipment for future development and necessities for immediate consumption. The remedy was to increase domestic production of textiles, cement, sugar, and chemicals, and to undertake extensive electric power, irrigation, and reclamation projects by mobilizing private capital. But the immediate effect was inflationary. The people had to wait for the benefits and products to come from projects and plants only under construction at that time. Many persons seemed prosperous with new jobs, increased land values, and cash savings, but until new factories could deliver goods to the markets at lower domestic prices, the rising cost of living seriously hurt everyone on low incomes or fixed government salaries.

So high was the resentment fanned by the opposition parties as the country approached its ninth general election, set for May 2, 1954, that many government officials and observers felt sure that the People's party would return to power. Some of them even changed their allegiance and ran as opposition candidates. The party in power was finally provoked to retaliate. The Democratic Prime Minister had, for harmony's sake, refrained from carrying out a party convention decision of 1952, to reclaim for the national treasury all lands, buildings, and sums of money taken "illegally" from central, provincial, and municipal government ownership by the People's party during its single-party rule. When the People's party, two years later, implied doubts of the legal right of the Democratic government to rule the country, that government decided to take the postponed step and hastily passed a law to seize property "illegally acquired by the People's party." This hasty action, without first convincing the public of the reasons for an action generally deemed legitimate but seemingly timed solely to embarrass the opposition financially and morally on the eve of the general elections, brought condemnation on the government even from some of its own party members.

This was enough to shake the Democratic party's confidence in victory in the elections. Some of its members wanted the controversial proposals, such as those to encourage foreign capital to invest in Turkey and to insure advantages for investors in oil developments, held over until after the elections. The Democratic leaders, however, insisted on going to the electorate with both laws already passed. But they also wanted the electorate to vote an endorsement of them, and so reintroduced them as a plank in the party platform. (The voters gave the desired endorsement.) While the laws were under intense discussion in the Assembly, another chance for distortion of government motives presented itself.

The President of the United States officially invited the President of Turkey to visit the United States. I was one of four editors who accompanied President Bayar on his tour of America in January, 1954. In contrast to my student recollections of American ignorance and prejudice concerning Turkey and my own embarrassment from them, I took extraordinary pleasure in the cordial demonstrations of friendship for Turkey and appreciation of Turkey's conscientious and courageous service for stability in a free world. Turkey now seemed to mean to many Americans the only reliable and understanding ally in the common cause of nonaggression and freedom, and the only ally appreciative and grateful for American co-operation. But, alas, many opposition papers in Turkey misrepresented the tour as a hidden election scheme and a maneuver for American interference in internal Turkish politics.

Upon my return to Turkey, I made a hurried tour with Prime Minister Menderes to our eastern provinces. The tour convinced me of the people's general enthusiasm and gratitude for the government's help to the rural population. To see at political meetings, in Turkey, women with one child on the back, another held on the hip, and a third by the hand was a remarkable sight. The people of the Black Sea coast, used to living on cornbread and exposed to famines, were grateful for

271

wheat shipped and sold to them at two-thirds of the price their government had paid to the wheat growers elsewhere. The purchase and distribution of food by the government helped all areas of the country.

Turkey's 1954 election, the second wholly free and honest popular vote, again fooled the prophets. They had consistently foretold a People's party victory or very large gains. But the opposition had been fooling itself when it believed that its destructive and opportunistic tactics and its underground activities would win votes. The Democratic party won a more sweeping victory than in 1950, gaining 505 seats out of 546. The People's party won only 31 seats; the Republican party of the Nation, 5; independents, 5; and a new Peasant party, none.

The re-elected government set to work with fresh energy to carry forward its industrial program and the development of natural resources in order to raise production and consumption to proper levels and in proper balance. Although the problem of suspended payments of foreign debts was still unsolved, various European firms poured in offers of five- to twelve-year credit for equipment purchases by Turkey. Then, too, the Prime Minister accepted an invitation to Washington to exchange views on Turkish-American relations and world problems. I, with another newspaper editor, accompanied him. His well-publicized visit afforded more gratifying evidence of international confidence in Turkey.

After the Prime Minister had ended his American visit and returned to Turkey, I took part in a three-week North Atlantic Treaty Organization (NATO) trip in Canada, including its Pacific and Arctic regions. I was pleased to make better known to the Turkish public this potentially most important country which already enjoys world esteem.

Yugoslavia was my next destination, in order to be present at the signing of the Balkan military alliance of Yugoslavia,

Greece, and Turkey. I was amazed to find Yugoslavia not only freed from the yoke of Moscow, but rapidly emancipating herself from all narrow dogmatism, xenophobia, and police pressures. Her wise decentralization, increasing self-criticism, decreasing bureaucratic tendencies, and melting pot policy, by consent of all elements, to insure equality for all citizens (Croat, Serb, Slovene, and minorities) seem to promise one of the strongest national structures in Europe and a bulwark against Muscovite ideology.

My country still has to face many difficulties, but it is consistently contributing to expansion of the free world in new directions. Faced with an unfortunately uncompromising opposition by the People's party in its determined grasp for power, and with the risk of being caught unawares and weak by predatory Russia, the Democratic party government, following its second victory at the polls, erred in the direction of limiting liberty to gain order. But, at first, this did not lessen my conviction that its general direction would always be democratic and liberal.

23: SETBACKS

AND AGAIN OPTIMISM

THE RE-ELECTION of the Democratic party after the test of its first four years in office led me to assume that a long, happy period was in sight for Turkey. It seemed obvious to me that the government would use its secure position to carry out its progressive program of private initiative and individual liberty, and I foresaw stability and tolerance in every sense and in every field.

As an incorrigible optimist I once more overlooked the fact that stupidity remains the determining factor in shaping history. The victorious government used its freshly won advantage to take revenge on its opponents. It undertook to insure itself a third victory (in the 1958 elections) by amending the electoral law and modifying or passing other laws to block opposition. These moves towards authoritarianism produced deep dissatisfaction, not only in the opposition but also in independent citizens who had chosen to support the Democratic party in previous elections.

On the economic side, the government's daring efforts to equip the country overnight with harbors, roads, hydroelectric and thermoelectric power stations, silos, factories, and so on, which had at first served to inject new life, began to show diminishing returns. Financial commitments and production schedules could not be met. No attention was paid to saving the national credit outside or inside of the country. The fact was that some European governments continued to guarantee mid-dle-term credits for more new ventures in Turkey in order to secure outlets which would increase employment in their own industries, and this created the popular illusion that Turkey's credit was sound. Meanwhile, the exchange rate of the Turk-ish lira on the black market fell to less than one-third of its official rate. Waves of inflation rose. The cost of living became unbearable.

The acute conflict with Greece over the agitation on the island of Cyprus for *Enosis* (union with Greece) greatly sharp-ened the politico-economic crisis in Turkey. Moscow knew how to take advantage of dormant Panhellenic imperialism. By play-ing on the "Big Idea" recurrent in Greece, for reconquest of Istanbul and re-establishment of the Byzantine Empire, and by using the tendency of the Orthodox church in Athens and Cyprus to play a political role, Moscow was quick to spread communism among the Greek-speaking populace of Cyprus and to create violent agitation in Greece for the annexation of Cyprus. Turkey, after nearly three centuries of ruling Cyprus, had temporarily ceded it to Great Britain in 1878, during the Russo-Turkish war, to gain protection against a rear attack by Russia. The British acquired permanent possession of it in World War I. Cyprus is only forty-five miles from the Turkish coast, hence the same short distance from Turkey's present naval base at İskenderun (Alexandretta) and the air base at Adana, where, in case of conflict, the forces of Turkey and her allies would join. The distance from Cyprus to the Greek main coast is thirteen hundred miles. Cyprus has a Turkish population of one hundred thousand, which Turkey cannot consent to place under Greek rule, in view of the disastrous experiences of one hundred thousand Turks left under Greek rule in western Thrace following World War I. Furthermore, the coast of Asia Minor is already closely paralleled by a chain of Greek-occupied islands. If Cyprus were added to the chain, the blockade of Turkey would be complete.

These considerations and the fact that this resurrection of old Panhellenic imperialism revived memories of the atrocities committed during the Greek invasion of Turkey, 1919–22, over-shadowed the conciliatory and co-operative gains achieved by Atatürk and Venizelos and aroused vehement Turkish opposition to the Greek aspirations. For some time the government in Turkey succeeded in preventing serious counterdemonstrations against Greek propaganda and violence. However, the situation afforded an all too favorable opportunity for Moscow to undermine the Turkish-Greek alliance and with it this vital southeastern wing of the North Atlantic Treaty Organization. A bomb planted near the house in Salonika where Atatürk was born, followed by provocative reports of the bomb's explosion, suddenly brought the agitation in Turkey to an incendiary pitch. The result was riots in Istanbul and İzmir on the night of September 6, 1955. Widespread excesses were elaborately planned, and the violent destruction of property was out of hand for several hours; then martial law was proclaimed. But feelings in Turkey on both the Cyprus issue and the government's mistakes did not quiet down. The once popular Democratic party government fell in disgrace. Dissident Democrats formed a new Freedom party. The Prime Minister had to reconstruct his cabinet, and the Assembly rescinded or modified certain restrictive laws. Once more Turkey was embroiled in serious domestic and foreign troubles.

At first glance the whole outlook seemed to be discouraging. With many other Turkish patriots of independent and objective minds, I have been inclined to consider this question: "Has it been worth while to devote a life to the struggle for ideals, only to arrive at such disappointment and to witness again and again a return of stupidity as the maker of history?"

My pessimistic mood was suddenly deepened by the arbitrary suspension of *Vatan* for fifteen days on the pretext that it went too far in criticizing the government. This had not happened in Turkey since 1944, and I had hoped that such measures were permanently a part of the past.

My afterthoughts, however, have brought to light reasons to cheer up again. Do we not have to pay a price to attain real democracy, to benefit from liberty, and to develop faith in the future? Are all our troubles not forging a better destiny for the Turkish nation as a reliable guardian of the free world in its dangerous frontier area? And, then, what would journalism of the kind I am devoted to mean without confidence in a better future, and without the spirit of struggle and self-sacrifice to make constructive dreams and lofty ideals come true? The cause of liberty anywhere requires constant care and vigilance. It is an aim difficult to attain and worth any sacrifice. Even if one cannot enjoy personally and permanently the fruits of such a struggle, the determination of making efforts in that direction constitutes its own reward.

A turn for the better came promptly. The government adopted a budget limiting new financing to the completion of projects under way and to balancing credit. Some increases in production promised relief from consumer shortages and inflation. But foreign problems increased because of the 1956 crises in the neighboring Arab states and Israel, linked with the Cyprus issue and with NATO and the United Nations.

At no point can a writer "adequately" close the story of a nation reshaping its own destiny, for changes continue during the publication and the reading of a book such as this. I can bring to an end only the narrative of my share in my nation's life.

While international, national, and personal struggles continue as Turkey's destiny unfolds, I still enjoy life intensely. I can be considered one of the best-liked and most-hated persons in Turkey. My consistent crusade against reaction and communism, and the price of my life which I so nearly paid for my ideals in Malatya, are credited by thoughtful Turks to be vital factors in changing the country for the better. On the other hand, the forces of evil consider me their worst enemy. A new catastrophe may befall me at any moment, but I don't care. I discount any adverse happening like a soldier on an actual battlefield, because I have decided it is worthwhile to expose one's life to any danger in return for basic gains for one's country and for a cause dear to the free world.

In retrospect, I can best summarize my feelings by quoting Nasreddin Hoca. Asked the meaning of happiness one day, Hoca replied, "When God wants a man to be very, very happy, he makes him lose his donkey, then lets him find it again."[1] In this sense I have been a very happy man indeed, because I have repeatedly lost my donkey but have always found it again.

I have used this life of continual lively struggle to emancipate myself from fear, conceit, lust for money, and personal ambition for titles and power of office. I have made some enemies but many friends. The initial harmony in my marriage developed through the years; besides, there has been close friendship, mutual esteem, and pleasurable co-operation between my wife and myself as fellow writers on the same paper. I have just one son, Tunç, who, after studying in the Lincoln Progressive School in New York, Robert College in Istanbul, the University of Istanbul, and Queens College in North Ireland, and after making a start as a conscientious dramatic critic on my paper, graduated from the School of Drama at Yale University. He became a playwright and dramatic art critic on my paper—his dream since childhood. He has also proved his mettle as a political ob-

[1] In Nasreddin Hoca's day, and today for most peasants, the man who loses his donkey loses his only means of transportation, and thereby loses also his means of earning a living.

server by his dispatches from eastern and southern Africa as *Vatan*'s special correspondent covering the acute Mau Mau troubles in Kenya and the racial problems in South Africa. Indeed, as a journalist he is showing qualities exceeding mine. At this writing, he is again in America, this time on the staff of the Turkish Information Office in New York. My other "child," the newspaper, *Vatan*, seems to be well established and enjoying the esteem and confidence of the public.

The results of the almost incredible—nay, almost miraculous—events in Turkey during the first half of the twentieth century, of which I have told here the inside story, now will receive the test of time. Fundamental ideals of a democracy of political equality for citizens, representative government, and freedom of religion and the press, with collective security and equal rights for sovereign states in the world, should perpetuate the sympathetic relations already established between the United States of America and Turkey. The hard-earned freedom of the modern Turkish press, in spite of all the forces of reaction and self-seeking that work against it, survives temporary defeats and stands as historical evidence of the effectiveness of a responsible journalistic crusade for ideals of national health and world peace. Finally, Turkey's dangerous position on Russia's border has seasoned her in understanding Russia's ways. Although no longer a great empire posing a threat or counterbalance to Russia's power, the Turkish Republic contributes even more than her share to the protection of the other peace-loving countries by her moral and military resistance to Russian aggression and her will for collective security.

Yes, this seems a happy climax for my life work. When I was born long years ago on the last Friday of Ramazan, the Muslim holy month of fasting, a day which coincided with Kadır Day, the Day of Fate, at the hour when the muezzins were calling from the minarets for the midday prayer, all agreed that such a favorable combination of omens was very rare, and that it foretold a most happy and successful life. When I look back on my life of excitement, danger, and last-minute escapes from disaster, I find no reason to question that prophecy. I rejoice that my son and his generation, and my paper *Vatan,* will carry on in Turkey, a country sure to occupy an outstanding place among the progressive, liberal, peace-loving nations of the world.

235, 236, 265, 279; *see also* American, Americans
"United States of Europe": 237
U.S.S. Scorpion: 56, 65
University of Istanbul: 34, 55, 278
Urfa, Turkey: 66
Üzmez, Hüseyin: 257, 258–59, 261

V.E. Day: 221
Vahdeti Dervishes: 88
Vakit (newspaper): 43, 57 ff., 135
Van Kleefens, Eelco N.: 234
Varlik Vergisi: see taxes
Vatan (*Fatherland*) (newspaper): 3, 151, 154, 188, 191, 198, 214, 220, 223, 224, 225, 226, 228, 230, 236, 247, 252, 261, 264 n., 266, 279, 280; founded by Yalman, 135; suspension of, by Eastern Tribunal, 186; publication of, resumed in 1940, 186 ff.; suspended for 45 days, 189–90; suspended for 90 days, 193–94; financial success of, after reinstatement, 194–95; suspended by Turkish cabinet, 208–209; publication of, resumed, 215; suspended for 15 days, 277
Vatan Publishing Company, Ltd.: 186
Vatican, The: 136
Veils: of women, 55; abandoned, 175
Venizelos, Eleutheros: 66, 276
Versailles Conference: 217
Vlachs: *see* Romanians

Wallace, Henry: 191
War criminals, trial of, at Nuremberg: 232–33
War of Independence (against

Greece): 117, 127, 130, 132, 144, 241, 262
War of Tripoli: 88
Warsaw, Poland: 39
Washington, D.C.: 43, 213, 272
Welles, Sumner: 191
Wellington Koo, K. V.: 234
Western calendar: 55
Western democracies: 267
Western powers: 33, 134, 200, 201, 227
Western press: 129
White Russians: 69
Wichita Eagle: 32
Wilhelm II, Kaiser, of Germany: 40, 61
Williams, Talcott: 27 ff.
Wilson, Woodrow: 74, 77, 78, 121, 122, 127; Fourteen Points of, 71
Women: emancipation of, 173; veils abandoned by, 175
World Students' Conference: 28
World War I: 25, 28, 31, 32, 39, 45, 46, 48, 55, 56, 68, 80, 87, 88, 110, 114, 115, 116, 126, 127, 134, 173, 180, 183, 201, 203, 214, 275; aerial warfare in, 36–37
World War II: 25, 28, 31, 48, 64, 100, 113, 167, 183, 210

Yalçin, Hüseyin Cahid: 20, 193, 264 n.
Yale University, School of Drama: 278
Yalman, Ahmed Emin: birthplace of, 9; boyhood home of, 10; conservative uncle of, 11–13; father of, 12–13; schooling of, 13–14; publishes *The Intention,* 18; becomes a journalist, 19–20; enrolls in law school, 20; goes to Italy, 25; as student in U.S., 26 ff.; im-

293